# NON
# OBVIOUS

## Also by the Author:

*Personality Not Included: Why Companies Lose Their
Authenticity–and How Great Brands Get It Back*

*Likeonomics: The Unexpected Truth Behind Earning Trust,
Influencing Behavior, and Inspiring Action*

*ePatient: 15 Surprising Trends Changing Healthcare*
(with co-author Fard Johnmar)

*Always Eat Left-Handed: 15 Surprising Secrets
For Killing It at Work and in Real Life*

*The Non-Obvious Guide to Small Business Marketing
(Without a Big Budget)*

# ABOUT THE NON-OBVIOUS TREND SERIES

For the past nine years, the *Non-Obvious Trend* Series has been one of the most widely-read curated annual predictions about business and marketing trends in the world, reaching well over 1 million readers and utilized by dozens of global brands.

Each new annual edition features 15 original trend predictions alongside detailed insights on how to use those trends to evolve your business or fast-track your career.

*Non-Obvious* has been translated into 10 languages globally, with new editions to be released throughout the coming year.

For more details about booking private workshops, keynote speaking engagements, training, or custom print editions of books from the series, visit www.nonobviouscompany.com.

# PRAISE FOR *NON-OBVIOUS*

"

*"Non-Obvious* is a sharp, articulate, and immediately useful book about one of my favorite topics: the future. With actionable advice and entertaining stories, Rohit offers an essential guidebook to using the power of curation to understand and prepare for the future of business."

**—DANIEL H. PINK,** author of *To Sell Is Human* and *Drive*

There are very few books I read hoping that no one else around me will. They're the books that are so insightful, so thought provoking, and so illuminating that they provide a powerful competitive advantage. *Non-Obvious* is one of those. Pass on it at your own peril.

**—SHIV SINGH,** former SVP Global Head of Digital at VISA and co-author of *Savvy: Navigating Fake Companies, Fake Leaders and Fake News*

This is one of those rare books that delivers insights that are useful and to help illuminate where business is going. It's a great read.

**—CHARLES DUHIGG,** author of the bestseller *The Power Of Habit*

The insights in Rohit's *Non-Obvious Trends* are an invaluable guide to understanding our customer's customer. His predictions are useful and highly anticipated within our group across the globe every year. As a B2B marketer and leader, this is one of my rare must-read recommendations for my entire team.

**—NAVEEN RAJDEV,** Chief Marketing Officer, Wipro

It doesn't take a crystal ball to predict that digital is the future. Rather than tell you what you already know, Rohit sets his sights on something much more important: helping you adopt a more curious and observant mindset to understand the world around you. If you believe in a lifetime of learning, read this book!

**—JONATHAN BECHER,** President, San Jose Sharks and Former Chief Marketing Officer, SAP

**"**

A lot of books promise to help you see things differently, but Rohit's book actually delivers. His insightful blend of visual thinking and business strategy shows you how to find meaningful patterns that others miss. A real mind-opener.

—**SUNNI BROWN,** author, *Gamestorming* and *The Doodle Revolution*

Shatter your magic crystal ball, and toss out the tea leaves. In this book, Rohit shows us how and where to find the future trends that will shape your business, your brand, and even your own decision-making.

—**SALLY HOGSHEAD,** *New York Times* bestselling author of *How the World Sees You*

Lots of books tell you to "think different," but *Non-Obvious* is one of the few books that actually teaches you how to do it. Whether you are trying to persuade clients, motivate a team, or just impress a demanding boss, *Non-Obvious* can help you succeed. I've already purchased copies for my entire team.

—**JOHN GERZEMA,** *New York Times* bestselling author of *The Athena Doctrine*

The best books approach their topic with a spirit of generosity. Rohit's new book offers insight into the business and cultural trends that matter. And why they do. And what actions they might inspire. But more than that, it also generously teaches you how to develop your own process, for evaluating the trends that matter and those that don't. Also, it's well-written. Which makes it a joy (and not a chore!) to read!

—**ANN HANDLEY,** Chief Content Officer, Marketing Profs

*Non-Obvious* is simple, elegant, and powerful: one of those intensely engaging books that I couldn't put down. Every year, I use the ideas in this book to help my team see new opportunities and out-think our competition.

—**HOPE FRANK,** Chief Marketing and Digital Officer + Futurist

"

Rohit Bhargava's *Likeonomics* is the gold standard on understanding the social economy. His new book had me at "predict the future," but there's much more than that in here. It's about seeing the world in a new way—plus a powerful argument for how curation can change your organization.

—**SREE SREENIVASAN,** former Chief Digital Officer,
the Metropolitan Museum of Art

Rohit provides a goldmine of ideas and trends that will shape the future of marketing and product development. Read this book to get in front of the herd.

—**GUY KAWASAKI,** Chief Evangelist of Canva,
Author of *The Art of the Start, 2.0*

Our industry is all about the future—the future of kids, the future of schools, the future of education. In the admissions office, the ability to recognize and leverage that future is an indispensable skill. In *Non-Obvious*, Rohit provides us the tools we require to perform those functions with precision and get better at predicting what will be important tomorrow, based on improving our observations of today.

—**HEATHER HOERLE,** Executive Director,
the Enrollment Management Association

Seeing things that others don't is perhaps the highest form of creativity that exists. Unlock the *Non-Obvious* approach, and you can write your ticket to success in any field.

—**JOHN JANTSCH,** author of *Duct Tape Marketing* and *Duct Tape Selling*

In *Non-Obvious*, Rohit shares valuable tips, tricks, methodologies, and insightful curated trends to help readers navigate the future. Recommended!

—**ROSS DAWSON,** Chairman, Future Exploration Network

Very few people understand the world of digital business better than Rohit, and I have introduced my clients to his ideas for years. His new book is a must-read resource for learning to see patterns, anticipate global trends, and think like a futurist every day!

—**GERD LEONHARD,** author and keynote speaker, Basel, Switzerland

*Non-Obvious* should be called "oblivious," since that's how you'll be if this book isn't on your shelf. I actually wish some of Rohit's predictions wouldn't come true ('Selfie Confidence!?' Nooo!) . . . but usually, they do. He's the best at this, and this book shows you why.

—**SCOTT STRATTEN,** four-time bestselling author, including the 2014 Sales Book of the Year: *UnSelling*

Artfully lacing stories together to pull out simple yet powerful trends, Rohit offers a blueprint for making trend identification a key component of your business strategy. The format of his book makes it easy for the novice to adopt these principles, and for the expert to glean pearls of wisdom. While the title is *Non Obvious,* your next step should be obvious: read this book today!

—**JOEY COLEMAN,** Chief Experience Composer at Design Symphony

*Non-Obvious* is a powerhouse 'must read' for corporate executives, marketers, and product and service developers. Rohit Bhargava provides valuable, entertaining, and easily understood sideways insights into critical trends shaping the near future. He lifts the lid on the myths surrounding the dark arts of trend prediction, and offers very practical guidance on how to spot, curate, and capitalize on Non-Obvious trends.

—**ROHIT TALWAR,** global futurist and CEO at Fast Future Research

# NON OBVIOUS

## ROHIT BHARGAVA

IDEAPRESS
PUBLISHING

**IDEAPRESS**
PUBLISHING

Published in the United States by Ideapress Publishing.

**IDEAPRESS PUBLISHING** | WWW.IDEAPRESSPUBLISHING.COM

Non-Obvious® is a registered trademark of the Influential Marketing Group.
*All other trademarks are the property of their respective companies.*

Cover Design by Jeff Miller/Faceout Studios
Cover Photo by Javier Pérez
Interior Design by Jocelyn Mandryk
Cataloging-in-Publication Data is on file with the Library of Congress.
ISBN: 978-1-940858-66-1   ISBN: 978-1-940858-52-4 (e-book)

**SPECIAL SALES**

Ideapress Books are available at a special discount for bulk purchases for sales promotions or corporate training programs. Special editions, including personalized covers and custom forewords, are also available. For more details, email info@ideapresspublishing.com or contact the author directly.

*To my parents–for always giving me
a chance to see the world in my own way...
even if it wasn't always non-obvious.*

# How To Read This Book...

## Part 1—HOW TO CURATE TRENDS

→ Learn how to predict trends for yourself with our signature "Haystack Method" approach.

## Part 2—THE 2019 NON-OBVIOUS TRENDS

→ Read our 15 latest trend predictions along actionable advice on how to use them.

## Part 3—THE TREND ACTION GUIDE

→ Further your non-obvious thinking with advice on what to read and do next.

## Part 4—APPENDIX WITH 100+ PAST TRENDS

→ Explore and apply our past trend predictions, rated and analyzed for accuracy every year.

**To see all online resources referenced in this book, visit:**
**www.nonobviousbook.com/resources**

# Contents

*Part IV*

# PREVIOUS TREND REPORT SUMMARIES
## (2011-2018)

# The 2019 Edition -
# What's New and Non-Obvious?

—

This is a book about learning to predict the future.

Every year, my team and I spend hundreds of hours reading thousands of stories, conducting dozens of interviews, attending and speaking at nearly 50 events, reading or reviewing more than 100 new books, and then combining all that research to identify 15 trends that will change the world in the coming year.

Whether you have read a previous edition of this book or not, this new edition features much more than just new trend predictions. Here are the updates you'll find in the book this year:

- ✓ Optimized interior design with new charts and images
- ✓ Updated appendix featuring ratings of over 100 past trends
- ✓ Additional images of my trend-curation method
- ✓ A new guide to notetaking and effectively saving ideas
- ✓ And, of course, 15 more trends for 2019!

While it will be tempting to focus on the new, I highly encourage you to check out the past and previously predicted trends, as well. You will find the answer there to the one question everyone asks: "Did your predictions come true?" The other thing you might discover, though, is that new trends don't make old trends irrelevant.

Rather, trends are meant to describe an accelerating idea, and if those past predictions were actually "non-obvious" when predicted, then they may become more obvious over time—but still ring true.

Whether you actively seek to understand the future or find yourself curious about the past, this book will help you indulge that curiosity and channel it toward creating new and interesting ideas.

The most important thing I hope you will take from it, though, is the belief that there is real value in being more open-minded, accepting people who think differently than you do, and seeing the world in more "non-obvious" ways.

The world needs your empathy and leadership now more than ever. I can't wait to see what you come up with.

Rohit Bhargava
Washington, D.C.
January 2019

## PART I

—

# The Art of Trend Curation

# INTRODUCTION

*"I am not a speed reader, I am a speed understander."*
— ISAAC ASIMOV, Author, Historian, and Biochemist

Nearly 150 years ago, the Dewey Decimal Classification System ambitiously introduced a method to break down the published volumes of the world into ten main categories. Isaac Asimov has written at least one book on nine of them.

In his prolific lifetime, he wrote nearly five hundred books on topics ranging from his beloved science-fiction series to a two-volume work explaining the collected literature of William Shakespeare. He even wrote a reader's guidebook to the Bible.

Though he was celebrated for his science fiction, Asimov never defined his work using a single category. When asked to name his favorite book, he often joked, "the last one I've written." He cannot be described only as a scientist or theologian or literary critic.

He was, without question, a writer and thinker with an incredible curiosity for ideas. In fact, he used this curiosity to maintain his grueling schedule of publishing, which, at its peak, resulted in about fifteen books per year. His secret, if there was just one, seemed to be his ability to juggle multiple projects at once.

When he became stuck during writing (which, indeed, happened to him, just as it does to any writer), Asimov would simply move on to one of his other in-progress projects. He never stared at a blank sheet of paper.

He credited his ability to focus on so many areas at once to his voracious appetite for reading and his capacity as a "speed understander." What if you could become a speed understander like Asimov?

I believe we all can.

The simple aim of this book is to teach you how to notice the things that others miss. I call this "non-obvious" thinking, and learning to do it for yourself can change your business and your career.

The context within which I'll talk about this type of thinking is business trends. For better or worse, most of us are fascinated by trends and those who predict them. We anticipate these predictions as a glimpse into the future, and they capture our imagination.

There's only one problem—too many trends are based upon guesswork or lazy thinking. In other words, they are obvious instead of non-obvious.

This book was inspired by the landslide of obvious ideas with which we are surrounded and our desire to do something better with them.

In a world where everyone is one click away from being a self-declared expert, learning to think differently is more important than ever. Observing and curating ideas can lead to a unique understanding of why people choose to buy, sell, or believe anything.

A non-obvious trend is a unique, curated observation about the accelerating present.

Unlike many other far-future predictions, the trends and methods in this book are designed to help you right now. There are plenty of people who can tell you what the world might be like twenty years from now. Sadly, many of those are guesses or wishful thinking. How many trend forecasters do you think predicted the rise of something like Twitter back in 2006? Exactly zero.

Yet this doesn't mean curating trends (or honing your ability to predict them) is useless. The most powerful trends can offer predictions for the short-term future based upon observing the present. The truth is, knowing the short-term future is more valuable than you may think.

## Why Does Trend Curation Matter?

Most of our life decisions happen in the short term, though we may describe them differently. You choose to start a business in the short term. You choose who to marry in the short term. You change careers from one role to the next, all in the short term.

Long-term decisions start in the short term, so understanding how the world is changing in real time is far more valuable in your day-to-day career and life than trying to guess what will happen in the world twenty years from now.

When I speak at industry events, I often describe myself first as a "trend curator." The reason I use this term is because it describes my passion for collecting ideas and taking the time to see the patterns in them to describe the world in new and interesting ways. In this book, you will learn the exact step-by-step method I use, and how to become a trend curator yourself.

The result of all of my idea collection is that for the past eight years, I have published an annual list of fifteen trends that will shape the business world in the year to come. Across that time, I have advised some of the largest brands in the world on business strategy, taught several courses at Georgetown University, and been invited to speak at events in thirty-two countries around the world.

All of this gives me the valuable chance to gain firsthand insight into dozens of different industries and to study media, culture, marketing, technology, design, and economics with an unfiltered eye. Adding to these real-life interactions, I also read or review dozens of books and buy magazines on everything from cloud computing to Amish farming methods.

My philosophy is to collect ideas the way frequent fliers collect miles—as momentary rewards to use for later redemption.

## Why I Wrote *Non-Obvious*

When I first started writing an annual list of predictions in 2011, my intent was to share trends as ideas that didn't have a home with any project I was working on at the time in my role at a large marketing agency. In 2015, the first edition of this book expanded beyond the trends themselves to feature an inside look at my process for curating trends and detailed instructions on how people could learn to curate their own ideas.

The book is divided into four parts.

Part I is dedicated to sharing my methods of trend curation, which I have usually only taught in depth through private workshops or with my students in class. You will learn the greatest myths of trend prediction, the five essential habits of trend curators, and my own step-by-step approach to curating trends, which I call the Haystack Method.

Part II is the 2019 edition of the Non-Obvious Trend Report, featuring fifteen new ideas that will shape business in the year to come. Each trend features supporting stories and research, as well as an outline for why that trend matters and concrete ideas for how to apply the trend to your own business or career.

Part III is filled with tips on making trends actionable, including a short description of workshops you can host yourself to bring these trends to life in your organization. In this section, I also discuss the importance of anti-trends, and how to use "intersection thinking" to see the patterns between industries and stories.

Finally, Part IV is a candid review of 105 previously-predicted trends from the past eight years, along with an honest assessment and rating for how each one performed over time—all sourced from a combination of conversations with industry insiders and a review panel of trusted colleagues.

You can choose to read this book in the order it's presented, or you can skip back and forth between trends and techniques. Whether you choose to focus on my predictions for 2019 or jump to the last part to see how previous trends rated, this book can be read in short bursts or all at once.

Either way, like Asimov, you don't need to be a speed reader.

Being a speed *understander,* however, is a worthy aspiration. It's my hope that this book will help you get there.

# 01

≋

## THE NORWEGIAN BILLIONAIRE:

# Why Most Trend Predictions Are Spectacularly Useless

—

In 1996, Christian Ringnes was a billionaire with a first-world problem—he was running out of space for his favorite collection.

As one of the richest men in Norway, Ringnes is well known as a flamboyant businessman and art collector whose family started the country's largest brewery more than a hundred years ago. In his hometown of Oslo, Ringnes owns several restaurants and museums, and has donated more than $70 million for the creation of a large sculpture and cultural park, which opened in 2013.

In his heart, Ringnes is a collector. Over the decades, he has built one of the largest private collections of art in the world. Yet his real legacy may come from something far more unique: his lifelong obsession with collecting mini liquor bottles.

This fixation began for Ringnes at the age of seven, when he received an unusual present from his father: a half-empty mini liquor bottle. It was this afterthought of a gift that led him on a path toward amassing what is recognized today as the largest independent mini-bottle collection in the world, with more than 52,000 miniature liquor bottles.

Unfortunately, his decades-long obsession eventually ran into an insurmountable opponent—his late wife, Denise.

As the now-legendary story goes, Denise wasn't too pleased with the disorganization of having all these bottles around the house. After years of frustration, she offered him an ultimatum: either find something to do with all those bottles, or start selling them.

Like any avid collector, Ringnes couldn't bear the thought of selling them, so he created a solution perfectly suited to his wealth and personality.

He commissioned a museum.[1]

## "To Collect Is Human."

Today, his Mini Bottle Gallery, located in downtown Oslo, is one of the world's top unique museum destinations, routinely featured in irreverent travel guides and global lists of must-see Scandinavian tourist attractions. Beyond providing a place for Ringnes to store his collection, the gallery, which has a restaurant, is also a popular venue for private events.

It was here, while in Oslo for a conference dinner that included a tour of the Mini Bottle Gallery, that I got my first personal introduction to Ringnes and his story. "

———

*"I have 52,500 different miniature bottles in a museum in Oslo. They're completely useless... [but] once you get fascinated by something, you want it and then you start collecting".*

— CHRISTIAN RINGNES,
Founder, the Mini Bottle Gallery

———

The museum lived up to its quirky reputation.

The entrance is a bottle-shaped hallway leading to an open lobby with a champagne waterfall. As you move through over 50 unique installations spanning three floors, each features its own composed soundtrack, customized lighting, and even some unique smells. Like all great museum experiences, the rooms of the Mini Bottle Gallery are carefully curated.

The mini bottles are grouped into themes ranging from a brothel-inspired Room of Sin with mini bottles from De Wallen (Amsterdam's red-light district) to a Horror Room featuring liquor bottles with trapped objects such as mice and worms floating inside.

There's a Jungle Room, a Room of Famous Persons, and rooms themed around sports, fruits, birds, circus performers, and the occult. There's even a room featuring the iconic porcelain series of the Delft Blue KLM houses, a series of tiny Dutch rowhouse-shaped liquor bottles given away to passengers by KLM Airlines for more than five decades.

Across all of these rooms, the tour mentions that the gallery typically has more than 12,000 bottles on display. Apart from the scope of the themed rooms, one of the most interesting elements of this story is what the gallery does with the bottles that aren't on display.

## An Accidental Trend Curator

Like any other museum, the Mini Bottle Gallery never uses its entire collection. Instead, they only display about 20 percent of Ringnes's full collection at any one time, carefully keeping the rest in storage. This thoughtful curation adds value to the experience of seeing the bottles.

# Curation is the ultimate method of transforming noise into meaning.

If you consider the amount of media any of us is exposed to on an average day, the quest to find meaning amid the noise is a challenge we all know personally. Navigating information overload requires the same discipline as deciding which bottles to put on display so the ones visitors see can tell a better story.

Without curation, themes would be indecipherable, and the experience would be overwhelming and downright noisy.

It was only on my flight home from Oslo after the event that I realized how important curation had become to my own work.

Just a few months earlier, I'd published the first edition of my *Non-Obvious Trend Report*, inspired by an idea to publish an article from the many ideas I'd collected over the past year, but had never written about. What I was already doing, without realizing it, was collecting intriguing ideas and saving them in perhaps the most disorganized way possible—by writing them down randomly, printing them or ripping them out of magazines, and then stashing everything in a well-worn folder on my desk.

In producing that first report, my ambition had been to describe patterns in the stories I had collected that went beyond the typical obvious observations I was always reading online. My goal was to find and develop insights that others either hadn't yet noticed, and that were not getting the attention they warranted.

To get a different output, sometimes you need a different input.

On that flight home from Norway, I realized that my accidental method for getting different input—collecting ideas for a year and waiting months before analyzing them—could be the very thing that would set my insights apart and make them truly non-obvious.

The *Non-Obvious Trend Report* (my annual list of fifteen trends) was born from this desire to collect underappreciated ideas and connect them to predictions about the future.

## The Underappreciated Side of Data

Now, if you happen to be an analytical person, this process will hardly seem rigorous enough to be believable. How can collecting ideas and waiting possibly be a recipe for developing genuine insights? What about firsthand research, surveys, and focus groups? What about trend panels and using a global army of trend spotters? What about the data?

While it's easy to assume that data means putting numbers into a spreadsheet or referencing some piece of analytics published in a journal—the truth is, data has a forgotten side that has little to do with devising experiments and far more to do with training your powers of observation.

When you think about the discipline that goes into scientific research to produce raw data, research can seem like a task only performed by robotic perfectionists. The truth of scientific research, just like the truth behind many equally complex areas of study, is that experiments aren't the only way to gather data—nor might they even be the most accurate.

Trends, like science, aren't always perfectly measured phenomena that fit neatly into a spreadsheet.

Discovering trends takes a willingness to combine curiosity with observation and add insight to create valuable ideas that you can then test to ensure they are valid.

The one thing that I don't believe describes this method is, ironically, the one term that comes to many people's minds as soon as the art of predicting the future is mentioned: *trend spotting*. The term itself is a symbol of the biggest myths we tend to believe about those who predict or describe the future.

Let's explore these myths and the reasons behind their popularity.

## The 5 Myths of Trend Spotting

Trend spotting is not the key to predicting the future.

Unfortunately, the bias toward trend-spotting has created an unreasonable portrait of the type of person who can put the pieces together and anticipate the future. Consider this infuriatingly common definition for what it takes to become a so-called trend spotter:

———

*To become a trend spotter, someone usually receives extensive education and training in the industry he or she is interested in working for. After receiving a thorough grounding...the trend spotter could start working in company departments which predict trends.*[2]

———

The assumption that you need to be working in "company departments which predict trends" is just plain idiotic—and wrong.

I believe anyone can learn the right habits to become better at curating trends and predicting the future for themselves. You just need to develop the right habits and mindset.

Before we start learning those habits, however, it's important to tackle the biggest myths surrounding trends and explain why they miss the mark so badly.

## Myth #1 TRENDS ARE SPOTTED

The concept of trend spotting suggests that there are trends simply sitting out there in plain sight ready to be observed and cataloged like avian species for birdwatchers. The reality of trends is far different. Trend spotters typically find individual examples or stories. Calling the multitude of things they spot the same thing as trends is like calling ingredients such as eggs, flour, and sugar the same thing as a cake. You can "spot" ingredients, but trends must be curated from these ingredients to have meaning.

## Myth #2 TRENDS ARE PREDICTED BY INDUSTRY EXPERTS

It's tempting to see industry expertise as a prerequisite to being good at curating trends, but there's also a predictable drawback: blind spots. The more you know about a topic, the more difficult it becomes to think outside your expertise and broaden your view. There's no single area of expertise required to curate trends, but psychologists and business authors have long pointed to this "curse of knowledge" as a common challenge to anyone seeking to build any type of expertise.[3] To escape this, you need to learn to engage your greater curiosity about the world beyond what you know, and learn to better empathize with those who don't share your depth of knowledge.

## Myth #3 TRENDS ARE BASED ON "HARD" DATA

When it comes to research, some people rely only on numbers inserted into a spreadsheet as proof, and they conveniently forget that there are two methods to conducting research: the quantitative method and the qualitative method. Qualitative research involves using observation and experience to gather mainly verbal data instead of results from experiments. If you are uncovering the perfect pH balance for shampoo, you certainly will want to use quantitative research. For curating trends, you need a mixture of both, as well as the ability to remember that research data can often be less valuable than excellent observation.

## Myth #4 TRENDS ONLY LAST FOR A SHORT TIME

The line between trends and fads can be tricky. Although some trends seem to spotlight a currently popular story, good ones need to describe something that happens over a span of time. Fads, in comparison, describe an idea that's popular in the short term, but doesn't last. Great trends do reflect a moment in time, but they also describe more than a fleeting moment.

## Myth #5 TRENDS ARE HOPELESSLY BROAD PREDICTIONS

Perhaps no other myth about trends is as fueled by reality as this one. The fact is, we encounter hopelessly broad trend predictions in the media all the time. Therefore, the problem comes in concluding that trends should be broad and all-encompassing. Good trends tend to be more of the opposite: they define something that's concrete and distinct, without being limiting.

For example, someone once asked me after an event if I had considered the rise of 3D printing as a trend. I replied that I had not, but the maker movement well-described trend  focusing on the human desire to be a creator and make something (which 3D printing certainly enables)—was a worthwhile trend. The point was, a trend is never a description of something that just exists—like 3D printing.

Instead, a trend must describe what people do, or believe as a result. Once you know that the maker movement describes the human desire to make something, for example, you can think about how to offer that type of fulfillment to your customers in how they interact with you. IKEA has benefitted from this trend for years,because people often feel a disproportionate emotional connection to furniture they have to work to assemble themselves. Psychologist have dubbed this the "IKEA effect."

Now that I've shared the most common myths about trend predictions, let's consider why so many trend predictions involve self-indulgent guesswork or lazy thinking. What, exactly, makes them so useless?

To answer this question, let me tell you a little story.

## Why Most Trend Predictions Are Useless

A few years ago, I picked up the year-end edition of *Entrepreneur* magazine, which promised to illuminate trends to watch in the coming year. Earlier that same week, a special double issue of *BusinessWeek* magazine had arrived in the mail, making a similar promise.

It was the end of the year, and the trend season was in full swing.

Similar to New Year's resolutions to lose weight, trend forecasting is popular in December (one of the reasons each annual edition of *Non-Obvious* is usually published in December, as well). Unfortunately, the side effect of this annual media ritual is an abundance of lazy predictions and vague declarations.

For entertainment, I collect these year-end trend forecasts and keep them as standing memorials to the volume of pitiful predictions that bombard us as we look to the year ahead.

Here are a few of the worst-offending, most obvious "trends" I've seen. For the sake of kindness, I haven't tagged them with sources or authors:

- ✓ "It's all about the visuals."
- ✓ "Streaming video content."
- ✓ "The Year of Drones has arrived. Really."
- ✓ "Content marketing will continue to be the place to be."
- ✓ "Fantasy sports"

✓    "Virtual reality"

✓    "Change will be led by smart-home technology."

Virtual Reality? Really?

Not to ruin the suspense, but I don't believe any of these should be described as trends. Some are just random buzzwords, or the names of platforms. Others are hopelessly broad, useless—and, yes, obvious.

None of them fit my trend definition of a unique idea describing the accelerating present.

Meanwhile, all of us as media consumers read these predictions with varying levels of skepticism. To better understand why, let's review the four main reasons most trend predictions fail the believability test.

## Reason #1 NO OBJECTIVITY

If you sell drones for racing, declaring 2019 the "Year of Racing Drones" is clearly self-serving. Of course, most bias isn't this easy to spot, and objectivity is notoriously difficult for any of us. Our biases are based on our expertise and the world we know. This is particularly true in business, where we sometimes need to believe in an industry or brand in order to succeed. The problem is that losing objectivity usually leads to wishful thinking. Just because we want something to be a trend doesn't make it one.

## Reason #2 NO INSIGHT

Trends need to do more than repeat common knowledge. For example, saying that "more people will buy upgraded smartphones this year" is obvious—and useless, because it lacks insight. The biggest reason that most trend predictions share these types of obvious ideas is because it's easier to do so. Lazy thinking is always easier than offering an informed and insightful point of view.

## Great trends are never obvious declarations of facts that most people already know.

Instead, they share new ideas in insightful ways while also describing the accelerating present.

### Reason #3  NO PROOF

Sharing a trend without specific examples is like declaring yourself a musician by simply buying a guitar. Unfortunately, many trend predictions coast in a similar way on the power of a single story or example. Exceptional examples and stories are powerful components of illustrating why a trend matters. They are necessary elements of proving a trend. Finding just one example and declaring something a trend without more evidence is usually a sign that a so-called trend is based on little more than guesswork.

### Reason #4  NO APPLICATION

Perhaps the most common area where many trend predictions fall short is in the discussion of how to apply them. It's not enough to think about trends in the context of describing them. The best trend forecasts go further than just describing something that's happening. They also share insights on what it means, and what you can or should do differently as a result of the trend. In other words, trends should be actionable.

## How to Think Differently About Trends

Now that we have examined the many myths and reasons for failure, let's focus on one of the key ingredients that makes a non-obvious trend:

# Non-obvious trends focus on the intersection of multiple industries, behaviors, and beliefs.

Over the next two chapters, you'll learn a step-by-step technique that can help you think differently about trends and escape the trap of lazy thinking that leads to obvious ideas. In doing so, you'll immediately find yourself having more insights than your peers around you, and seeing the connections between industries and stories in a way that most people don't.

The key to the method you're about to learn is a willingness to go outside your usual sources of information and open your mind to unconventional ways of thinking and brainstorming. As a result, you'll become better at spotting the connections between the things you read, what you see, and the conversations you have.

There's magic to be found in thinking like a trend curator. Let's talk about how to find it.

02
≋

# THE CURATOR'S MINDSET:

# Learning the 5 Essential Habits of Trend Curators

---

*"You never learn anything by listening to yourself speak."*
— SIR RICHARD BRANSON, entrepreneur and
Founder of the Virgin Group

Across decades of research with grade-school students, interviewing professional athletes, and studying business leaders, renowned Stanford psychology professor Carol Dweck has developed an elegant way to describe why some people manage to exceed their potential while others peak early or never achieve the same success.[1]

According to Dweck, it all depends on your mindset.

People with *fixed mindsets* believe that their skills and abilities are set. They see themselves as either being good at something or not good at something, and therefore tend to focus their efforts on tasks and in careers where they feel they have a natural ability.

People with *growth mindsets* believe that success and achievement are the result of hard work and determination. They see their own (and others') true potential as something to be defined through effort. As a result, they thrive on challenges and often have a passion for learning.

When it came to setbacks, people with a growth mindset are more likely to treat failure "like a parking ticket instead of a car wreck."[2] They're more resilient, have more self-confidence, are less focused on getting revenge for any perceived wrong, and tend to be happier.

Despite the many benefits of adopting a growth mindset, the sad reality is that as soon as children become able to evaluate themselves, some of them become afraid of challenges and failure. They become afraid of not being smart. This is a tragedy, because it's a limitation that they will continue to impose upon themselves into adulthood, sometimes without realizing it.

—

*I have studied thousands of people...and it's breathtaking how many reject an opportunity to learn.*
— CAROL DWECK (from *Mindset*)

—

The first and most important key to becoming a better collector of ideas and thinking more innovatively is the deceptively simple decision not to limit yourself.

What if you were capable of more than just a narrowly-defined list of things you believe you are naturally good at? Learning to curate ideas into trends, like playing an instrument or becoming more observant, is a skill that's within your grasp to learn and practice—but only if you venture outside of your mental comfort zone and adopt a growth mindset.

Does this mean anyone can transform themselves into a professional flamenco guitarist or a full-time trend forecaster with enough practice? Not necessarily. Aptitude and natural talent still play an important part in succeeding at anything on a professional level.

Yet the past decade of my work with thousands of executives and students at all levels of their careers has proven to me that the skills required for trend curation can be learned and practiced, just as the growth mindset can be taught and embraced. When you learn these skills and combine them with the right mindset, they can inform your own view of the world and power your own future success.

After understanding your mindset, the next step on your path to predicting the future is learning five core habits. To start learning them, let me share a story of the most famous art collector most people had never heard of—until he passed away.

## The World's Most Unknown Art Collector

By the time eighty-nine-year-old Herbert Vogel died in 2012, the retired New York City postal worker had quietly amassed one of the greatest collections of modern art in the world.

Vogel and his wife, Dorothy, were already local legends in the world of art when Herbert passed away. News stories soon after his death told the story of five large moving vans showing up at the Vogels' rent-controlled, one-bedroom Manhattan apartment to pick up more than five thousand pieces of art. The Vogel Collection, built over decades, was offered a permanent home as part of the archives and collection at the National Gallery of Art in Washington, D.C.

The Vogels had always said the only thing they did was buy and collect art they loved.[3]

This passion often led them to find new young artists to support before the rest of the world discovered them. The Vogels ultimately became more than collectors. They were tastemakers, and their fabled collection, featuring the work of hundreds of artists, including pop artist Roy Lichtenstein and post-minimalist Richard Tuttle, was the envy of museums and other private collectors around the world.

The same qualities that drive art patrons like the Vogels to follow their instincts and collect beautiful things are the ones that make great curators of any kind. Museums and the art world are a fitting place to start when learning how to be a curator.

## The Rise of "Curationism"

Museum curators organize collections into themes that tell stories. Whether they're quirky, like the ones told in the Mini Bottle Gallery, or an expansive exhibit covering eighteenth-century pastel portraits at the Metropolitan Museum of Art, the goal of curation is always to take individual items and examples and weave them together into a narrative.

# Curators add meaning to isolated beautiful things.

I'm inspired by curators—and I'm clearly not alone. The business world has turned toward the longtime practice of curation with such growing frequency that even artists and art critics have noticed.

In 2014, art critic and writer David Balzer published a book with the brilliant title *Curationism* (a play on "creationism") to examine how "curating took over the art world and everything else." His book explores the evolution of the curator as the imparter of value, and what the future of curation looks like when so many from outside the art world (or without the usual training) start to use the principles of the field for their own purposes.

Though the book is an academic read intended mainly curatorial circles, Balzer cautions that this rise in curationism could inspire a "constant cycle of grasping and display" in which we never take the time to understand what the individual pieces mean.

In other words, curation is only valuable if you follow the act of collecting, with sufficient moments of quiet contemplation to truly understand what it all means.

This combination of collection and contemplation is central to the ability to effectively curate ideas and learn to predict the future.

## The 5 Habits of Trend Curators

I realize that calling yourself a "curator" of anything can seem like a stretch.

*Curator* is a job title often applied to someone with years of expertise in the study of history or the evolution of a particular industry, but curators today can come from all types of backgrounds.

Some focus on art and design, while others may look at history or anthropology. Some have professional training and degrees, while others are driven by passion alone, like Herbert and Dorothy Vogel. No matter what their background, every one of them exhibits the same types of habits that help them to become masters at adding meaning to collected items.

Curation doesn't require you to be an expert, a researcher, or an academic. Learning these five habits will help you put the power of curation to work to help you discover better ideas and use them to develop your own observations about the rapidly accelerating present.

## THE 5 HABITS OF TREND CURATORS

01 **Be Curious**
Always asking why, investing in learning, and improving knowledge by investigating and asking questions.

02 **Be Observant**
Learning to notice the small details in stories and life that others may ignore or fail to recognize as significant.

03 **Be Fickle**
Moving from one idea to the next without becoming fixated or overanalyzing each idea in the moment.

04 **Be Thoughtful**
Taking time to develop a meaningful point of view and consider alternative viewpoints without bias.

05 **Be Elegant**
Seeking beautiful ways to describe ideas that bring together disparate concepts in a simple and understandable way.

## How to Be Curious

Ask questions about how things work, and approach unfamiliar situations and/or topics with a sense of wonder.

Bjarni Herjulfsson could have been one of the most famous explorers in the history of the world.

Instead, his life has become a cautionary tale about the historic consequences of a lack of curiosity. In the year A.D. 986, he set off on a voyage from Norway with a crew to find Greenland. Blown off course by a storm, his ship became the first European vessel in recorded history to see North America.

Despite the pleas of his crew to stop and explore, Herjulfsson refused, and guided his ship back on course to eventually find Greenland. Years later, he told this tale to a friend named Leif Erikson, who became inspired, purchased Herjulfsson's ship, and took the journey for himself. Erikson is now widely remembered as the first European to land in North America—nearly five hundred years before Christopher Columbus landed in the Bahamas and "discovered" America.[4]

Herjulfsson, on the other hand, has been mostly forgotten, and his story illustrates exactly why curiosity matters: it's a prerequisite to discovery. Humans are naturally curious. The challenge is to continually find ways to allow yourself to explore your curiosity without it becoming an ongoing distraction.

When noted chef and food pioneer Ferran Adrià was once asked what he likes to have for breakfast, his reply was simple: "I like to eat a different fruit every day of the month." Imagine if you could do that with ideas. Part of being curious is wanting to consume stories, ideas, and experiences to earn greater knowledge of the world, even if that knowledge doesn't seem immediately useful.

## 3 Ways to Be More Curious Today

→ **Consume "brainful media."** Sadly, we are surrounded with brainless media, including reality shows featuring unlikeable people doing unlikeable things (sometimes on islands, sometimes in our backyards). While they can be addictively entertaining, brainless media encourages vegetation instead of curiosity. Curiosity is fueled by consuming media that makes you think, such as a short documentary film or an inspirational seventeen-minute talk from TED.com.

→ **Empathize with magazines.** One of my favorite ways to see the world through someone else's eyes is buying niche magazines to learn about unfamiliar topics. Simply walking into the magazine section of a bookstore offers plenty of options. For example, *Modern Farmer, Model Railroader,* and *House Beautiful* are three vastly different magazines. Flipping through the stories, advertisements, and imagery in each will do more to take you outside of your own world than almost any other quick-and-easy ten-minute activity.

→ **Ask bigger questions.** A few years ago, I was invited to deliver a talk at an event for the home interior paint industry. It's an industry I know very little about, so it was tempting to show up, deliver my keynote, and then leave. Instead, I stayed, and walked around the exhibit hall asking questions. In less than thirty minutes I learned about how paint is mixed and which additives are typically used. I heard about the industry debate between all-plastic cans versus steel, and the rise of computerized color-matching systems. Thanks to that small investment of time on my part, the talk I gave was far more relevant.

## Be Curious: What to Read

→ **Historical fiction.** Every great piece of historical fiction was inspired by a writer who found a story from the past that was worth sharing with the world. By reading books such as Erik Larson's *The Devil in the White City* (about murder at the 1893 Chicago World's Fair) or Simon Winchester's *The Professor and the Madman* (about the creation of the Oxford English Dictionary), you can give yourself a wonderful gateway to start thinking about the world in unexpected ways.

→ **Curated compilations.** There are many books that bring together real-life stories or essays to help you think about new and interesting topics. A collection of shorter topics and stories is sometimes far easier to use for engaging your curiosity than a longer book. For example, the *This Will Make You Smarter* series edited by John Brockman, or any book by *You Are Not So Smart* podcast host and psychology buff David McRaney is a perfect, bite-sized way to inspire your curiosity without requiring a huge time investment.

## How to Be Observant

# Pay attention to the world, and train yourself to notice the details that others miss.

I was invited not long ago to a formal dinner connected to an event in New York. The venue was a beautiful restaurant, and after our meal, the waiter came around to take our dessert orders from one of two set menu options. Less than ten minutes later, a team of six people, not including our waiter, came and delivered all the desserts to our large table of thirty people, getting each order perfectly right without saying a word to anyone.

As they delivered the desserts, I started to wonder how that one waiter who took our orders had managed to relay all those choices perfectly to a team of six in such a short time.

By observing the wait staff for a moment, I quickly figured out the simple trick our head waiter had used. If you had picked dessert option one, he had placed a dessert spoon on the table above your plate. If you picked option two, he placed the spoon to the right of your plate.

When the team of food runners came to the table, all they needed was the "code" to decipher the spoon positioning and they could deliver the desserts to the right people with ease and accuracy.

Perhaps you already knew that spoon trick, but imagine if you didn't. Simply observing it gives you a glimpse into the little processes that we rarely pay attention to that keep the world moving along. Now, you might be thinking, "who cares how waiters deliver dessert"?

Of course, understanding how dessert is delivered will hardly change your life, but imagine that moment multiplied out to a thousand different situations. Observation of details can lead to understanding something insignificant, but it can also lead to your next big business idea.

**VISIT THE NON-OBVIOUS RESOURCES CENTER ONLINE TO:**

Watch me share this story live in a video!

Learning to be more observant isn't just about seeing the big things. Instead, it's about training yourself to pay more attention to the little things. What can you see about a situation that other people miss? What can the details you're noticing teach you about people, processes, and companies that you didn't know before?

This is the power of making observation a habit.

## 3 Ways to Be More Observant

→ **Explain the world to children.** If you're fortunate to have children in your life, one of the best ways to hone your skills of observation is to explain the world around you to them. For example, when one of my kids asked me recently why construction vehicles and traffic signs are orange, but cars that most people drive aren't, it forced me to think about something I would otherwise have easily ignored, even if I didn't have the perfect answer to the question.[5]

→ **Watch processes in action.** Many interactions in life, from how the coffee shop makes your latte to who gets an upgrade on a flight, are controlled by a scripted process. the next time you engage with one of these processes, pay attention to the details. What does a typical interaction look like? How does it differ from person to person? Learning not to ignore these common processes in everyday life is great training for being more observational in situations where it really matters.

→ **Don't be observationally lazy.** Aside from being really good at capturing our attention, our devices can keep us from seeing the world around us. Rather than switching to autopilot to navigate daily tasks, like walking down the street or buying groceries while trying to avoid any and all eye contact, train yourself to put your phone down, see the world, and maybe even have a conversation.

## Be Observant: What to Read

→ *What Every Body Is Saying,* **by Joe Navarro.** If you need to learn the art of interpreting body language or detecting lies, a former FBI agent like Joe Navarro is probably the ideal teacher. In this book, Navarro shares some of his best lessons on how to spot "tells" in body language and use them to interpret human behavior. His work on situational awareness is a perfect supporting book to teach you how to be more observant.

## How to Be Fickle

# Resist the urge to fully understand or analyze ideas in the moment you save them.

People often cast the idea of being fickle as a bad thing. When we hear the word, we tend to think of all the negative situations in which we abandon people or ideas too quickly, but there is an upside to learning how to be purposefully fickle.

On the surface, this may seem counterintuitive. After all, why wouldn't you take the time to analyze a great idea and develop a point of view? There are certainly many situations when you do this already.

But you probably never do the opposite. A key element of becoming an idea curator is saving ideas for later digestion. As you will see in Chapter 3, where I share my specific methods for curating trends, this concept of saving an idea so I can return to it later when it may have more value is a fundamental part of the method I use for trend curation.

Often, the connection between ideas will only come from the discipline of setting them aside and choosing to analyze them later, when you have more stories and added perspective to see the connections. Being fickle isn't about avoiding thought— it's about freeing yourself from the pressure to recognize connections immediately, and making it easier to come back to an idea later for analysis.

## 3 Ways to Be More Fickle

→ **Save ideas offline.** There are countless digital productivity tools, such as Evernote, but they can be hard to manage and navigate when you need them. Instead, I routinely print articles, rip stories out of magazines, and put them all into a single trend folder that sits on my desk. Saving ideas offline allows me to physically spread them out later to analyze more easily.

→ **Use a timer.** To avoid the temptation to overanalyze an idea in the moment, set a timer as a reminder to go back. It will help you to clear your mind in the interim. The other benefit of using a timer is that it can force you to evaluate things more quickly, and just focus on the big picture.

→ **Take notes with a sharpie.** I mark the many articles and stories I find throughout the year with a few words to remind me of the theme of the article or story. I use a Sharpie marker, because the thicker lettering stands out and subtly encourages me to write less. This same trick can help you to make only the most useful observations in the moment, and save any others for later.

## Be Fickle: What to Read

→ *The Laws of Simplicity,* **by John Maeda.** Maeda is a master of design and technology, and his advice has guided many companies and entrepreneurs toward building more amazing products. In this short book, he shares some essential advice for learning to see the world like a designer and how to reduce the noise in order to see and think more clearly.

→ *How to Make Sense of Any Mess,* **by Abby Covert.** I have read many books on the art of organizing information, but this one, with its smart reasoning and simplified approach, is one of my favorites. The author is an information architect who goes by the pseudonym "Abby the IA." She shares methods based on more than ten years of teaching experience that are worth adopting and sharing with your entire team.

## How to Be Thoughtful

# Take the time to reflect on a point of view before sharing it in a considered way.

In 2014, after ten years of writing my business and marketing blog, I decided to stop allowing comments. For some readers, this seemed counter to one of the fundamental principles of blogging, which is to create dialogue.

The reason I stopped was simple. I had noticed a steady decline in the quality of the comments. What was once a robust discussion involving thoughtfully-worded responses had devolved into a combination of thumbs-up-style comments and spam.

Thanks to anonymous commenting and the ease of sharing knee-jerk responses, comments had lost their thoughtfulness— and people were starting to notice. Thus, I turned off the comments.

The web is filled with this type of "conversation": angry, biased, half-thought-out responses to articles, people, or media. Being thoughtful is harder to do when the priority is to share a response in real time. Yet people who are routinely thoughtful are the ones who gain and keep respect. They add value instead of noise... and you can be one of them.

# 3 Ways to Be More Thoughtful

→ **Wait a moment.** The beauty and challenge of the Internet is that it occurs in real time. It's easy to think that if you can't be the first person to comment on something, your thoughts are too late. That's rarely true. "Real time" shouldn't mean sharing a comment off the top of your head within seconds. Take your time before writing a comment or sharing a link, and consider what you're about to say—and whether you'd still be proud to say it twenty-four hours from now.

→ **Write, and then rewrite.** When it comes to being thoughtful with writing, the most talented writers take time to rewrite their thinking instead of sharing the first thing they write down. The process of rewriting can seem like a big-time commitment, but the fastest form of writing is dialogue—so, when in doubt, write it like you would say it.

→ **Embrace the pauses.** As a speaker, becoming comfortable with silence took me years to master. It's not an easy thing to do. Yet when you can use pauses effectively, you can emphasize the things you really want people to hear, and give yourself time to craft the perfect thing to say.

# Be Thoughtful: What to Read

→ *Brain Pickings,* **by Maria Popova.** Popova describes herself as an "interestingness hunter-gatherer," and she has one of the most popular independently-run blogs in the world. Every week, she publishes articles combining lessons from literature, art, and history on wide-ranging topics like creative leadership and the gift of friendship. The way she presents her thoughts is a perfect aspirational example of how to publish something thoughtful week after week.

# How to Be Elegant

Describe concepts in more beautiful, deliberate, and simple ways.

Jeff Karp is a scientist inspired by elegance . . . and jellyfish.

As an associate professor at Harvard Medical School, Karp's research focuses on using bio-inspiration—inspiration from nature—to develop new solutions for all types of medical challenges. His eponymous Karp Lab has developed innovations such as a device inspired by jellyfish tentacles to capture circulating tumor cells in cancer patients as well as better surgical staples inspired by porcupine quills.

Nature is filled with elegant solutions, from the way forest fires spread the seeds of certain plants to the way termites build porous structures with built-in heating and cooling.

I believe it's this idea of simplicity that's fundamental to developing elegant ideas. As Albert Einstein famously said, "Make things as simple as possible, but not simpler."

A good example of things described beautifully can be found in what talented poets do. Great poetry has simplicity, emotion, and beauty, because superfluous words are edited out of the verse. Poets are masters of elegance; they obsess over language, and understand that less can mean more.

You don't need to become a poet overnight, but some of these principles can help you get better at creating more elegant descriptions of your own ideas. To illustrate how, here's the process I used to name my trends in previous reports.

## 3 Ways to Think More Elegantly

→ **Start with the obvious.** One of the most popular trends from my 2015 *Non-Obvious Trend Report* was something I called "Selfie Confidence." The name was a play on *self-confidence*, and was written to force people to see something they were already familiar with in a new way. Selfies are often criticized as demonstrations of narcissism, but the trend counterintuitively suggested the idea that selfies might contribute to helping people to grow their self-esteem.

→ **Keep it short.** One thing you'll notice if you look back on any of the previous years' trends (including this year) is that the title for most trends is no longer than two words. Elegance often goes hand in hand with simplicity, and this usually means using as few words as possible.

→ **Use poetic principles.** Poets use metaphors and imagery instead of obvious language. In Chapter 3, you'll get an inside look at how I use techniques borrowed from poetry as part of the naming process I use every year for trends. A quick scan of past trends will also illustrate how I've used these principles to describe trends like "Preserved Past" or "Lovable Unperfec-tion."

## Be Elegant: What to Read

→ *Einstein's Dreams,* **by Alan Lightman.** This book, writ-ten by an MIT physicist and one of my favorites, creatively imagines what Einstein's dreams must have been like, and explores them in a beautiful way through short chapters with interesting assumptions about time and space. This is not a book of poetry, but it'll introduce you to the power of poetic writing while offering the most elegant description of the nature of time that you'll ever read.

→ **Any book by Dr. Seuss.** This may seem like an odd sugges-tion, but Dr. Seuss had a great talent for sharing big ideas with simplicity and elegance. You probably already know some of his brilliance: "Today you are you, that is truer than true. There is no one alive who is youer than you." Reading his work, though, will remind you of the power of finding just the right words while inspiring you to do more with less.

## Why These 5 Habits?

Do these five habits for learning the art of idea curation seem a bit surprising? The fact is, the process of how I came to these five involved an exercise in curation, as well.

Over the past several years, I've read interviews with professional art curators about how they learned their craft. I have bought more than a dozen books written by trend forecasters, futurists, and innovators. I have interviewed dozens of top business leaders and authors. I have carefully studied my own behavior. I have tested the effectiveness and resonance of these habits by teaching them to my students at Georgetown University and professionals in private workshops.

Ultimately, I selected the five habits presented here because they were the most helpful, descriptive, easy to learn, and effective once you learn to put them into action.

As a recap before we get started with a step-by-step approach to curating trends, let's do a review:

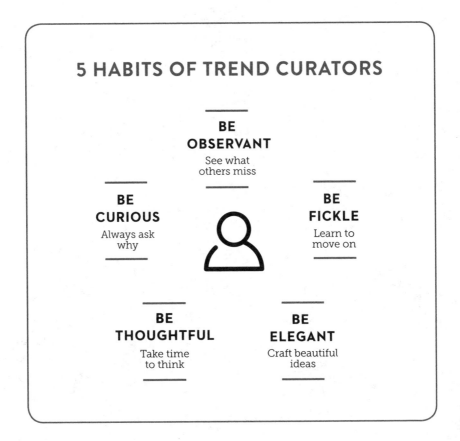

# 5 HABITS OF TREND CURATORS

**BE OBSERVANT**
See what others miss

**BE CURIOUS**
Always ask why

**BE FICKLE**
Learn to move on

**BE THOUGHTFUL**
Take time to think

**BE ELEGANT**
Craft beautiful ideas

## 03

≡

THE HAYSTACK METHOD:

# How to Curate Trends for Fun and Profit

——

*"The most reliable way to anticipate the future
is to understand the present."*
— JOHN NAISBITT, Futurist and Author of *Megatrends*

In 1982, a book called *Megatrends* changed the way
governments, businesses, and people thought about the future.

Author John Naisbitt was one of the first to predict our evolution
from an industrial society to an information society, and he did
so more than a decade before the advent of the Internet. He also
predicted the shift from hierarchies to networks, and the rise of the
global economy.

Despite the book's unapologetic American-style optimism, most
of the ten major shifts described in *Megatrends* were so far ahead
of their time that when it was first released one reviewer glowingly
described it as "the next best thing to a crystal ball." With more than
14 million copies sold worldwide, it's still the single bestselling book
about the future published in the last forty years.

For his part, Naisbitt believed deeply in the power of observation to understand the present before trying to predict the future (as the opening quote to this chapter illustrates). In interviews, friends and family often described Naisbitt as having a "boundless curiosity about people, cultures, and organizations," even noting that he had a habit of scanning "hundreds of newspapers and magazines, from *Scientific American* to *Tricycle*, a Buddhism magazine" in search of new ideas.[1]

John Naisbitt was, and still is (at a spry ninety years old), a collector of ideas. For years, his ideology has inspired me to think about the world with a similarly broad lens, and has helped me to develop the process I use for my own trend work, which I call the Haystack Method.

## Inside the Haystack Method

It's tempting to describe the art of finding trends with the cliché of finding a "needle in a haystack." This common visual reference brings to mind the myth of trend spotting that I discounted in Chapter 1. Uncovering trends hardly ever involves them sitting in plain sight, just waiting for us to spot them.

The Haystack Method is a process in which you start with a gathering stories and ideas (the hay), then use them to define a trend (the needle).

In this method, the work comes from assembling the information and curating it into groupings that make sense. The needle is the insight you apply to this collection of information in order to describe what it means—and to curate information and stories into a definable trend.

While the above describes the method with metaphors, to learn how to do it for yourself, we need to go deeper...starting with the story of why I created the Haystack Method in the first place.

## Why I Started Curating Ideas

The Haystack Method was born out of frustration.

In 2004, I was part of a team that was starting one of the first social-media-focused practices within a large marketing agency. The idea was that we would help big companies figure out how to use this new platform as a part of their marketing efforts.

The aim of our team was to help brands work with influential bloggers, because in 2004 (prior to Facebook and Twitter), "social media" mainly referred to blogging. There was only one problem with this well-intentioned plan—none of us knew very much about blogging.

So, we did the only thing that seemed logical to do: each of us started blogging.

In June of that year, I started my "Influential Marketing Blog" with the aim of writing about marketing, public relations, and advertising strategy. My first post was on the dull topic of optimal screen size for web designers. Within a few days, I ran into my first challenge: I had no plan for what to write about next.

How was I going to keep this hastily-created blog current with new ideas and stories, when I already had a full-time day job that wasn't meant to involve spending time writing a blog? I realized I had to become more disciplined about how I collected ideas.

At first, I focused on finding ideas for blog posts, usually collected by scribbling them into a notebook or emailing them to myself. Then I decided to include ideas from the daily brainstorming meetings I attended. Pretty soon, I expanded to saving quotes from books and ripping pages out of magazines.

Those first four years of blogging helped me land my first book deal with McGraw-Hill. Several years later, in 2011, the desire to write a blog post about trends based upon ideas I had collected over the years led me to publish the first edition of my *Non-Obvious Trend Report*.[2]

My point in sharing this story is to illustrate how the pressure to find enough ideas worth writing about consistently on my blog helped me to get better at saving and sharing ideas that people cared about. Blogging helped me become a collector of ideas, which is the perfect introduction to the first step in the Haystack Method.

# The Haystack Method

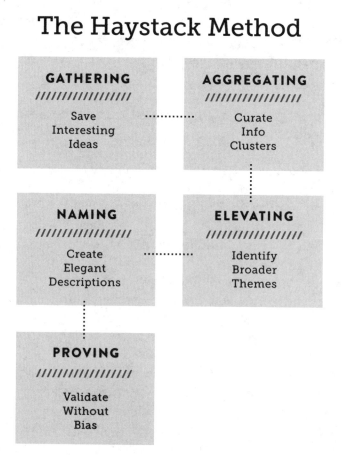

# Gathering is the disciplined act of collecting stories and ideas from reading, listening, and speaking to different sources.

Photo: Sources used for gathering information.

Do you read the same sources of media religiously every day? Or do you skim social media occasionally, and sometimes click on the links your connections share to continue reading? Regardless of your media diet, chances are you encounter plenty of interesting stories or ideas. The real question is: do you have a useful method for saving them? The key to gathering ideas is making a habit of saving interesting things in a way that allows you to find and explore them later.

My method involves always carrying a small passport-sized notebook in my pocket, and keeping a folder on my desk to save media clippings and printouts. By the time you read these words, that folder on my desk will have changed color, and will probably already be labeled "2020 Trends." In my process, I start the clock for my annual *Non-Obvious Trend Report* every January and complete it each December (see Part II of this book). Thanks to this deliverable, I have a clear starting and ending point for each new round of ideas I collect.

You don't need to follow as rigid a calendar timetable as I do, but it is valuable to set a specific time for yourself to review and reflect upon what you have gathered in order to uncover the bigger insights (a point we will explore in subsequent steps).

## IDEA SOURCES: WHERE TO GATHER IDEAS

✓ Personal conversations at events or meetings
✓ Listening to live speakers or TED Talks
✓ Entertainment
✓ Books
✓ Museums
✓ Magazines and newspapers
✓ Travel!

This list of sources might seem, well, obvious. It's rarely the sources of information themselves that will lead you toward a perfectly packaged idea or trend. Rather, mastering the art of gathering valuable ideas means training yourself to uncover interesting ideas across multiple sources, and becoming diligent about collecting them. One thing that will help is learning to take better notes. See the chart on the following page for some tips on how to do it.

# *THE*
# NON OBV/OUS
## GUIDE TO NOTE TAKING

Don't lose your best ideas.
Learn to curate them.

___

## 3 Essentials of Idea Curation

Focus on memorable insights
Insert noteboxes for easier skimming
Think in terms of intersections

___

## Example Noteboxes
### (Or Use Your Own)

To organize your notes, draw one of these noteboxes with
a key phrase inside it as a visual reminder.

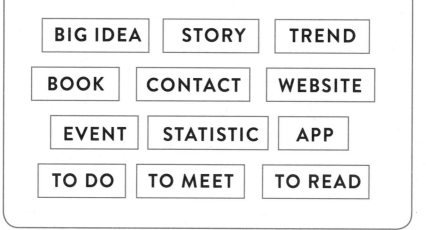

| | | |
|---|---|---|
| BIG IDEA | STORY | TREND |
| BOOK | CONTACT | WEBSITE |
| EVENT | STATISTIC | APP |
| TO DO | TO MEET | TO READ |

# Tips & Tricks: How to Gather Ideas

→ **Start a folder.** A folder on my desk stores handwritten ideas I find interesting, articles ripped out of magazines and newspapers, printouts of articles from the Internet, brochures from conferences, and the occasional odd object (like a giveaway from a conference or a brochure received in the mail). This folder lets me store things in a central and highly visible way. You might choose to create your own folder digitally or with paper. Either way, the important thing is to have a centralized place where you can save ideas for later digestion.

→ **Always summarize.** When you're collecting ideas on a longer time scale (i.e., over the course of an entire year), it's easy to forget why a story seemed significant in the first place. To help yourself remember, get into the habit of highlighting a few sentences or writing down a few notes about your thoughts on the idea (usually using a Sharpie pen—which is also suggested in Chapter 2). Later, when you're going through your gathered ideas, these notes will be useful in recalling what originally sparked your interest.

→ **Seek concepts, not conclusions.** As we learned in Chapter 2, a key habit of good curating is the ability to be fickle. In practice, this means not getting too hung up on the need to quantify or understand every idea you save in the moment. Many times, the best thing you can do is to gather something, save it, and then move on to your next task. Perspective comes from taking time and having patience.

*Step 2* **AGGREGATING**

# Aggregating involves taking individual ideas and grouping them together to uncover bigger themes.

Photo: Example of aggregating possible trend topics.

After gathering ideas, the next step is to combine the early results of your observation and curiosity with some insights about how ideas might fit together. Using a series of questions can help you do that. Here are a few of my favorites.

At this stage, a common trap is to start grouping all the stories from one industry together. Resist the temptation to do that, and try aggregating based on insights and human motivations instead.

In this second step, it's not important to come up with a fancy name for your ideas, or even to do extensive research around any one them. Instead, the aim is to start building small clusters of ideas that bring together stories into meaningful groupings.

## Tips & Tricks: How to Aggregate Ideas

→ **Focus on human needs.** Sometimes, focusing on a bigger underlying human emotion can help you see the basis of the idea and why it matters. For example, the basic human need for belonging fuels many of the activities people engage in online, from posting social comments to joining online communities. The key is to connect the ideas you have gathered with the basic human needs behind them.

→ **Recognize the obvious.** Along the path to uncovering "non-obvious" insights, there's some value in recognizing (and even embracing) the obvious. In a grouping exercise, for example, you can often use the obvious ideas (like multiple stories about new wearable technology products) as a way of bringing things together; later, you can work on discovering the non-obvious insights between them.

→ **Follow your intuition.** When you train yourself to be more observant, you might also find that you start to develop a feeling for stories that are interesting or somehow feel significant—even though you may not be able to describe why. Embrace that intuition, and save the story. In later phases of the Haystack Method, you can try to connect this story to a broader idea.

## *Step 3* ELEVATING

# Elevating involves finding the underlying themes that connect groups of ideas to describe a single, bigger concept.

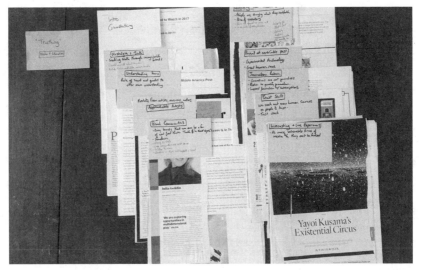

Photo: Examples of groups of stories elevated together for a trend.

If you've gone through gathering and aggregating ideas, this is the point at which you'll probably confront the same problem I do every year: there are too many possibilities!

When I go through my annual exercise of curating trends, the first time I aggregate my ideas into clusters, it usually yields between seventy and a hundred possible trend topics. That's far too many, and a clear sign that there's more work to be done.

How do you know what to focus on in order to build out into a trend? The goal in this third step is to try and take a broader view, and connect your smaller clusters of ideas together into larger ones that describe even bigger and potentially more powerful ideas. More than any other step, this is where the breakthroughs and inspiration usually come.

---

### ELEVATING QUESTIONS:
### HOW TO THINK BIGGER ABOUT IDEAS

✓ What interests me most about these ideas?

✓ What elements could I have missed earlier?

✓ What is the broader theme?

✓ How can I link multiple industries?

✓ Where is the connection between ideas?

---

This third step can be the most challenging phase of the Haystack Method, because the process of combining ideas can also lead you to unintentionally make them too broad (and, by definition, too obvious). Your aim in this step, therefore, should be to elevate an idea to make it bigger and more encompassing of multiple stories, without losing its uniqueness.

For example, when I was producing my *2014 Non-Obvious Trend Report* I, came across an interesting healthcare startup called GoodRx, which had a tool to help people find the best price for medications. It was simple, useful, and the perfect example of an evolving shift toward empowering patients in healthcare, which I wrote about in my earlier book, *ePatient 2015*.

At the same time, I was seeing retail stores like Macy's investing heavily in creating apps to improve their in-store shopping experience; and a number of fashion services like Rent the Runway, designed to help people save time and money while shopping.

On the surface, a tool for saving on prescriptions, an app for a department store, and an optimized tool for renting dresses don't seem to have much in common. I had, therefore, initially grouped them separately. While elevating trends, though, I realized that they all were all characterized by the underlying intent of helping to optimize a shopping experience in some way.

I grouped them together as examples of a shared trend, which I called Shoptimization. The trend described how technology was helping consumers optimize the process of buying everything from home goods and fashion to medical prescriptions.

In the next step, I'll discuss techniques for naming trends (including how I named Shoptimization but for now, my point in sharing this example is to illustrate how elevation can help you make connections across industries and ideas that may have initially seemed disconnected and meant to fall into different groups.

The difference between aggregating ideas and elevating them may seem slight, but there are times when I manage to do both at the same time, since the act of aggregating stories can help to broaden my conclusions about them.

In the Haystack Method, I choose to present these steps separately, because most of the time, they do end up as distinct efforts. With practice, though, you may get better at condensing these two steps together.

# Tips & Tricks: How to Elevate Your Ideas

→ **Use words to elevate.** When you have groups of ideas, sometimes boiling them down to a couple of words can help you see the common themes between them. When I was collecting ideas related to entrepreneurship, for example, a word kept emerging to describe the growing ecosystem of on-demand services for entrepreneurs: *fast.* It was the theme of speed that helped me to bring the pieces together to eventually call that trend "Instant Entrepreneurship."

→ **Combine industry verticals.** Despite my own cautions against aggregating ideas by industry sector, sometimes a trend ends up heavily focused in just one sector. When I see one of these idea clusters predominantly focused in one industry, I always try to find another batch of ideas I can combine it with. This often leads to bigger thinking and helps to remove any unintentional industry bias I may have held earlier in the process.

→ **Follow the money.** With business trends, sometimes the underlying driver of a trend is who will make money from it. Following this trail can sometimes lead you to make connections you might not have considered before. This was exactly how studying a new all-you-can-read ebook subscription service and the growth of cloud-based software led me to write about the trend of "Subscription Commerce" several years ago.

## Step 4 NAMING

Naming is the creative art of describing a trend in an easily understandable and memorably branded way.

Photo: Sources used for names and word lists.

Naming a trend is a little bit like naming a child—you think of every way that the name might unintentionally be dooming your idea to a life of ridicule, and then you try to balance that with a name that feels right.

Naming a trend involves the choice of sharing a specific point of view in a way that names for kids generally don't. Great trend names convey meaning with simplicity—and they're memorable.

For this reason, naming a trend is often my favorite part of the Haystack Method, but it is also the most creatively challenging. It's focused on that critical moment when you brand an idea that will either stick in people's minds as something new and important, or be immediately forgotten.

The title for my second book, *Likeonomics*, came from one of these trend-naming sessions. The concept took off immediately, because people understood the idea and the name was just quirky enough to inspire a second look. Finding the right name for an idea can do that.

An effective title can inspire people. It can help a good idea capture the right peoples' imaginations and urge them to own and describe it for themselves. Of course, that doesn't make naming any easier to do.

In fact, naming a trend can take just as long as any other aspect of defining or researching a trend. In my method, I try many possibilities. I jot down potential names on Post-it notes and compare them side by side. I test them with early readers and clients. Only then do I finalize the names for the trends in each of my reports.

> ## NAMING QUESTIONS:
> ## HOW TO ENSURE YOU HAVE
> ## AN EFFECTIVE TREND NAME
>
> ✓ Is the name not widely used or already well understood?
> ✓ Is it relatively simple to say out loud in conversation?
> ✓ Does it make sense without too much additional explanation?
> ✓ Could you imagine it as the title of a book?
> ✓ Are you using words that are unique and not clichéd?
> ✓ Does it build upon a topic in an unexpected way?

So, how did 2019's trend names turn out? The full list is outlined in Part II and the backlist of trend names is included in the appendix, but here are a few of my favorite trend names from previous reports, along with a little of the backstory behind the development and selection of each:

→ **Virtual Empathy (2016 + 2018).** During a time when virtual reality was a hot topic, the underlying theme behind VR was how it managed to amplify a sense of empathy in anyone who used it. As a result, I paired the term "virtual" with "empathy" instead, to create a new way of thinking about the powerful effects of virtual reality.

→ **Experimedia (2015).** The name for this trend came together quite quickly after finding several articles all talking about how social experiments were creating a new category of media stories. Putting "experiment" together with "media" works because the prefix of "experiment" remains unchanged, and a new ending creates a word that engages people's curiosity while still being clear enough that you could guess the meaning.

→ **Obsessive Productivity (2014).** As the life-hacking movement generated more and more stories of how to make every moment more productive, I started to feel that these tools and advice about helping each of us optimize every moment were bordering on obsession. The naming of this trend was easy, but to me, it worked, because it combined a word most people associate as negative (obsessive) with one that is usually discussed as a positive (productivity). I used the same principle to name "Fierce Femininity" in 2017.

While there are many ways inspiration can strike as you name your own ideas, the following tips and tricks share a few of the techniques that I tend to use most often in naming and branding the trends in my reports.

## Tips & Tricks: How to Name Your Ideas Powerfully

→ **Mashup.** Mashups take two different words or concepts and put them together in a meaningful way. Likeonomics is a mashup between likeability and economics. Shoptimization is a mashup between shopping and optimization. Use of this technique can make an idea immediately memorable and ownable, but it can also feel forced and artificial if not done artfully. There is a reason I didn't call my book Trustonomics. The best mashups are easy to pronounce, and are as close to sounding like the original words as possible.

→ **Alliteration.** When naming a brand, this technique is commonly used, and the virtues are obvious: think Coca-Cola and Krispy Kreme. The idea of using two words beginning with the same consonant is one I have used for trends such as "Muddled Masculinity" (see Chapter 5) and "Disruptive Distribution." Like mashups, it can feel forced if you put two words together that don't belong, but the technique can lead you toward a great trend name.

→ **Twist.** The technique involves taking a common idea or obvious phrase and inserting a small change to make it different. The name should employ a term that's already commonly used, and then twisted a bit to help it stand out. One of my favorite examples was a trend from 2015 called "Small Data" to counter all the discussion about big data. The "Unperfection" trend, which was first published in 2015, used a similar method—just enough of a twist on the actual word *imperfection* to feel new and different.

## Step 5  PROVING

Evaluate your ideas and and seek out more research to make the case for why an idea describes the accelerating present.

Photo Credit: Tech.co (Tech Cocktail Sessions DC)

Though my Haystack Method relies heavily on analysis of stories and ideas that have been published, there is also a consistent thread of conversations, speeches, and interviews that inform the trend-spotting process. I'm lucky to be able to speak at fifty or soevents every year, and my team and I routinely deliver dozens of workshops at companies in almost every industry.

The result of these interactions is a consistent stream of ideas as well as the opportunity to interview the visionary keynote speakers I'm sharing the stage with. This allows me to test new trend ideas and approaches with some of these groups before publishing the new trends.

I believe trends are curated by observing behavior, identifying patterns, and assembling the pieces of a puzzle. You can't make a puzzle by showing someone a piece and querying them about what they think the rest of the puzzle might be.

I don't mean to discount the value of focus groups or surveys as input. The truth is, the more analytical or scientific your stakeholders and audience, the more likely it is you'll need some of this type of data to support your curated trends. I'm neither a behavioral psychologist nor a market researcher, however. There are people who are excellent at this, and I would much rather read their research and have a conversation with them—and then use those insights to inform my curation of trends and help to prove them in this final phase of the Haystack Method.

The framework my team and I use (and teach our clients to use) to prove ideas is based on a formula of looking at three critical elements: idea, impact, and acceleration.

# Elements of trends

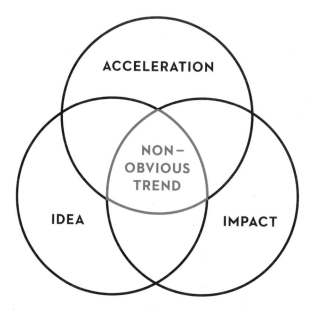

1. **Idea.** Great trend ideas are unique descriptions of a shift in culture, business, or behavior in a concise enough way to be meaningful without being oversimplified.

2. **Impact.** Impact comes when people start changing behavior, or companies start to adapt what they are selling or how they are selling it.

3. **Acceleration.** The last critical element is how quickly a trend is affecting business and consumer behavior, and whether that's likely to grow.

Since we started publishing our trend research, this is the central filter my team and I have used to measure trend concepts and determine whether they are provable. To do this, one technique we use is to consistently ask five questions as we finalize our trend list.

> ## PROVING QUESTIONS:
> ## HOW TO QUANTIFY A TREND
>
> ✓ Is the trend idea unique enough to stand out?
>
> ✓ Has anyone published research related to this trend idea?
>
> ✓ Is the media starting to uncover examples, or focus on it?
>
> ✓ Are there enough examples across industries?
>
> ✓ Is the trend likely to continue into the foreseeable future?

In your own efforts to curate trends, when you go through this list of questions—it's possible you'll find that some of the trend ideas you've curated, analyzed, elevated, and even created names for may not satisfy all these criteria.

Unfortunately, you have now reached the toughest step in the Haystack Method: leaving behind trends that you cannot prove. Abandoning ideas is brutal, especially after you have become attached to them. It probably won't help that in this chapter, I've already advised you to name them before proving them, which seems logically wrong. You never name something you're going to leave behind, right?

Well, as true as that may be, the problem is that you need to name the trends before you can assess their importance. The process of naming helps you understand what a trend is and how you might prove it, but it doesn't mean you're finished.

This is the phase of the process in which I find discipline. It forces me to go back and either do more research or sometimes even change the original concept of the trend to make it broader or narrower.

Grading all the past identified trends (see appendix) was eye-opening when my team and I first decided to add it to the 2016 edition of the book. It was clear that the trends where we had more discipline in the proving phase were the ones that fared better over time. Those were the best ideas, and the ones that you can and should aspire to have, too.

## Tips & Tricks: How to Prove Your Trend Ideas

→ **Focus on diversity.** One of the biggest mistakes people make in trend curation is only seeking out examples in a single industry, category, or situation. If a trend is going to have a large impact on how business is done or how consumers behave, it should be supported by examples or cases in other industries.

→ **Watch your biases.** Nothing will cloud your judgment more quickly than finding a trend that somehow helps your own industry, product, or career. This is a tricky subject, because part of the intention of curating your own trends may be to specifically support a product or belief. Yet it's also where many of the trends that are oversimplified or just plain wrong come from. Non-obvious trends don't have apparent industry biases, and are not gratuitously self-serving.

→ **Use authoritative sources.** When it comes to the examples and research you've found to support a trend, the more authoritative sources you can find, the better. What this means in practice is using examples that people may recognize, or finding research from reputable organizations or academic institutions. These sources can make the difference between selling your vision and having your audience question your conclusions because they don't believe your sources.

Let's bring the five elements of the Haystack Method to life through a step-by-step analysis of how the process helped define a trend from a past report.

The following description takes you through all five steps of the Haystack Method to gather, aggregate, elevate, name, and prove a single trend from the 2015 *Non-Obvious Trend Report:* "Engineered Addiction."

## Case Study: *Engineered Addiction*
## How to Curate a Non-Obvious Trend

### *Step 1* GATHERING

One of the earliest stories I saved, more than a year before this trend was published, was about Dong Nguyen, the creator of the mobile game Flappy Bird, which became one of the most downloaded apps of the year in 2013. After millions of downloads, Nguyen suddenly removed the game from the iTunes and Android stores. In the interview I had saved, he shared how his unusual move had fueled a consuming worry that the game was negatively affecting people's lives because it had become "addictive."

His unexpected choice seemed significant—though I wasn't yet sure exactly why—so I saved it. Months later, I read a book called *Hooked,* by Nir Eyal, which explored how Silicon Valley product designers were increasingly building "habit-forming products." This seemed to describe perfectly what Nguyen had unintentionally done (and felt so guilty about). I saved that idea, too.

### *Step 2* AGGREGATING

At the end of that year, I began the process of aggregating ideas to start to identify trends. This was the moment when I started seeing a pattern in examples that seemed to focus on some type of addictive behavior. The Flappy Bird story was about game design that seemed to lead to addiction. The book *Hooked* was about product design, and using it to create addictive habits in people. As I grouped these ideas together, I focused on the role that interface design seemed to be playing in creating all these addictive experiences. I stapled these stories together and put an index card on top, upon which I wrote the words "Addictive Design" with a black Sharpie. It was a guess about what I thought the trend could be.

## Step 3 **ELEVATING**

When I stepped back to look through my initial list of possible trend ideas (which usually numbers about seventy-five, once I make it through the first two phases of the Haystack Method), there were several other trend concepts that seemed potentially related to this idea of Addictive Design.

One of them was a grouping of stories all about the use of gamification techniques to help people of all ages learn new skills. For that group, I had an index card on top that said "Gamified Learning. Inside were stories about the Khan Academy using badges to inspire learning, and a startup called Curious that was making learning addictive by creating bite-sized pieces of education on interesting topics.

Another group of ideas was inspired by a book I had read earlier that year called *Salt Sugar Fat* by Michael Moss, which had focused on the idea of addiction related to food. The book exposed how snack foods, such as Oreos and Cheetos, had been created to offer a "bliss point" that mimicked the sensations of addiction in most people.[3] Along with the book, I also had several other articles with similar themes that were grouped together and stapled with an index card labeled "Irresistible Food."

In this third phase of elevation, I realized that what seemed like three unique ideas (Gamified Learning, Addictive Design, and Irresistible Food), might actually be elements of a single trend. This broader idea seemed to describe a growing instance in which experiences and products of multiple types were increasingly being created to be intentionally addictive.

I put all the stories for each of these three aggregated concepts together and called the elevated grouping "Ubiquitous Addiction."

## Step 4 **NAMING**

Now that I had examples as disparate as food manufacturing and online learning, it was time to pick a name that would effectively describe this trend. I had already come up with several to consider. As I reviewed, I dismissed "Addictive Design," because it was too small and didn't describe the food-related examples. "Gamified Learning" was also tossed aside as too obvious and niche. The elevated name "Ubiquitous Addiction" also didn't exactly roll off the tongue, and seemed to imply that more people were getting addicted to things than in the past, which I didn't believe properly described the trend.

None of the earlier names worked, and I knew I needed something better.

The final clue as to what the name of the trend could be came from another interview article I read featuring Nir Eyal. In the article, he described himself as a "behavioral engineer." This idea of "engineering" instead of just design immediately seemed far better suited to describing what I felt the trend was.

After testing a few versions of the word "engineering" in the title of the trend, I settled on "Engineered Addiction" as the most descriptive and memorable way to describe this trend and all of its components.

## Step 5 **PROVING**

Once the name was in place, I had a way to talk about and share the trend to test it further. I already knew that I had stories across multiple industries, and that the trend had several dimensions. To get even more proof, I sought out further examples and research intentionally focused upon addictive products and experiences that had been "engineered."

My research led me to a recently-published Harvard study showing why social media had become so addictive for so many, and then later to a body of research from noted MIT anthropologist Natasha Dow Schüll, who spent more than fifteen years doing field research on slot-machine design in Las Vegas.[4]

Her book, *Addiction by Design,* exposed the many ways casinos use the experience and design of slot machines to encourage addictive behavior.

Together, these were the final elements of proof that would help me tell this story completely.

Engineered Addiction made my 2015 Non-Obvious Trend Report; and, ultimately, it became one of the most talked-about trends that year.

## Avoiding Future Babble

Now that we have gone through the process of curating trends, I want to share a final caution: the dangerous potential for the majority of trend forecasting to sink into nonsense.

Despite my love of trends and belief that any of us can learn to curate them, the fact remains that we live in a world frustrated with predictions, and for good reason.

Economists fail to predict activities that lead to global recessions. Television meteorologists predict rain that never comes. And business-trend forecasters are perhaps the worst offenders, sharing glassy-eyed predictions that seem either glaringly obvious or naively impossible.

In 2011, journalist Dan Gardner wrote about this mistake-ridden obsession with the future in his insightful book, *Future Babble.* Gardner illuminated the many ways in which so-called experts and pundits have led us down mistaken paths and caused more harm than good.

He builds his argument based upon the widely known but rarely heeded research of psychologist Philip Tetlock, who spent more than twenty years interviewing all types of experts and collecting 27,450 of their predictions and ideas about the future. Tetlock then analyzed these predictions against verifiable data, and found that the experts' predictions were no more accurate than random guesses.[5]

When Tetlock confronted some of these experts on how flawed their predictions had been, he found that the experts who fared worst were the ones who had struggled with uncertainty. These "hedgehogs," as Tetlock describes them, were overconfident, often described their mistaken predictions as being "almost right," and generally held an unchanging worldview.

---

*"At least 50% of pundits seem wrong all the time.*
*It's just hard to tell which 50%."*
— DAN GARDNER (from *Future Babble*)

---

On the other side were experts who didn't follow a set path. They were comfortable with being uncertain, and accepted that some of their predictions could be wrong. These experts were "foxes," and their defining characteristics included modesty about their ability to predict the future and willingness to express doubt about their predictions.

How can you tell which predictions to trust and which to discount? And how can you improve the accuracy of your own predictions?

# The Art of Getting Trends Right (and Wrong)

I shared Dan Gardner's caution about the dangers of false certainty and skepticism with regard to future predictions for a reason. If you are going to build your ability to curate trends, you must also embrace the idea that sometimes, you will be wrong.

In Part IV, you will see a summary of previous trends along with a corresponding letter grade and a retrospective analysis of their longevity.

Some of them are embarrassingly off the mark.

The reason I share them candidly anyway is partly to illustrate Gardner's point. I want to be as honest with you as I try to be with myself and my team after each year's report. Foxes, after all, are comfortable with uncertainty, and know they may sometimes be wrong. I know I'm sometimes wrong, and I guarantee that you will be, too.

Why write a book about predicting trends and describe the entire process if we might be wrong at the end of it? A fear of failure should not hold you back from applying your best thinking and exploring big ideas. More importantly, the Haystack Method may be a way to curate trends, but it's also a way to think about the world that involves finding more intersections and avoiding narrow-minded thinking.

Learning to predict the future, in other words, has a valuable side effect: it can make you more curious, observant, and understanding of the world around you. It's this mental shift that may ultimately become the greatest benefit of learning to see and curate trends.

Oscar Wilde wrote that "to expect the unexpected shows a thoroughly modern intellect."[6] *Non-Obvious* is about helping you to build this type of modern intellect, through noticing the things others miss, thinking differently, and curating ideas to describe the accelerating present in new and unique ways.

Now that we've achieved that, let's turn our attention to the trends for this year.

## PART II

—

# The 2019 Non-Obvious Trend Report

**What is a trend?** *A trend is a unique curated observation about the accelerating present.*

**Culture & Consumer Behavior:** Trends in how we see ourselves and patterns in popular culture.

**STRATEGIC SPECTACLE**

**MUDDLED MASCULINITY**

**SIDE QUIRKS**

**Marketing & Social Media:** Trends in how brands are trying to influence and engage consumers.

**ARTIFICIAL INFLUENCE**

**RETROTRUST**

**B2BEYOND MARKETING**

**Media & Education:** Trends in information impacting how we learn, think or are entertained.

**FAD FATIGUE**

**EXTREME UNCLUTTERING**

**DELIBERATE DOWNGRADING**

**Technology & Design:** Trends in innovation, technology and product design impacting our behavior.

**ENTERPRISE EMPATHY**

**INNOVATION ENVY**

**ROBOT RENAISSANCE**

**Economics & Entrepreneurship:** Trends in business models, industry or the future of work or money.

**GOOD SPEED**

**OVERWEALTHY**

**PASSIVE LOYALTY**

04

# Strategic Spectacle

## What's the Trend?

—

Brands and creators intentionally
use spectacles to capture attention
and drive engagement.

The most controversial rocket launch of the past decade took
place on January 21, 2018, from a comparatively tiny launchpad
in New Zealand.

After days of weather delays, a U.S.-based aeronautics company
called Rocket Lab finally launched a long-awaited test flight
for their newest rocket: the Electron. Although the company
had originally announced the rocket was carrying three small
commercial satellites, days after the successful launch, its CEO
Peter Beck came clean. There was a fourth passenger on the
Electron: a 3-foot-tall, 23-pound spherical satellite covered with
76 reflective panels designed to reflect sunlight back to Earth. The

Humanity Star, as Beck called it, promised to be "the brightest thing in the night sky." Beck did not put it into orbit to fulfill some deep scientific purpose. He simply did it "to get people to look up."[1]

The response was swift and harsh.

Some scientists immediately decried Beck's move, calling the Humanity Star their worst fear, an example of light pollution and space graffiti. Others compared it to putting a disco ball in space. Many questioned whether it was ethical to place this performance-art-installation-meets-clever-marketing thing into the night sky—a domain belonging to no one, and unavoidable by everyone.

The controversy, though, died down quickly as the satellite fell out of orbit earlier than planned and burned in the atmosphere upon reentry, as expected. Less than a month later, Elon Musk's Space X launched their much larger Falcon Heavy rocket and put its payload—an actual Tesla roadster sports car—into orbit around the sun. The news grabbed headlines around the world.

Over the past year, we have been tracking more and more organizations and people who intentionally create spectacles like these to attract predictable attention. Welcome to the age of the Strategic Spectacle, in which more industries than ever will resort to leveraging big stunts and engaging experiences like these to attract attention and make a bold statement.

## Immersive "Museums"

After Mary Ellis Bunn and Manish Vora announced the opening of the Museum of Ice Cream in Manhattan—a pop-up venue featuring whimsical ice-cream-themed interactive exhibits—tickets sold out within three days. Over the course of a month, lucky ticketholders eagerly awaited their chance to to swim in a pool of ice cream sprinkles, walk through a gallery of suspended plastic bananas, and climb on a giant ice cream sandwich swing. It was a huge sensation.

Some critics rightly noted that the Museum of Ice Cream was hardly a museum, but rather a colorful collection of themed backdrops. Visitors did not walk away with a deeper understanding of much of anything. They did, however, take lots and lots of photos. Designed specifically to be as Instagram-friendly as possible, the Museum of Ice Cream's colorful, picture-perfect galleries were, predictably, popular fodder for sharing on social media—and drove big engagement and word of mouth from visitors hungry to share unique selfies with their followers.

Since the museum's short run in Manhattan in 2016, Bunn and Vora have expanded to new locations, including Los Angeles and Miami Beach, and in 2018, even opened a permanent installation in San Francisco. According to them, more than 250,000 people went through the exhibit in Miami Beach, and around 1,700 visit their San Francisco location every day. Though they won't reveal revenues, it is estimated that this attendance rate could amount to revenues of $20 million for their first two years of operation.[2]

Over the past year, this tactic to deliver the perfect setting for the ultimate selfie has fueled the openings of what one critic called "Instagram-optimized funhouses,"[3] each hoping to wow visitors with ever more colorful and Instagrammable spectacles. Among them, the Happy Place—a multi-sensory collection of 13 colorful rooms "designed to evoke feelings of happiness"—opened its doors in Los Angeles.

In Tokyo, the popular Kawaii Monster Café offers an eccentric, anime-inspired restaurant with a colorfully cartoonish menu and a devoted staff dressed as popular cosplay characters. It has become a destination for Japanese diners and tourists alike, with dance parties, multicolored alien-themed desserts, and plenty of strobe lights for effect.

Kawaii Monster Cafe in Tokyo, Japan

Each of these experiences appeals to people's consistent desire to share happy and unique moments to fuel their hunger for social reinforcement online. The more people visit and have this "unique" experience, the more everyone wants to have that same experience for themselves, take the same photo, and share in the same spectacle.

These pop-up "art" installations are not only creating Strategic Spectacles by launching Instagram-bait experiences, they are also bridging the divide between art experience and retail destination. In the summer of 2018, for example, the Museum of Ice Cream's founding team created a pop-up "grocery" in New York's Chelsea neighborhood called the Pint Shop, which offered merchandise, tastings, and museum-branded apparel.

# Experiential Retail

The shift toward maximizing the spectacle in the retail environment, exemplified by the Museum of Ice Cream's new pop-up grocery venture, is one we have been tracking and writing about since 2011. We first described it as the *Culting of Retail* trend and followed it in 2012 with a trend we named *Retail Theater*. Today, the concept of the retail environment as a place in which theater and spectacle co-exist is common.

Similar to the immersive experiences offered by pop-up "art" installations, Samsung's flagship store in New York City was conceived as an interactive playground for shoppers. In the massive 56,000 square foot store, visitors can participate in a virtual reality ride, hang out in a DJ booth, lounge in comfortable living-room-like settings, or even catch a free concert. Unlike most other retail destinations, the point of Samsung 837, as it is called, isn't really to sell anything. At least not directly. The point is to use a *Strategic Spectacle* to generate attention by encouraging people to try the products, and hopefully share their experience of doing so with their friends through social media.

In many ways, Samsung 837 found its roots in a retail trend we wrote about in 2015: *Reverse Retail*. That trend described how many online-only retailers were creating brick-and-mortar stores to satisfy customers who wanted to see, touch, and feel products prior to buying them. The clothing retailer Bonobos, for example, opened branded "Guideshops"—showrooms where customers could try clothing on before placing the order online. Online mattress retailer Casper has been aggressively investing in opening retail locations, mainly in shopping malls across the United States, and plans to open more than 200 physical stores in the coming months.[4]

## Reverse Retail & the Omnishopper

All of these physical stores aren't just driving purchases online, either. A group of consumers one recent study dubbed "omnishoppers"[5] are researching products online and then buying them in-store, providing even more evidence that the physical retail experience is far from dead.

Far from the glitz of Samsung's New York-based hub, midwestern retailer MartinPatrick3 provides a good example of a traditional retailer that has garnered significant attention by creating one of the most unique retail experiences in the country. Located in the hip outskirts of the Twin Cities in Minnesota, the store sells an unusual combination of products: furniture alongside men's suits and interior design services.

The store itself—housed in an 130-year-old warehouse that used to be a streetcar company—delights customers with its beautiful and careful design, as well as its bar and in-house barber shop where customers can relax. What sets it apart is the idea that a retail experience doesn't need to focus on just one vertical or one experience. Instead, creating one that operates almost like a tiny city block, with a bar and barber shop built in, is a recipe for something that people will want to return to over and over again—and rave about.

In an age in which every consumer says they want an experience, one can argue that physical stores where brands can captivate their customers have become more important than ever—whether they are trying to sell their products there, online...or not at all.

## Live Experiences

After delivering a keynote at an event last year, I was having drinks with a group of attendees when suddenly, several people's phone alarms went off simultaneously. It was 9 p.m., and those alarms meant it was time to play HQ Trivia.

Launched in late 2017, HQ Trivia is a mobile trivia game "airing" on weekdays at 3 p.m. and 9 p.m. The format of the game is simple: you compete with other players to correctly answer 12 multiple-choice questions of increasing difficulty. Get them all right, and you'll automatically split the cash prize for that day with all other players receiving a perfect score.

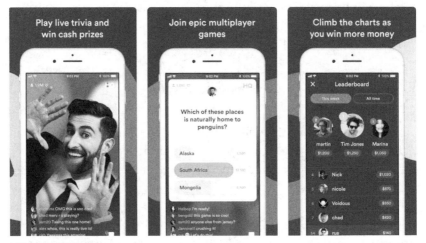

HQ Trivia Mobile App

What's fascinating about the meteoric rise of the game is how it has demonstrated that at a time when almost all entertainment is available on demand, people will still set their alarms and tune in real-time for the right kind of engaging live experience.

This willingness to engage in live experiences isn't limited to mobile apps, either. To promote the release of the movie musical *The Greatest Showman,* Twentieth Century Fox broadcasted a live commercial featuring an elaborate performance by its star, Hugh Jackman, his film co-stars, and more than 150 dancers. The live ad helped to propel fan enthusiasm, and generated enough word of mouth to turn the film into a runaway hit.

These two live experiences illustrate how *Strategic Spectacles* can help creators and organizations alike to leverage attention in the moment to drive engagement, enthusiasm, and anticipation.

I realize that throughout this chapter, it will be tempting to apply a negative judgement to the idea of creating a "spectacle" in the first place. The word itself is generally used somewhat negatively. Yet ironically, when something is described as "spectacular," it is always good. Spectacles can have a similarly dual effect. Some may feel manipulated and overly produced, while others can inspire awe in a good way. The point in this chapter is not to grade them as good or bad, but rather to realize that they (and the reactions they inspire) are being done *strategically.*

## Art as Spectacle

Like the creators of the live commercial for *The Greatest Showman* and the colorful pop-up venues, artists are also creating spectacles by leveraging live experiences in the development of their work.

In early October 2018, a painting by the anonymous British street artist Banksy was sold at auction for $1.4 million. Seconds after the sale was complete, the bottom half of the work passed through a shredder concealed within the frame. Originally entitled *Girl with Balloon,* the piece was retitled *Love is in the Bin,* and the buyer, a female European art collector, decided to keep the work anyway. Her decision may have been influenced in part by the fact that most critics agreed that its value was likely already higher than the price she paid to acquire the piece.

While some dismiss Banky's artwork as a mere stunt to subvert the established art world, Sotheby's head of contemporary art declared the painting historic: "the first artwork in history to have been created live during an auction."[6] Whether the painting goes down in history as a prank or a respected piece of art, the spectacle undeniably earned Banksy something quite rare, for most artists: attention from the mainstream.

The elusive Parisian street artist known only to his fans as Invader doesn't create spectacles with stunts designed to shock the art world. Instead, he does so with his unusual art "game:"

about once a week, he installs a piece of street art somewhere around the world and announces it to his more than 40,000 Instagram followers, along with the hashtag #invaderwashere and an approximate location.

Example of Invader's street art (Photo Credit: Lorie Shaull, Flickr)

The unspoken challenge issued with each image is to find that installation, take a photo using a GPS-enabled phone, and post it before the art is found or stolen by thieves eager to sell it. Those who successfully post a photo earn points to increase their rank among players—and bragging rights.

Both Banksy and Invader have an intuitive understanding of the power of *Strategic Spectacle* to attract and sustain attention for their art. More importantly, they both use it intentionally to make fans out of ordinary people (who might not otherwise be interested in art) while retaining their mystique.

# Why It Matters

When deciding what to call this trend, we chose our words very carefully. When we say something is "spectacular," we usually mean that it is memorable and worthy of our attention. As I shared earlier, the word "spectacle" can have either positive or negative connotations. Some may question whether the Museum of Ice Cream or Invader's street art are as worthy of our attention as the Smithsonian or the Getty Museum,for example; but by creating a spectacle in a deliberate way, they have nonetheless captured it.

The need to develop a *strategy* for creating spectacle is a natural result of a crowded media landscape. The harder it is to stand out, the more audacious creators need to be. Yet the implication of this trend is not that those who yell the loudest in a desperate attempt to be heard over the din will win. In a world in which *Strategic Spectacles* proliferate, the most frequent winners will be those who direct their teams' creativity toward using spectacle to convert momentary attention into longer-lasting engagement.

## How to Use This Trend

✓ **Engage in flip thinking**—The most effective spectacles are those no one else is doing, and that may even run counter to what everyone else does. No artist would ever destroy his or her own painting. Most stores don't invite people to come in and try products without buying them. This type of counter-intuitive thinking works, because it demands to be noticed.

✓ **Don't forget the strategy**—The challenge isn't to create a spectacle, but rather to create one that is *strategic,* and moves the needle where it matters for *your* business. The founders of the Museum of Ice Cream didn't just create a whimsical installation about ice cream. They strategically crafted each installation to satisfy visitors' desire to take unique selfies and post them on social media-generating significant word-of-mouth that resulted in sold out exhibits.

05

# Muddled Masculinity

## What's the Trend?

—

The rising empowerment of women and reevaluation of gender itself are causing widespread confusion and angst about what it means to be a man today.

When I was in middle school, my favorite book series was *Sweet Valley High,* which followed the lives of Jessica and Elizabeth Wakefield, identical twins from the fictional town of Sweet Valley, California.

*Sweet Valley High* was the brainchild of author Francine Pascal, who eventually built what the *L.A. Times* called "a one-woman publishing industry," hiring ghostwriters to write nearly two hundred books in the series. At its peak in 1985, 18 books in the series were listed on Waldenbooks' Top 20 Titles for young adults. Often called "teen Harlequins," these books were highly popular at the time, and inspired young readers to turn to books instead of TV.

Young *female* readers, that is.

As Pascal told the *L.A. Times* in an interview, "The truth is, boys read until about age 12, then they go outside and don't come back in until they are about 18."[1] I remember loving to go outside, so my younger years did resemble the first part of her statement... but every time I came back in, it would be to read another story about the romantic adventures of Jessica and Elizabeth.

I also I remember, with some embarrassment, how odd it was for a young boy to be checking out five or six *Sweet Valley High* books at a time from the library. On more than one occasion, I'm sure the librarian assumed I was getting them for my nonexistent sister. A boy reading about love, relationships, and high school drama was out of the ordinary in the late 1980s.

In the time since, our perspectives on gender roles have shifted dramatically. Women continue to break through old-fashioned gender roles and make strides in the workforce, business, and culture—even as the #MeToo movement sheds light on how much further we still have to go as a society in this regard. (Readers of the 2017 edition of this book will recall that I wrote extensively about the increasing celebration and empowerment of fiercely independent women in the past trend prediction *Fierce Femininity*).

Even the very idea of gender is being reevaluated, a trend I called *Ungendered,* and which I explored deeply in the 2018 edition of this book. For a look at the previous 100+ trend predictions from our team, along with transparent ratings of how they fared over time, turn to Part IV of this book.

Our perspective on male gender roles—particularly how we perceive masculinity and fatherhood—remains fairly confused. Sadly, decades later, a young boy checking out *Sweet Valley High* books at the local library will likely *still* get a few raised eyebrows.

That's why it is fitting that in 2019, we turn our attention to men—specifically, a trend we've been tracking called *Muddled Masculinity.* Put simply, changes to male gender roles and ideals of masculinity are emerging with a speed similar to the dramatic changes to female gender roles, but often with less clarity. The result is that more men (and boys) are feeling confused and anxious about what it means to be a man today—a fact that we believe will affect every workplace, team dynamic, and conversation with men as customers, colleagues, and members of the community.

## The Confusing Ideal of Masculinity

In June 2018, the opinion-polling website FiveThirtyEight commissioned a survey of 1,615 adults who identify as men. They wanted to find out whether the recent media attention given to gender inequality and sexual harassment at work (symbolized by the hashtag #MeToo) has changed men's thinking on masculinity.

The results were conflicted. Fifty-three percent of surveyed men said it was important for them that others see them as masculine. Forty-nine percent reported always trying to pay the bill when out on a date. More than half felt that, in the wake of the #MeToo movement, it was a *disadvantage* to be male at work, as "they are at a greater risk of being accused of sexual harassment."[2]

The survey results suggested that even as other parts of our culture are in the midst of a reckoning over gender roles and inequality at work, many men continue to feel the same pressures of society to adhere to a traditional and outdated ideal of what it means to be a man. In a powerful piece for *The Atlantic*, writer Sarah Rich points to the Boy Scouts of America as an example of how boys are still directed toward traditional ideals of masculinity at an early age.

Recently, the Boy Scouts of America made the decision to allow girls to join its organization. But there was no similar conversation about whether boys might be allowed to join the ranks of the Girl Scouts. As Rich asks, would any boy even want to? We've been encouraging girls to embrace aspects of themselves that have traditionally been called "masculine,"and to be unafraid of enjoying activities like learning how to tie knots or building a pinewood racing car (both activities traditionally done by Boy Scouts).

The same understanding, though, is rarely extended to boys who might choose the more social or artistic activities typically offered to Girl Scouts, like being a "social butterfly" or learning how to be a screenwriter (both badge-earning activities offered to Girl Scouts).[3]

Approaching gender equality by focusing exclusively upon empowering girls unintentionally reinforces the idea that girls who embrace more traditionally masculine behaviors, such as being assertive and courageous, will be more successful, while boys who embrace more traditionally feminine behaviors, such as being kind and cooperative, will not.

"When school officials and parents send a message to children that 'boyish' girls are badass but 'girlish' boys are embarrassing, they are telling kids that society values and rewards masculinity, but not femininity,"[4] Rich concludes. When boys get this message, it reinforces the confusing belief that there is only one way to be a boy (and, by extension, only one way to act like a man). And that way doesn't involve engaging in any activity that is seen as being "for girls." Especially not reading teenage romance novels.

## Doofus Dads and Masculinity Reinvented

If men learn to embrace a traditional ideal of masculinity when they are boys, they continue their education through the media. They learn how men are expected to talk and behave from what they see on advertisements, on TV, and in pop culture. And all too often, what they see are images of toxic masculinity.

According to the Good Men Project, toxic masculinity is:

—

*"...a narrow and repressive description of manhood, designating manhood as defined by violence, sex, status and aggression... where strength is everything while emotions are a weakness."*[5]

—

The good news is, things might be changing. Some brands are recognizing the dangers of such a version of masculinity, and hope to counter it through their advertisements.

"Is it okay for guys not to like sports?"

"Is it okay to wear pink?"

"Is it okay to be emotional?"

These are just some of the questions highlighted in a widely praised advertising campaign from the men's grooming brand Axe (also known as Lynx in the U.K., Ireland, Australia, and New Zealand). In the commercials, these and other, similar questions— all derived from actual web searches—are narrated by a voiceover on top of images of various men. They illustrate just how conflicted guys are today about the messages they receive about what it means to be a man.

As Rik Strubel, Global Vice President at Axe, said in a statement about the campaign, "We can't just tell guys to be themselves without addressing the underlying cultural issues and restrictive definitions of manhood holding them back in the first place. It not only hurts guys, it hurts everyone."[6]

In 2017, the brand also partnered with the Brazilian advocacy group Promundo to publish a study called *The Man Box,* which examined young men ages 18 to 30 in the U.S., the U.K., and Mexico—and found that most men still feel pushed to live in the "man box—a rigid construct of cultural ideas about male identity. This includes being self-sufficient, acting tough, looking physically attractive, sticking to rigid gender roles, being heterosexual, having sexual prowess, and using aggression to resolve conflicts."[7]

By spotlighting the so-called "Man Box" (and its corresponding "rules," like the one below), the brand was trying to encourage guys to think outside of it.

RULE #2:

## "GUYS SHOULD KEEP THEIR EMOTIONS TO THEMSELVES"

Lynx/Axe Ad - "Man Box"

While Axe is at the forefront of brands trying to denounce toxic masculinity and help men navigate what it really means to be a man, other brands continue to reinforce outdated stereotypes of men and masculinity. Perhaps nothing exemplifies this more than the countless ads showing "helpless" dads in childrearing or domestic activities. Whereas women are getting more gender-shifting messages from advertisers (you can do anything!), men often continue to get the message that they are incompetent, lovable doofuses when it comes to domestic matters.

The double standard sends a damaging implicit message: why even try, when you are going to be ridiculed and screw up anyway? Just leave it to the women, who are so good at this stuff....

Even though there's widespread dissatisfaction with these stereotypes, the ads endure. A recent survey from MDG Advertising found that 85 percent of fathers said they knew more than advertisers give them credit for, and 74 percent of millennial fathers felt advertisers and marketers were "out of touch with modern family dynamics."[8]

## Stuck-at-Work Dads

Men don't just receive confusing messages about what it means to be a father from the media. They receive them at work, too. Over the past few decades, we have debated and dismissed the stereotype of the "stay-at-home mom," but the stereotype of the "stuck-at-work-dad," who is required to remain at work from 9 to 5 (at least) has barely been revisited. Even today, in dual income households, fathers are still expected to primarily provide for the family, according to Pew.[9] Meanwhile, mothers are disproportionally expected to balance work with kids' doctors' appointments and grocery shopping.

Women, of course, have fought hard and long for their place in the workforce. And that fight has been supported by networking groups that help mothers with work-life balance as well as evolved workplaces that understand that sometimes, schedules have to accommodate the needs of moms who must care for a sick child or attend a school function. These are all positive shifts for women and families.

Unfortunately, the same understanding is often not yet offered equally to dads. Many men still work in environments in which it is not culturally acceptable to leave early to attend a school function. "Boasting about your latest diaper victory isn't yet a normal part of guy talk," writes Brittany Levine Beckman in Mashable. "Even taking paternity leave can still be perceived as weak."[10]

The result is that men are increasingly being expected (and willing) to be supportive, equal partners and emotionally available fathers—but struggle to balance those demands with sometimes hostile workplaces that don't accommodate them or make it acceptable for them to prioritize their kids and family above work.

## The Gender-Fluid Man

Traditional ideals of masculinity have imposed significant limitations on how modern men express themselves. But there are encouraging signs that the reevaluation of these ideals is underfoot on multiple levels, particularly as society starts decoupling gender from the choices we make—from what we wear to what we call ourselves to what we buy.

One of these signs is the growing number of trailblazers who are challenging us to reimagine gender roles in general. Jaden Smith, for example, has become a symbol of the fashion-forward man who refuses to be confined by traditional clothing choices. He cites Batman and Poseidon as design influences, and famously wore a skirt for a Louis Vuitton photo shoot. I also wrote about Smith in last year's discussion of the *Ungendered* trend. The son of actors Will Smith and Jada Pinkett Smith, he speaks often about his gender fluidity and his hope to break down gender lines while helping others to do the same—or at least to revaluate where those lines should or should not be drawn.

Another pioneer doing groundbreaking work to challenge typical gender conventions is Los Angeles-based teacher and relationship expert John Wineland. He founded The New Men's

Work Project, which helps men to rethink traditional ideas around intimacy and open up and better communicate with others (particularly women) by being more connected and vulnerable.

One more small sign that our ideas of gender may, indeed, be shifting come from considering the evolution in popular baby names in the United States. In 1910, only 5 percent of American babies named "Charlie" were girls. Over 100 years later, more than half of the babies with that name were girls.[11] A broader analysis by Quartz showed that American names in general have become less gendered since the 1920s: baby names are increasingly used for either boys or girls, whereas before, those names would have been assigned primarily to one gender.

## Why It Matters

For much of the past decade, our traditional understanding of gender roles has been continually challenged and broken down. The main focus, however, has been on reconceiving female gender roles; and the secondary focus has been on the reinvention of gender itself. Understanding or reevaluating male gender roles—or masculinity—has taken a distant third for too long.

Every organization on the planet is faced with workplace challenges and conversations related to interactions between men and women. These are shaped by societal norms, political overlays, media programming, and how we were all raised. The fact is, organizations that can utilize a better understanding of how to help men and women deal with *Muddled Masculinity* will have greater harmony and teamwork, less workplace conflict, and the ability to build a stronger workplace culture.

In the coming year, we expect more introspection and discussion of the role of men in culture and what it means to remain a good man, as well as a reevaluation of how we portray and appreciate fatherhood in the workplace. A single new definition of masculinity is unlikely to emerge; after all, so much of the process of reevaluating gendered roles is about freeing them from limiting expectations. As a result, we anticipate that this trend, *Muddled Masculinity*, will continue to evolve and be important to watch.

## How to Use This Trend

✓ **Encourage the nonconforming**—When men or boys express a passion or curiosity for exploring traditionally feminine things, it is up to all of us to find ways to encourage them, and to avoid making quick judgements. In our experience, creating permissioned, fun, safe experiences at work that allow men (and women) to explore new perspectives can build powerful bonds across genders and teams while igniting new and innovative ideas. To reinforce these experiences, consider using non-conforming images and messaging when portraying men—and their relationship with women—to help encourage nonconforming views of masculinity to come out into the open.

✓ **Innovate with compassion**—We frequently see organizations investing in training for innovation, creativity, and even mindfulness. What about compassion? One of the biggest takeaways from the trend of Muddled Masculinity is that both men and women have to unlearn traditional gender roles and see the world a bit differently. The companies we have studied and worked with that do invest in compassion are the ones who are able to shift their culture based upon trends like this one far more effectively.

## 06

# Side Quirks

## What's the Trend?

—

A global shift toward individualism drives people to follow their passion, start a side business, and appreciate quirks in one another.

A coffee mug can be a nearly universal symbol of individuality.

This simple insight is one that the team at the online arts and crafts marketplace Etsy uncovered as they prepared several years ago to launch their first global brand advertising campaign. The campaign introduced the tagline "Difference Makes Us," and featured an assortment of unique and quirky products (like coffee mugs), which were sold directly to consumers by artistic enthusiasts.

Describing the vision behind the campaign, Etsy CCO Paul Caiozzo said, "An important part of this message is: did you know that something as simple as a coffee cup can reflect what creativity means to you? And on Etsy, there are 200,000 different coffee cups—new, old, antique, used, vintage—that you can get."[1]

With more than 25 million buying and selling users, Etsy also happens to be the ultimate place for anyone to explore their *Side Quirks*. It provides the perfect introduction to this trend. The site allows consumers to find the ultimate product to express their individuality, and supports aspirational entrepreneurs in generating income from their passion.

The real secret of the site's success, though, might be a global shift that has been decades in the making.

## Rise of Individualism

Social scientists describe the societies of the world as holding two seemingly opposite worldviews. "Collectivist" societies value family and group goals over the needs of the individual. In collectivist cultures like India, China, Korea, Mexico, Japan, and most of Africa, the "rules" of society promote working with others, selflessness, and caring for larger extended families.

"Individualistic" cultures, like the USA, Australia, South Africa, and most of Europe, generally celebrate individual achievement, and encourage people to rely on themselves and focus on their immediate families.

Although those classifications have long been accepted as fact, recently, researchers have started to test these assumptions.

The groundbreaking World Values Survey (WVS), for example, has measured people's values and beliefs across the world since 1981. One of the architects of the survey, social scientist Ron

Inglehart, has said that the mission of the WVS is to measure everything from support for gender equality to attitudes toward family, national identity, and culture.

One of the key findings from the survey over the past two decades has been a rising shift toward individualism globally.[2]

In some highly individualistic cultures like the United States and many parts of Europe, this has also led to a corresponding rise in entrepreneurship from people who are taking their *Side Quirks* and using them to start new businesses—a phenomenon many people are now describing as a "side hustle."

## Side Hustles

Catherine Baab-Muguira offers the following description of the appeal of the "side hustle" in a piece for Quartz online:

———

*"The side hustle offers something worth much more than money: a hedge against feeling stuck and dull and cheated by life...in the best-case scenario, your side hustle can be like a lottery ticket, offering the possibility—however remote— that you just might hit the jackpot and discover that holy grail of gigs. The one that perfectly blends money and love. The one that's coming along any day now."[3]*

———

Baked into this description is a sense of hope and optimism for the future fueled by the side hustle. It offers a purpose that work often does not—and does it in a way that offers a more fulfilling life without quitting your day job.

Whether you use it inside the company or as an entrepreneur, the side hustle is an example of how *Side Quirks* are affecting careers, how companies attract and retain employees, and the way we think about work for people of all ages.

Though the side hustle is often equated with a millennial mindset, it is important to note that one of the fastest-growing groups embracing this idea are people over 50 years old. To embrace this shift, the AARP now offers a frequent stream of articles and advice, both online and in their monthly magazine, on how to make money on the side while exploring all sorts of unrequited passions for hobbies they might have had earlier in life—from graphic design to saddle-making.

Our past trend of *Optimistic Aging* was inspired in part by the growing desire of those over 50 not to only remain active in their retirement, but also to accomplish this by starting a second career or an entrepreneurial venture on the side.

The side hustle is a positive implication of the *Side Quirks* trend; however, there is another side to consider. This becomes apparent when we turn our attention across the world to a shift taking place in many traditionally collectivist societies, like Korea, Japan, and China.

## Korean Honja, Japanese Hikikomori, & Chinese Individualism

While individualistic societies tend to celebrate the success of the individual and the "quirk" that helps them stand out, in other places, this shift toward increasing individualism is leading to some disturbing results. Perhaps nowhere is this more apparent than in the case of the *hikikomori* in Japan.

The term *hikikomori* is used in Japan to define a reclusive subgenre of (mostly) men who haven't left their homes or interacted with others for at least six months. A recent Japanese cabinet survey estimated that well over 500,000 young Japanese aged 15 to 39 could be described as *hikikomori,* though some say the real number could be twice as many, since their reclusive nature makes them hard to count.

Some have been driven to their solitary existences by failing to live up to societal or parental expectations. Others retreat after being unable to cope with some big conflict. This isolation, ironically, may itself be a way to express originality, according to photographer Maika Elan, who published a rare photo essay and interview of the *hikikomori* for *National Geographic* magazine. In the interview, she explains:

———

*"In Japan, where uniformity is still prized, and reputations and outward appearances are paramount, rebellion comes in muted forms, like hikikomori. "[4]*

———

Part of what makes this type of existence appealing is easy access to the Internet and technology, which allows *hikikomori* to retreat into the digital world. In China, the rise of individualism is having a different effect. When former J. Walter Thompson Asia-Pacific CEO Tom Doctoroff was interviewed about the state of individualism in China, he described the youth of China in this way:

———

*"Young people in China use the Internet as much more of an emotional engagement with their own identity. They feel they have opportunities to express themselves in ways that they never could in the real world."[5]*

———

In China, the path for rising individualism goes through the Internet. In South Korea, individualism is creating a rising comfort that people are finding through time spent alone.

In late 2016 a well-known Korean jobs portal called Saramin asked 1,593 male and female users between the ages of 20 and 30 years old about their preferences and habits. When asked whether the spread of "individualistic culture" and wanting to enjoy more "me time" was a positive thing, 86 percent responded yes.[6]

Despite the fact that in Korea, going out alone was once considered the behavior of a social outcast *(wangda)*, a new vocabulary has emerged in recent years to describe a slew of activities that used to be taboo, but are now growing in popularity.

On a recent visit to Asia, a Korean colleague of mine shared that *honbap* is the Korean word for eating alone, *honsul* for drinking alone, and *honyeong* for going to the movies alone. "Hon" is the first syllable from the word *honja* (which means to do something alone in Korean), and an online search for "hon" activities now yields hundreds of results. In the survey, most respondents felt that technology and social media (often described as "selfie culture," which we explored in our 2016 trend *Selfie Confidence*) had enabled more independent thinking and less desire to conform among Korea's youth.

What can the Japanese *hikikomori,* the growth of *honja* activities in Korea, and the way Chinese citizens find and explore their identities online tell us about the power of *Side Quirks?* In some cultures, the quirk may not be exploring a hobby for pleasure,but rather driving people to spend more time alone,which can be empowering for some and isolating for others.

## Twee Revolution and Generation Z

The final element of this trend to consider is how individualism is impacting the sense of identity among young people. These successors to the millennial generation who are just now entering their teenage years are increasingly being called Generation Z.

In his book *Twee: The Gentle Revolution in Music, Books, Television, Fashion, and Film,* former *Spin* magazine writer Marc Spitz introduces an alternate term for this generation, which he calls "Twee," and defines their cultural mindset as "the utter dispensing with of 'cool' as it's conveniently known, often in favor of a kind of fetishization of the nerd, the geek, the dork, the virgin."[7]

Whether you prefer the term Twee or Generation Z, this new cohort (generally between 5 and 19 years old) differs from their older millennial cousins and siblings in a few important ways. Most notably, according to a research report from the consultancy Sparks & Honey, they have global social circles, are concerned about and aware of the world, and far more likely to come from blended cultural backgrounds.[8]

This mixed background creates a curious duality: they want to fit into the group and feel connected, but also try to retain enough personality quirks to stand out. While children of their parent's generation might have been ridiculed for bringing ethnic foods to lunch, they use it to stand out and embrace their heritage.

This desire for a unique self-identity and embracing of *Side Quirks* extends to the traditionally binary descriptor of gender, as well. Gen Z are driving the shift toward a world where the options for gender are now unlimited

## Why It Matters

There used to be a global divide between cultures that celebrated individualism and those that did not. Among those that did, people were encouraged to find success as an individual, but not necessarily encouraged to celebrate the quirks of their personalities that made them unique in the first place. These passions and behaviors were once described in a derogatory manner as quirks. Now, quirks have a new positive meaning, and more people are finding joy in embracing these previously-hidden elements of their personalities.

In some cases, *Side Quirks* are leading people to start businesses or volunteer for causes they believe in. In other situations, they are just leading people to feel more independent and comfortable spending time alone, without the necessity of having others around. While some cultures will continue to struggle with this shift, leaving behind troubled groups like the Japanese *hikikomori,* we believe the broader effect of this trend will be more consumer empowerment, greater self-esteem, and the flexibility and freedom to do the things you always wanted to do, at work or otherwise.

## How To Use This Trend

✓ **Show your quirks to connect**—When leaders want to build trust, they are often best served by showing some vulnerability. Showing your quirks can be a great way to build connections. This might mean sharing a hobby or having a side interest that becomes a reason to connect. Either way, *Side Quirks* can give people a reason to believe in and trust you more deeply.

✓ **Stand for something**—Inherent in the idea of showing your quirks is being willing to take a stand on behalf of what you think. This is a powerful strategy that allows brands to stand out, and one that you will routinely see beloved brands employ. *Side Quirks* are not just to be embraced in people, but can also bring a brand to life, creating more human and emotional connections with customers.

*Note: This trend was originally published in the 2017 Non-Obvious Trend Report, and is included in this new trend report with revised examples and new insights.*

# Artificial Influence

## What's the Trend?

—

Creators, corporations, and governments use virtual creations to shift public perception, sell products, and even make fantasy into reality.

Sixteen-year-old pop music superstar Hatsune Miku got her first big break as the face of voice synthesizer software developed by the Japanese company Crypton Future Media. The software allows anyone to write original songs, which Miku then brings to life by singing them. As music creators started generating music and sharing it on YouTube, Miku's performances went viral. Videos featuring her crossed the 100-million-views mark. The Japanese sensation was even invited to open for Lady Gaga, and has launched her own (mostly sold-out) series of live events known as the Hatsune Miku Expo in cities around the world.

Yet her rapid, crowdsourced rise to fame isn't the most interesting thing about Miku. What really sets her apart is that *she isn't real.*

Miku is an anime character designed by manga artist Kei Garo at the request of Crypton Future Media. Through a Creative Commons license, anyone can use her voice and image to create music, as long as they don't make money on their creations. Since she was first developed as a *vocaloid,* over 170,000 sounds have been created for Miku. She's earned millions of fans who share posts about her on social media, follow her from concert to concert, and even start fan clubs dedicated to her.

Hatsune Miku

More importantly, she's become a huge franchise for Crytpon Future Media. Since her popularity has soared, the company has brokered deals for Miku to co-brand or endorse products like the Toyota Corolla, and even to become a spokesperson for the city of Sapporo, where she was "born."

Over the past two years, there has been a dramatic increase in the prevalence of these sorts of "digital celebrities" and avatars like Miku.

Another example is Shudu, striking, dark-skinned digital supermodel created by London-based fashion photographer Cameron-James Wilson. Explaining why he chose to create her, Wilson said, "I am just a creative person, and to me, she is what the most beautiful woman in the world would look like." After a photo of Shudu wearing Fenty Beauty's lipstick went viral, Wilson reportedly received offers to partner up with brands, which quickly made her more than a piece of digital art.

As these virtual celebrities gain the trust and adoration of millions of followers, they are also becoming important influencers. Most promise that they will only promote brands they authentically like and believe in, though of course, that is fairly meaningless when each of their "opinions" is programmed by their creators.

—

*"We live in such a filtered world now, where real is becoming fake. I wanted to create something that is fantasy toward becoming more real."[1]*
— CAMERON-JAMES WILSON, creator of Shudu

—

Virtual celebrities are only one manifestation of how some technologies are blurring the line between what's real and what is fake around us. Their prominence is raising some big questions about the nature of influence itself, and who to believe. They are also at the heart of an emerging trend we call *Artificial Influence*.

## Holographic Celebrities

When thousands of people are already paying to see concerts of a completely fabricated digital personality like Miku, it's easy to imagine they might also be willing to pay to see a holographically resurrected one.

In October of 2018, the father of the late singer Amy Winehouse announced a concert tour to be launched in 2019 featuring a hologram of his daughter onstage. A digital avatar of Winehouse, who died in 2011 at the age of 27, will "perform" some of her most popular songs, accompanied by a live band, real backup singers, and lots of special effects.

According to her father, "fans have been clamoring for something new from Amy, but really, there isn't anything new."[2] With Base Entertainment, the company producing the virtual simulation, he is hoping the avatar will satisfy her fans' desire to continue connecting with her and her music.

Other experiments with holographic celebrities are reinforcing the power of *Artificial Influence,* as well. In the past year alone, these have included the appearance of deceased rapper Tupac Shakur at Coachella, Michael Jackson at the Billboard Music Awards, and others. In another sign of the optimism around this idea, the L.A.- based firm Hologram USA is even trying to create the world's first hologram theater right in the heart of Hollywood, where founder Alki David plans to bring artists like Whitney Houston and Buddy Holly, and comedians like Andy Kaufman and Redd Foxx. Soon, this same technology that brings dead celebrities back to life could also be used to allow simultaneous appearances by living artists in which they could actually perform in two (or more!) locations at once.

As more computers act and perform like humans thanks to artificial intelligence (the other AI!), they will increasingly blur the lines between what's real and what isn't, influencing us to do unexpected things—like pay for the chance to see holographic versions of our dead idols perform one more time.

## Deepfakes and a Gullible Audience

This past year, MIT named GANs (generative adversarial networks) to its prestigious annual list of "10 Breakthrough Ideas." Despite the complex name, the idea behind a GAN is actually fairly simple.

We already have computers that can look at a photo and determine if it's fake by comparing it to a huge database of real images. We also have computers that can generate new images based upon that same dataset of real images. What would happen if the computer generating the new images (known as the generator) could continue creating and refining images based upon the fake-or-real assessment of the other computer (known as the discriminator)? Eventually, the generator would come up with an image that the discriminator would rate as real.

The invention of the GAN was incredibly important in the field of AI. Some even described it as the closest we've come to finally giving machines an imagination.[3] Unfortunately, the rise of this technology is also offering an opportunity to more evil-minded players.

The term "deepfakes" is typically used to describe any doctored video or photo in which a person's face is superimposed on top of someone else's body to present a misleading scene. Perhaps fittingly, there are two industries in which you will find "deepfakes" most frequently: pornography and politics.

Around the end of 2017, a number of sexually-explicit videos featuring Hollywood stars began appearing online. With the help of AI technology, hordes of amateur coders had managed to swap the faces of these stars with those of performers in X-rated scenes. Most video hosting platforms have already banned these clearly unethical videos. And, by and large, deepfakes are low-quality and easy to spot.

Of course, the adult film industry is already thinking about how to leverage this technology in legal ways to add features their customers might want. Leading adult entertainment company Naughty America, for example, recently announced they would offer a service giving customers the ability to insert themselves (so to speak) into scenes with their favorite actors.

Outside of the adult industry, the potential to deploy deepfakes to influence political outcomes is far scarier and more problematic on a global scale. In 2016, deepfakes showing Filipina presidential candidate Leila de Lima in a series of compromising sexual situations were widely blamed for her loss to then-Davao

City Mayor (and current President of the Philippines) Roderigo Duterte. Many have argued that these deepfakes influenced voters by eroding their confidence in her.[4]

Many also believe that the ease with which the masses were manipulated by deepfakes was partly due to the relative dominance of Facebook in the country. Back in 2013, the social media platform launched Free Facebook in the Philippines, offering free access to the Internet. Almost immediately, for many Filipinos, Facebook *became* the Internet. The site offered a conduit to filtered news and limited access to the wider world. It also made it relatively easy for the same fake stories to spread quickly through the amplified echo chamber that had been created.

When your entire mainstream media is squeezed through one social media platform, *Artificial Influence*–such as content created by deepfakes–becomes inescapable, and lies become truth.

In addition to the digital platforms that enable *Artificial Influence* to spread, there's another growing factor that has a lot to do with its rise: the real-time nature of news, and the individuals who publish stories crafted to incite a reaction. We wrote about this trend, which we called *Manipulated Outrage*, in depth last year. At the time, we explained that these "news" creators have ulterior motives in sharing particular stories. Many players who engage in *Artificial Influence* have similar self-serving intent. Unlike the trend focused upon stoking outrage, though, these new efforts expertly employ individual creations as a more personal way to wield influence and shift how we think, particularly when it comes to marketing.

## Fake Influence & Crowdcasting

In June 2018, on the first day of Cannes Lion, a global conference for the advertising and marketing industry, Unilever CMO Keith Weed issued a bold mandate to the industry: get better at spotting and fighting influencer fraud, or lose millions in advertising revenue.

Weed was referring to the widespread practice among influencers to buy followers in an attempt to show higher numbers of fans– and therefore charge brands more to work with them. For his part, he promised that Unilever brands would not work with influencers who buy followers.[5] They would also prioritize partners who believe in increased transparency. These collections of fake followers are an important manifestation of *Artificial Influence,* because they add scale to content created by so-called influencers.

Fake influencers, unfortunately, are emerging not just in the digital world of social media, but in real life, too. For example, Surkus is an app that helps restaurants, bars, or any real-life venue create buzz by selecting and paying people to show up or stand in line, giving the illusion that the spot or event is trendy and well-attended. The app goes as far as "casting" specific people for these events according to their age, social-media engagement, and other characteristics. A *Washington Post* article about the company dubbed their work "crowdcasting," which is an apt description for what they do.[6]

The more examples there are of people getting paid to show up and pretend to be enthusiastic (or to follow and like an influencer even if they don't), the less people and consumers will believe what they see. The true danger of *Artificial Influence* as a trend is that it leads to erosion of consumer trust in what people see online or even in person, and makes them skeptical of *any* kind of influence.

## The Overquantification of Life

Last year, one of the most talked-about episodes of the dystopian Netflix hit show *Black Mirror* depicted a futuristic world in which everyone is assigned a social rating based upon how others rated their interactions with them. Entitled "Nose Dive," it centered upon a character played by Bryce Dallas Howard who is desperate to improve her rating. Her efforts, however, backfire, and her life falls into chaos.

This piece of science fiction was created to satirize what would happen to our relationships and to ourselves if we were judged and rated on everything we did. Next year, this dystopian reality will actually be implemented after years of anticipation.

The idea of assigning a social rating to people was first conceived in China in June of 2014. That year, the Chinese government announced it was building a *Social Credit System* (SCS) program to assign Chinese citizens scores based upon various behaviors. The ambitious aim of the SCS was to develop a "citizen score" that could eventually be used to determine everything from a citizen's eligibility for a mortgage to whom they could date. Though the system is currently only voluntary, all citizens will be required to participate in it by 2020.

This is an important example to consider within the context of the trend of *Artificial Influence,* because it represents a new example of a government exerting its own criteria upon who should be given influence (via ranking) in their society. More concerningly, the system could allow for influence to be taken away from those who dissent by shutting down everything from their mobility to how freely they can express their own ideas online.

The SCS in China may be an extreme example of social credit; however, there exist many daily examples of how social rankings are already used in our society today. You can rate an Uber driver after a shared ride, and that driver can rate you as well. After completing a peer-to-peer transaction online on a platform such as eBay, you usually have the chance to rate the other person. Every click of a like or love button is another form of social ranking.

Could all of these ratings lead us to present inauthentic fantasy versions of ourselves to the world? Could people game the system to generate real-world consequences—like getting an Uber driver kicked off the platform based upon a bunch of fake reviews?

Could citizens in China be given low ratings for small infractions, or infractions that shouldn't really be disqualifying criteria—say, a smoker being prevented from getting a mortgage?

As these rating systems proliferate, they will require us to ask all sorts of big questions about the real value of quantifying everything, and whether the actual way these systems are used will be fair or not.

## Why It Matters

Finding people, institutions, and products that are (or seem) trustworthy continues to be a challenge. According to the Edelman Global Trust Barometer, in 2018, the general population only trusted 52 percent of businesses and 43 percent of media.[7]

In order for individuals to stand apart and be counted among the trusted, the implications of this trend are that organizations must urgently find new ways to be believable and build trust and brand affinity. This will not come from desperately chasing innovation that aims to copy what other digital influencers are doing, or trying risky engagements with platforms that promise lots of social-media engagement from questionably ethical sources.

Instead, we believe it is possible to innovate with integrity and use the principles in this non-obvious trend to encourage higher levels of creative thinking. Digital celebrities, for example, have the potential to become powerful, trusted advocates for messages of good—akin to how animated characters like the long-running Smokey the Bear has been continually used since 1944 by the U.S. Government as a spokesperson (or, perhaps more accurately, a "spokesbear") to educate generations of Americans about their role in preventing wildfires.

In the coming year, it is likely that we will see both possible futures emerge from this trend. As *Artificial Influence* becomes more mainstream, consumers will make individual judgements about who is worth their time and attention and where their trust should be placed.

## How to Use This Trend

✓ **Don't Hide the Artificial Ingredients**—The more successful digital celebrities who have amassed millions of fans have done so by acting in genuine ways. They don't generally hide that they are not real, or try to manipulate their fans. Instead, they embrace their ephemeral nature and use it as proof of their authenticity. You can do the same, whether you are aiming to create your own digital celebrities or considering working with one. The more authentically and ethically you can use these technologies, the more you can reinforce your brand and engage customers and team members alike in non-obvious ways.

✓ **Forgive the Gullible**—It can be frustrating to see how many of the problems caused by *Artificial Influence* come down to simple human gullibility. People are generally lazy. They often believe the first headline they see, and don't ask deeper questions. Of course, none of us see *ourselves* in that light. *Other* people are the problem. Great innovators avoid the judgement, and instead try to rise above the artificiality and find ways to tap into the talent, creativity, and capabilities in their organization to help others do the same.

# RetroTrust

## What's the Trend?

—

Often unsure of whom to trust, consumers look back to organizations and experiences with brands that have a legacy, or those with which they have a personal history.

Thanks to the nature of what I do, a lot of curious things end up on my bookshelves or on the floor of my office. Among my growing collection of oddities—accumulated in the process of researching the latest edition of this book—is a magazine created for film and art lovers.

A year and a half after I bought this "limited-run" inaugural issue for $20, it is still sitting on my shelf. Within its 76 pages, I found stories about the booming independent magazine

MARKETING & SOCIAL MEDIA

culture, why artists continue to use film rather than digital to make movies, and the "power of the pencil." The mission of the magazine? To promote what it calls analog culture."

It's an unusual magazine, but what stands out about it most, and the reason I have kept it instead of discarding it, is the fact that the publisher is a brand that many people have mistakenly assumed was dead: Kodak.

It might be a surprise to learn that Kodak is still in business today. The company now generates more than half of its revenue from its commercial printing division. Selling film—what it was once known for—is a shrinking part of its business. By the numbers, the Kodak of today is a shadow of what it once was.

The brand's annual revenues have gone down nearly 90 percent since 1990. They have sold off or demolished more than half of the 200 buildings that once stood on their corporate campus in Rochester, New York, and have reduced their workforce by more than 100,000 employees over the past decade.

Yet Kodak Chief Branding Officer Dany Atkins sees a bright future for the company. Beyond launching their magazine, in the past year, the brand relaunched their iconic Super 8 cameras, announced they would be bringing back production of their Ektachrome film for diehard enthusiasts, and partnered with fashion retailer Forever 21 to create a line of streetwear featuring the storied brand's logo—an effort designed to appeal to teens obsessed with nostalgic 80s and 90s apparel.

———

*"I have this ambition to return Kodak to being one of the world's best-known, best-loved brands."*
DANY ATKINS, Chief Branding Officer, Kodak

———

Can a brand like Kodak, regularly dismissed as a casualty of the digital revolution, make a comeback?

It can, by tapping into its most underappreciated asset: trust. People have known and trusted Kodak for a long time. For those of us who didn't grow up digital natives, the brand is part of our history— we trusted its film to help us document our most important moments. The logo frequently appears on the back of our preserved photos from the past. It used to be printed on signs at famous landmarks, as an indication that you had made it to an ideal photo-worthy spot. Today, Kodak is trying to find a way to capitalize on that trust to make the brand more than an afterthought in our increasingly digitized world.

The reinvention of Kodak is one of an increasing range of stories of legacy brands reconnecting with their history that led us to uncover the trend of *RetroTrust* as a way to describe consumers' desire to connect with brands they trust because of their long history and legacies or their personal history with them.

## The Appeal of Retro Gaming

If you are on the hunt for old-school arcade machines, you can find an impressive collection at the Silverball Pinball Museum in Florida. The first time I visited on a recent trip to Del Ray Beach, I enjoyed the slightly surreal experience of playing on machines from the 60s and 70s that were older than I was. I'm not quite old enough to remember a time as a kid actually *playing* on pinball machines, though.

Silverball Museum - Del Ray Beach, Florida

I grew up in the 80s, when video games had just taken over from the old-school arcade machines—and it turns out that places to play these games are growing rapidly all over the world, thanks in part to the trend of *RetroTrust*.

Buenos Aires has seen significant growth in so-called "arcade bars," as 30- and 40-somethings aim to reconnect with their past and play games with friends.[2] A similar growth is happening in the U.S., where these destinations are increasingly known as "barcades:"adult retro arcades that serve alcohol and food.

One of the people working to modernize these new arcade experiences without causing them to lose their charm is an entrepreneur named Tyler Bushnell. To say gaming runs in Bushnell's blood would be an understatement. He is the son of legendary Atari cofounder Nolan Bushnell, and the cofounder of a startup, *Polycade*, which is introducing a retro arcade machine for the digital age.

The Polycade is the size of a small kitchen cabinet, and can be easily mounted onto a wall. Unlike current arcade machines that are heavy and difficult to move, the Polycade is much more easily transportable. And the 11 games it ships with are played on a built-in, 28-inch LCD screen. Their market, apart from trendy workplaces and well-to-do homeowners, is the increasingly popular barcades and so-called "micro-amusement parks" like Two Bit Circus, which was conveniently founded by his brother Brent Bushnell (who, predictably, was also an early customer for Polycade machines).

Bushnell's vision of bringing back retro gaming is shared by one of the largest gaming companies in the world.

## How Nintendo Mastered Nostalgia

Over the past few years, Nintendo has been tapping nostalgia for their games and consoles quite successfully. Back in 2016, the brand released their NES Classic, a gaming console with games most 40-something parents (like me!) would remember fondly from their youth. We previously wrote about this product launch in the chapter on the *Truthing* trend from the 2018 edition of this book, as well.

Nintendo is also leading the charge among console producers by blending the old with the new in their products—engineering *RetroTrust* into modern products and services. The latest, most versatile Nintendo Switch (which can be configured as a handheld mobile gaming device or as two detachable controllers for the console) has become the fastest-selling game console in U.S. history.

Earlier in the year, Nintendo released a series of cardboard kits that let kids build "accessories" for their Switch handheld console. These DIY kits—which will remind some of the model ships and planes they built in their childhood—include, for example, a motorcycle handle that allows the player to "steer" their kart in a Mario Kart game.

Nintendo DIY Kit for Nintendo Switch, 2018

With the NES Classic, as well as the Nintendo Switch and its Labo accessory kits, Nintendo is leveraging its considerable heritage as a toy and entertainment company to inspire trust in its latest gaming experiences.

In honor of the brand's widespread popularity, the 2016 handover ceremony for the Summer Olympics from Brazil to its 2020 destination of Tokyo even included a production that involved Japanese Prime Minister Shinzo Abe dressed as the beloved Nintendo character Mario. Despite the fact that it was not an official sponsor, Nintendo was unofficially the ambassador for Japanese culture to the world–and it delighted the fans who watched the ceremony worldwide.

In the 2018 report, we also introduced a trend we called *Touchworthy* to describe the growing desire among consumers for experiences they can touch and feel. In it, we cited an example of the growing popularity of familiar board games, which has continued to accelerate throughout the past year.[3]

What do these retro arcades, Nintendo's mastery of nostalgia, and the modern resurgence of board games tell us about the world today? These shareable experiences offer a striking alternative to the physically isolating experiences of our increasingly digital lives. Returning to the games and feelings of the past offers us a way to remind ourselves of a less complicated time when it seemed easier to know who you could trust.

This is a major opportunity for older legacy brands who are being disrupted by new entrants and seeking ways to fight back. As the examples in this category illustrate, in a time when trust has become harder to earn, people are looking toward the brands they grew up with for leadership and stability. As a result, this non-obvious trend of *RetroTrust* could offer a roadmap back to relevance for brands, if used strategically (see later in this chapter for how to do it).

This same phenomenon is driving a desire for people to reconnect with the artisans and professionals who make the things we consume.

## Why Craftsmanship Matters

The world's best umbrella isn't for sale at a retailer near you, and you won't find it on Amazon. In fact, the only way to get it is to travel to a tiny workshop in Naples, Italy, where generations of craftsmen from the Talarico family have been making umbrellas for more than 150 years. Today, these legendary umbrellas are hand-carved from local Italian wood by Mario Talarico and his nephew (an apprentice), and each one takes seven hours to make. The shop only sells 220 umbrellas a year—for the surprisingly approachable price of 200 euros each.[4]

A few hours' drive away, in the tiny Swiss town of Neuchâtel, Kari Voutilainen sits in his five-floor chateau working diligently on a watch. Voutilainen might objectively be described as the best watchmaker in the world, thanks to the many awards he's earned at prestigious watch shows, including five top prizes at the

Grand Prix d'Horlogerie Genève, the Oscars of watchmaking. He produces about 50 watches each year, has no marketing or sales staff, and his customers routinely pay anywhere from $75,000 up to half a million dollars for his creations. His customers frequently visit the workshop while he is making their watches.

"Real enthusiasts want to visit the place where their watch was made, and they want to know the person who created it," Voutilainen told *The New York Times*. "It gives them a story to tell, and that's something the bigger brands can't offer.[5]"

Across the world, there are craftsmen and craftswomen who, like Mario Talarico, produce beautiful artifacts steeped in deep history, tradition, and lore. Their families have been making them for generations and their long heritage has earned their work a strong reputation and the trust of customers. Other artistans are more recent entrants without deep family history, like first-generation watchmaker Voutilainen, but their process and attention to their craft offers a powerful story about a return to a time when products were handmade by someone you knew – another pathway to establishing *RetroTrust*.

This isn't the same as buying something off the shelf made in a faraway factory, assembled by robots, and inspected by humans. These are products you can trust, because often, you buy them directly from the person who made them. It is also a sign of a growing backlash against the increasingly faceless shopping we do online, and a yearning for a means of shopping with personal connection built in.

Like any other artisan, Talarico's and Voutilainen's success are manifestations of this prediction of *RetroTrust*, since these craftsmen effectively leverage their brand's history or their deep expertise to attract new customers and tell a story about the history, family, process, and quality of the products they make.

# The Power of Nostalgic Entertainment

When I was younger, I used to watch *He-Man,* the very popular cartoon set on the magical planet of Eternia. Every week, my brother and I would sit in front of the TV and cheer for our hero to defeat the evil Skeletor, then play with our action-figure set with the same characters.

He-Man Action Figure

Recently, I began watching *He-Man* again, this time with my kids. Like many other cartoons from the past, *He-Man is* back on the air, and will be coming to the big screen in a new live action movie planned for release in December 2019. (Hopefully, this movie adaption will be better than the 1987 version of *Masters of the Universe*, which has been suggested by some as a contender for the worst movie ever made).

The practice and pace of bringing back animated shows and movies from the past is increasing sharply. In this year alone, a live-action sitcom version of *The Jetsons* is coming to ABC, a reboot of the animated series *Where in the World is Carmen Sandiego?* will stream on Netflix, and a musical adaptation of Disney's *Aladdin* will be released in December 2019 with Will Smith cast in the role of Genie (made iconic by the late Robin Williams in the animated 1992 Disney version).

The factor driving this resurgence? Nostalgia. When thinking about watching a new show, it is hard to know whether it will resonate, be appropriate for your kids, or simply be worth your time and risk, given other options. Parents who grew up watching *these* animations remember them fondly. They are eager to introduce them to their children and create a shared experience by watching them together—just as I did by enjoying *He-Man* again with my kids.

Casting in these reboots is also going retro, with actors returning to roles that made them household names decades ago. In the past year, Sir Patrick Stewart announced he would return to play the role of Captain Jean Luc Picard in a new *Star Trek* series. Harrison Ford has returned to several of his iconic roles, including *Star Wars'* Han Solo, *Indiana Jones,* and *Blade Runner's* Rick Deckard.

There is even a growing number of actors returning later in life to roles that made them famous long ago—like the new version of *Fuller House* using the kids from the original show as parents in the reboot,or former 1970s *Wonder Woman* Lynda Carter returning to the superhero genre as part of the cast for the new *CW* hit show *Supergirl*. In addition, the popularity of a franchise like *Jurassic Park* or *Toy Story* continue to drive plans for new films—and this seems unlikely to change anytime soon.

Many actors are coming back to the roles (or genres) that defined them for the same reason we are seeing so many sequels and reboots of films from years (and sometimes decades) ago. In a world overwhelmed with viewing choices, people are naturally hesitant to risk trying out entirely new experiences. For those who are able to do it strategically, utilizing the non-obvious trend of *RetroTrust* could offer a powerful means of rising above the noise and earning focused attention.

## Why It Matters

When you look at consumers embracing retro video games and toys, reboots of older entertainment shows, or products made by real people with real craftsmanship, it's clear we are gravitating toward products with a history, or with which we have a history. As we've become more skeptical of brands' ulterior motives when they market to us, we've also become more uncertain about trying new things. The past we know is safe. *RetroTrust* is growing because putting our faith in products we recognize, or with which we have some prior experience, with helps us make decisions about what to pay attention to or buy.

This matters, both to companies with long histories and to newer ones without. For those that can leverage a legacy or tradition,storytelling is the key. Simply reprinting your logo on a product outsourced to a factory far away and offering a substandard experience will end up draining all the goodwill from that brand's legacy. Instead, legacy companies must reconnect with the attributes people fondly recall, and offer a consistent experience that reawakens passion in customers who will remember what the brand used to stand for and come back to give it another chance.

*RetroTrust* can also provide great value for newer or lesser-known companies that don't enjoy that same long legacy. Powerful storytelling can still help create innovative ways to share some aspect of the company's offerings (such as the founder's story) in order to create a similar emotional connection with customers.

## How to Use This Trend:

✓ **Focus on the backstory–** To create more trust and generate attention, organizations need to share powerful stories about what they do and who does it (or did it). When we have helped leaders to become more powerful storytellers, it often involves using trends like *RetroTrust* to communicate with methods that are highly relatable, safe, and familiar. Beyond communications, integrating the principles of *RetroTrust* into product/service design can also help to create innovations that better connect with consumers and have a compelling story built in.

✓ **Seek out opportunities for collaboration–**You don't need to have the legacy and history of a brand like Nintendo in order to use this trend effectively. For younger or less-established brands, strategic partnering can offer a smart way to build upon the trust and heritage of an older brand, and the older brands can find new relevance, ideas, and energy through teaming with a younger one, as well—much like Forever 21 and Kodak coming together on their branded line of apparel.

# 09

# B2Beyond Marketing

## What's the Trend?

—

B2B brands use non-traditional methods to embrace their humanity and reach decision-makers along with a broader audience.

The first time I wrote about this trend, martial arts actor Jean-Claude Van Damme had just done the "epic split." Our 2014 Trend Report had just been published, and there was something curious happening in the world of advertising.

The epic split, in case you haven't seen it recently, is an ad for Volvo trucks that involves Van Damme standing on the rearview mirrors of two large 18-wheeler trucks. The trucks are moving in reverse on a closed track, and they slowly move apart as Van Damme does his signature center split.

When the ad first debuted during the 2014 NFL Super Bowl, people were stunned. Did they really do that? (Yes, it was real.) As a marketing professional, I was curious. Why would the trucking division of an automotive brand spend millions of dollars to show an ad for a product that the majority of the people watching the game would never purchase?

**VISIT THE NON-OBVIOUS RESOURCES CENTER ONLINE TO:**

Watch this full ad with commentary!

At the time, I was working at a large marketing agency called Ogilvy, and most of our clients were also in business-to-business industries. There was a standard marketing playbook that almost all of them used. Go to trade shows, publish white papers, and host client events. Each of these was highly targeted, and they worked. Most importantly, they avoided waste.

Watching Volvo promote their "dynamic steering" feature on their trucks to a mass audience made no sense. Why would they intentionally waste their marketing dollars putting an ad like that on such an expensive stage?

Volvo Epic Split ad with Jean Claude Van Damme

# Fixing Failing Restaurants

Around the same time that Volvo was making headlines and resurrecting Van Damme's career, I started getting hooked on a reality TV show that seemed to be on every time I turned to the *Food Network* channel. The show was called *Restaurant Impossible,* and featured Chef Robert Irvine helping struggling restaurant owners in real time to fix their problems and renovate their restaurants.

The format of the show featured "before" stories of everything from fridges filled with rotten milk and old, brown produce to disorganized owners making convenience-store trips several times a day to pick up ingredients they failed to order in advance. Each time, as part of his process, Chef Robert transforms this dysfunctional food-ordering process by bringing in his preferred food supply partner Sysco Corporation.

Sysco is the perfect example of a dominant B2B business in its industry. Since 1970, the company has supplied food to restaurants, healthcare facilities, and other food-service providers. In 2018, the company had over $58 billion in sales, and more than 67,000 employees working to provide services to more than 600,000 customer locations around the world.

As a brand that sells directly to catering groups and restaurants, you would expect them to attend trade shows or run print ads in food industry magazines. Why would they spend the money to sponsor a mainstream *Food Network* show watched by millions of people who *don't* own a restaurant—and probably never will?

*Food Network* ratings data shows that one of the most popular times of the day for viewing is between midnight and 4 a.m. One possible explanation for the popularity of this late-night slot is that it overlaps with the times restaurant owners working long shifts are getting home and turning on their TV to decompress.

Network data also shows that more than 70 percent of independent restaurant owners watch the *Food Network* at least once a week.

While the audience for *Restaurant Impossible* may not have been only restaurant owners, those owners were *part* of the audience. That was the light bulb at the heart of the trend of *B2Beyond Marketing*.

If using mass-marketing techniques is effective in reaching your audience, then anyone else you reach are not wastage... they are a *bonus*.

Since this trend was initially researched and reported nearly five years ago, things have continued to evolve, and it has become even more relevant. Over time, the practice of B2B marketing as a category has increasingly involved more content creation, better storytelling, and a continuing evolution away from the mindset that all marketing for a B2B brand should only be seen by a niche audience.

The trend, in other words has escalated, and become even more relevant and important. Let's take a look at how, and shift our attention to a few more modern examples, starting with an unlikely B2B brand that has built a surprisingly large following on social media: the world's largest container shipping company.

## How the Boring Gets Interesting ... On Social Media

The maritime shipping brand Maersk Line uses content marketing across more than 30 different social media channels to bring the world of shipping containers and ocean liners to life. Across most of these channels, they have tens of thousands of follower, most of whom are not part of the maritime industry at all.

The content they share engages people while teaching them interesting facts about the industry. Several recent posts, for example, have included images of ships, videos about what life is really like on board, and plenty of other behind-the-scenes content showing how the maritime industry operates.

Social Media ad unit from Maersk to promote upcoming Facebook live session.

This content is not only humanizing the industry, but also offering a way for those who do work with Maersk to explain what they do to family and friends. It creates a shareable moment that allows the brand to improve its reputation, more effectively recruit top talent, and bolster a sense of pride among current employees in what they do everyday—and why it matters.

## Making Construction Equipment Fun

If you happen to be in a B2B business, at this point, you might be skeptical about exactly how all this storytelling will really impact the bottom line. Is the investment of time and resources in these activities really worth it?

The unique marketing strategy employed by construction equipment manufacturer Caterpillar may offer one clue that it does. Several years ago, the brand made a shift in marketing strategy to develop more advertising capable of creating a sense of awe among their audience and the general public. In one memorable piece, they featured machines facing off in an epic Jenga game, with the goal of removing 700-pound wooden blocks one by one from a tall stack until eventually, the entire stack collapsed. The video went viral, and has racked up more than 5 million views to date.

VISIT THE NON-OBVIOUS RESOURCES CENTER ONLINE TO:

Watch this full ad online!

The point, shares Caterpillar Global Brand Creative Director Archie Lyons, is "to take the Cat brand on the offensive. We are a large, Fortune 50 company... we want to go from cold, corporate, and conservative to human, relevant, and approachable."[1]

The video series clearly does that–but it has also faced some predictable B2B industry criticism. How valuable are branded videos like this, skeptics ask, when they are most likely to be seen and shared by people who are not prospective buyers or qualified leads?

Caterpillar "Built for It" Campaign

Lyons offers his own answer to this question: "The campaign is designed to reach people outside of our normal scope of customers. The viewer for these videos could be a teenage boy who likes to play Jenga, and he might show his mom and dad, or uncles, who may work in construction."

The value, in other words, comes from starting *conversations* from person to person—which may eventually lead to consideration, growing reputation, and eventually to purchase. As with many forms of brand marketing, tying the impact directly to a single sale is difficult. Could you really attribute an industry buyer purchasing a fleet of construction equipment to something like a viral YouTube video? Unlikely.

Most B2B marketing teams know that the buying cycle for their products is long. It takes months, and sometimes even years, to close a sale, and a lot of activities happen within that time. Customers see industry analyst reports, they look at the age and utility of their current solutions, they evaluate their options, and they watch quirky marketing videos. All have an impact on the eventual decision to buy.

In that context, it is easy to see how efforts like this could have real value. Generating attention for your brand, reminding a potential customer of what you do, getting them excited about your product features, and giving them a way to share what *they* do with family and friends outside of the industry are all important results from effectively using *B2Beyond Marketing*.

## Inside Intel

For more than two decades, Intel has had to get creative about their marketing. As an ingredient brand, they know the challenges of marketing to consumers who never buy their product directly. Over the past five years, the brand has been on a journey to use content marketing and cultivate an in-house team of journalists to produce highly engaging content that helps the brand stay relevant and reach people.

Today, their digital magazine platform, known as *iQ by Intel,* is a powerhouse—with hundreds of posted articles on everything from how technology is revolutionizing restaurants to a behind-the-scenes look at the VR experience related to the Steven Spielberg film *Ready Player One.* The brand has adopted the same mindset as a publisher, aiming to build a loyal audience over time and continually offer interesting and thoughtful content to keep them coming back.

In many ways, it is the opposite of the traditional white-paper strategy. Rather than create a few highly academic and technical reports and force people to "pay" by surrendering their email address for the purposes of lead generation, *B2Beyond Marketing* is driving brands to think like Intel: find something useful to say, and to offer it freely in a way that is interesting to people far outside your industry.

## Why It Matters

In Chapter 19, we will talk about the value of *Intersection Thinking.* A key argument for this is the idea that you can take lessons from outside your industry and apply them within to come up with new solutions and innovative ideas. This is a trend inspired by the idea that B2B brands can take and use inspiration from brands that sell to a variety of customers and industries.

The implication is that B2B brands can and should do more to get on the radar of potential customers before those customers even identify a need, and they can do this by using less traditional forms of media. The future of B2B marketing will be about creating better content, leveraging tactics and ideas that were once considered solely the realm of B2C brands, and ultimately building credibility by being more human.

# How to Use This Trend:

✓ **Make it fundamental**–When it comes to changing how we think about B2B marketing, much of the resistance comes from getting mired in the complexity of a feature or message. Yet Volvo didn't fret over whether people would know what "dynamic steering" was, or even whether they would care. Their real message was that Volvo technology can make driving surprisingly smooth–even if the driving experience happens to be two trucks going backward with an action superstar balanced between them. People got the message.

✓ **Get over the fear of wastage**–It is easy to think that making your content and marketing available to a broader audience will be too expensive and wasteful. When Sysco partnered with the *Food Network,* they didn't worry about how many non-restaurant owners might see their message. Instead, they focused on the fact that if they told their story simply (we reliably supply fresh food!), their target audience would get it, and act on it when they had a need.

*Note: This trend was originally published in the* 2016 Non-Obvious Trend Report, *and is included in this new trend report with revised examples and new insights.*

# 10

# Fad Fatigue

## What's the Trend?

—

Consumers get weary of innovations claiming to be the "next big thing," and assume none will last long.

Today, when people look for the latest tips on how to lose weight, or for the new popular "lifehack" to supercharge their productivity, they turn to the Internet. What the Internet usually delivers, however, is a mishmash of cutting-edge discoveries, half-baked theories, and celebrity-endorsed pseudoscience. Extracting what matters and what doesn't—or what matters for a short while *until* it doesn't—is not always easy.

There is a difference between a trend and a fad.

In every edition of this book, I am careful to distinguish between the two and it is a subject of constant discussion and debate among my team. In Part 1 of this book, I shared our definition of a non-obvious trend: a unique, curated observation of the accelerating present. Along with spotlighting and sharing meaningful trends every year, I often find myself cautioning readers against the overexcitement and misplaced faith that fads may inspire.

The enthusiasm around a "fad" is always intense and viral, and though it will, by definition, be short-lived, that can be hard to see in the moment. In Part 4 of this book, you will find a detailed appendix in which we transparently review and rate all of the previous trend predictions included in every year of this report. There are well over 100–and some of them have not stood the test of time.

Every year, these past ideas are tested through dozens of workshops with global clients and keynote presentations at events around the world. All of these live audiences engage with the trends, offer feedback, and provide the ultimate focus group with information to see what works, what lasts, and what doesn't.

## Why Do Some Trends Last Longer Than Others?

Looking back, what was it that caused some predictions to fare better than others? The secret usually came down to avoiding the distraction of smaller, fleeting examples of interesting innovation, and instead focus on bigger stories across multiple industries. The harder my team and I tried to find a pattern among stories of popular fads, the more apparent it became that these fads were not aligning to reveal a single broader shift or behavioral change. Instead, we realized that the speed of their rise was often accompanied by a faster fall from public conversation. If there was a bell curve for fad adoption, its range was looking a lot more like a giant tsunami than a small hill.

We asked a new question: could the roller coaster of attention itself be indicating what the broader trend might be? As we looked deeper, we discovered a deep sense of fatigue among consumers. People seemed to *assume* that any new discovery or "miracle" product would only last for a short while. The nature of this speedy expiry itself led us to describe a non-obvious trend we named *Fad Fatigue*.

To illustrate how prevalent this has become, it is fitting that we should start with one of the industries that has consistently brought us a stream of fads: home fitness.

## Fitness Fads

Like many people, I own a house filled with the remnants of failed fitness ambitions. I have a "twist board," which was supposed to tone my obliques, and a GRIPMASTER finger exercise tool to improve my grip strength for playing guitar. The intense P90x DVD set sits nearly untouched next to a DVD player that also rarely sees any use. Over the past few years, I have picked up stretch bands, foam rollers, and plenty of fitness tracking watches that run out of battery long before I'm able to use them consistently to track my health. And I'm not alone. The fitness equipment market alone is estimated to reach $12 billion by the year 2022,[1] and it is highly likely that much of that growth will come from replacing dormant at-home exercise devices and buying into quirky workout concepts.

While today, the Internet and social media seem to accelerate the spread of fitness fads, the truth is, they have been around since before many people reading this book were born. For example, earlier this year, *USA Today* published a fun article entitled "The Biggest Exercise Fad the Year You Were Born."[2] In my birth year, the "Leg Beauty Kit," a set of rubber resistance bands marketed to women to slim and tone their legs, ruled the day. It was followed a year later the by rise of "speed bag training." No doubt inspired by the release of the movie *Rocky*, men flocked to boxing gyms to get their arms in movie-star shape. The rest of the article highlights fads so outlandish, it seems inconceivable they were ever popular in the first place (e.g., the Thighmaster!).

The craze for new fitness ideas continues today, and they include everything from Parkour gyms (inspired by reality shows like *American Ninja Warrior*) and goat yoga, the practice of having baby goats climb on you while you do yoga poses. In case you're curious about the rationale for the latter, it is because (according to one expert) "it is impossible to be sad and depressed when you have goats around you."[3]

Goat Yoga Session, 2018 (Photo Credit: Central Washington University, Flickr)[4]

Clearly the fitness industry relies on fads. To be fair, part of the reason they work so well in this industry is because each new product or exercise craze offers something new to try, which has the positive side effect of giving people novelty as a tool for personal motivation to continue with their exercise regimen.

It also means no single product will last for very long reality the industry has embraced out of necessity, continually scrambling to launch new products before their customers discard the old ones. In a fad-driven industry, no one makes any money if you just stick to push-ups and squat jumps.

## Healthy Food Fads & Unusual Nutrition

It is a modern culinary tragedy that cauliflower is having its moment.[5]

My statement might be a bit biased. As some of my regular readers know, I am the self-appointed "Despiser-in-Chief" of cauliflower. Everything from its disgusting shape to its noxious smell has led to my longstanding disbelief that any non-starving human would willingly eat it. I have to admit that these days, my personal "cauliphobia," as I have sometimes called it, makes me an outlier. Cauliflower is now being mashed, riced, roasted, used as gluten-free pizza crust, and even turned into "cauliflower steaks." Yuck!

Yet for all the attention this horrible cruciferous vegetable is receiving right now, I can take solace in the fact that history suggests the attention won't last for long. When it comes to healthy food, as with fitness, our attention wanders frequently. Although some nutrition movements are rightly considered trends—like the shift away from eating meat and overly processed foods—many food manias around ingredients only enjoy their time in the spotlight for a short while. Quinoa, kale, sweet potato, and beets have all had their moments. And then they simply become ordinary ingredients once more. The one area of nutrition fads that accurately mirrors what has happened in fitness involves highly unusual items.

Today, there are plenty of news stories about the wonderous health benefits of activated charcoal (it traps toxins and chemicals in the gut, preventing their absorption!), algae capsules (boost your brainpower and prevent heart disease!), and acacia fiber (relieves pain and reduces fat!).

Some of these may well be real miracle treatments. Unfortunately, we are given so much conflicting advice, fueled by get-rich-quick online marketers and "advice" websites, that most of us end up completely confused. All the uncertainty that this *Fad Fatigue* trend describes is creating a golden opportunity for the few organizations that are able to tell a more concrete and authentic story to sustain their new product or service in the minds of customers, and rise above the here today, gone tomorrow bias affecting everyone else.

## Why People Don't Trust Science, Either

The comedy site Funny or Die captures this dynamic in a hilarious video about a "Time-Traveling Dietician." In the video, a dietician goes back to the 70s to warn an unsuspecting couple about all the developments and health discoveries made by scientists in the future. Every minute, he comes back with a conflicting piece of advice: don't eat eggs. Only eat the egg whites. Eggs are fine. Don't eat red meat. Eat lots of protein. Don't eat bread. Eat whatever, because the only thing that matters is genetics.

**VISIT THE NON-OBVIOUS RESOURCES CENTER ONLINE TO:**

Watch the full video online!

It is funny because it's true. The science around food and what we should or shouldn't eat seems to change daily, making us weary of all food claims in general—especially diets.

Our skepticism about which food health claims to believe or ignore is exacerbated by the fact that much of the justification for them—like the health benefits of the Mediterranean diet or intermittent fasting—rests on the fact that our ancestors ate that way (or didn't eat at all—though probably not voluntarily, in their case). The fact is, many of these diets may be effectivand almost of their arguments seem plausible. But there isn't always consensus in the medical research to support their claims. So who do we believe?

Complicating matters further is the tendency of many media outlets to take a small finding from a scientific research paper and sensationalize its implications in a link-baiting headline:" Chemical in McDonald's Fries Could Cure Baldness, Study Says!"[6] and "Drinking Too Much Coffee 'Could Shrink Women's Breasts.'"[7]

Each time we come across these manipulated messages, we lose a little more faith in anyone's ability to tell what is actually healthy and what isn't.

Most of us are tired of being burned over and over. We try to deal with this confusion by becoming more skeptical of new health claims (or more inclined to try them and move on to the next more quickly). Instead, we go back to the indisputable basics.

More sugar is bad. More vegetables are good. Eating less will keep you slim. A similar mentality is affecting how we approach work, as well.

## Workplace Health Fads: Sitting and Fidgeting

By now, you've probably heard the latest health maxim, "sitting is the new smoking."

Research has demonstrated that the amount of time people with desk jobs spend sitting can severely impact their long-term health.[8] Many businesses have created innovative products and services to address this problem. Flexible desks allow you to make your desk higher, so you can stand and work. Exercise ball chairs and other devices meant to improve the ergonomics of your seating promise to transform your posture and how you feel at work.

Outside of nutrition and fitness, the way we work has led to another fast growth area for plenty of fad-driven products. Popular products like fidget spinners and fidget cubes support those who need to address anxiety or attention challenges, and plenty of tech gadgets have come out recently to remind, prod, and shock us into sitting up straight, taking breaks, drinking more water, or using mindful techniques like meditation to become more productive in every waking moment.

Fidget spinner and fidget cube
(Photo Credit: www.fidgetcircle.com)

Like the products and ideas in other categories, few of these are likely to last a particularly long time,and each adds to the growing trend of *Fad Fatigue, which*describes how more and more of us continue to feel.

## Why It Matters

As consumers, we are used to seeing new health products or ideas hit the mainstream and rapidly gain popularity. What we may not appreciate is just how many industries (like fitness) depend on new fads appearing and disappearing. This cycle of fads is causing fatigue among consumers. We are tired of hearing about the latest and greatest health or fitness product,and are too skeptical to believe in them, precisely because we've heard so many similar proclamations before.

As consumers, we are used to seeing new products, business models, and experiences hit the mainstream and rapidly gain awareness and popularity—whether they include exercise, health, diet, office productivity or, frankly, any other industry. What we may not appreciate is how the non-obvious trend of

*Fad Fatigue* can affect any company seeking to innovate and create sustainable products, services, and experiences for their customers or employees.

This does not mean consumers are developing an immunity to falling for fads. Rather, people are getting tired of products and services more quickly—and they are moving on to the next just as quickly. This means it will be more important (and harder) than ever to keep customer attention focused on your current offering, and find ways to drive loyalty for your services, products, and company.

## How to Use This Trend:

✓ **Innovate with more strategy**—Often, companies will mistake invention for innovation. They are not the same thing. This common mistake can lead to shallow ideation, one-dimensional product/service ideas, and undifferentiated engagement with your customers. In other words, more *Fad Fatigue*. Instead, the most successful organizations we have studied (and often help to advise) challenge themselves to look beyond products to consider new approaches and business models that integrate greater purpose and deliver more robust experiences to delight their customers.

✓ **Build a gateway approach**—One way to leverage long-term value out of a fad or "short-term engagement" is to develop a plan for your next product/service, or an idea that builds on the success of the first fad. Ask yourself, how can I capitalize on the attention from this fad to deliver on my next product or service, and make it something that will last longer? One method we often use is considering how to widen the circle of a target audience to attract attention from *more* people, like late adopters and people who may have heard about the fad, but are unlikely to be the first to act upon it. This second circle of people can help you extend the life of a fad beyond its initial adopters, and potentially engage in a way that is more sustainable. It can build more loyalty, as well.

# Extreme Uncluttering

## What's the Trend?

—

To simplify daily life, people shed their excess "stuff," and seek pared-down experiences and ways to unclutter their digital identities too.

The annual ritual of writing this book has given me a disturbing tendency toward impulse purchases. If I hear about an interesting product, I usually try it. My justification, of course, is that these purchases are all part of the research for this book. The predictable problem is that it leads me to accumulate lots of stuff I don't need.

Though I may have used my annual research process as the perfect defensive rationale for my own clutter, I'm not alone in feeing like I have far too much of it. A lot of people share this uneasy relationship to excess "stuff," inspiring the steady rise in a cottage industry of organizational experts. Most famous among them is Marie Kondo, the Japanese author of the bestselling *The Life-Changing Magic of Tidying Up* (who we wrote about in the 2017 edition of this book). Kondo advises people to only keep those items that "spark joy," and get rid of the rest. Earlier this year, Swedish author Margareta Magnusson offered a more unusual take on the importance of decluttering. In *The Gentle Art of Swedish Death Cleaning,* she shares the principle of *döstädning* (dö meaning "death," and städning meaning "cleaning")—the act of cleaning or uncluttering as you become old in order to unburden your heirs of this task when you eventually die.

The trend toward simplifying our lives has morphed over the years, starting with the desire to declutter our excess stuff. We first reported on this in 2011, with a trend we called *Desperate Simplification.* Then, in 2016, we identified *Obsessive Productivity,* a trend that showed people simplifying everything in order to improve their productivity. The next year, we predicted another trend called *Mainstream Mindfulness* (which describes the rise of mindful practices and meditation in business as a method for decluttering our minds, fostering innovation, and increasing well-being). Finally, in 2018, we introduced *Data Pollution* (a prediction describing how much unnecessary and useless data companies and people are increasingly forced to manage).

This year, we've found that as people become more conscious and aware of the things they want around them, they develop an overwhelming sense of clutter in their daily lives, which drives them to make drastic changes. For some of us, this is leading to a process of decluttering our belongings—both physical and digital. For others, this is more of a mental journey that involves more mindful living and reducing life's distractions, or decluttering relationships that do not serve us.

We call this trend prediction *Extreme Uncluttering*–our term for describing the increasing number of people who are not just simplifying through reevaluation of the things they own, but also by removing the stressors or distractions, from noisy venues to in-your-face branding, that lead them to feel mental or emotional "clutter" in their daily lives.

## Uncluttered Venues, Uncluttered Experiences

One way people are choosing to declutter the distractions in their daily lives is by making more mindful choices about the venues they visit or support.

According to the 2018 Zagat National Dining Trends Survey, the top complaint reported by diners is the level of noise at restaurants.[1] More and more, people are feeling overwhelmed by overly stimulating environments such as loud cafés, bars, or eateries (often blaring with multiple unnecessary televisions reporting what I sometimes call "feel-bad breaking news." Several entrepreneurs are trying to find new ways to help restaurants deal with this problem and help people find the best restaurants for them. Apps like iHEARu and SoundPrint measure and rate the ambient noise levels of restaurants in real time, letting people decide whether to visit that venue or not.

In Spain, a campaign called "Comer sin Ruido" (Eat Without Noise) urges restaurants to promote a quieter dining environment. More than 50 restaurants have pledged to be less noisy as a result of the campaign, including several with Michelin stars.

Other restaurants are offering pared-down or "uncluttered" experiences, including the Dans Le Noir in Paris. This famous restaurant offers diners the opportunity to eat in a pitch-black room, allowing guests to focus their senses on the taste and texture of food, not on how the food or the environment around them looks. The idea that flavor—not appearances—should be the focus of an eating experience is also increasingly moving chefs in fine restaurants to a deliver a simpler and more elegant plating style. "It's really about letting the dish and ingredients speak for themselves," explains the executive chef of Bâtard in New York.[2]

The movement toward less-cluttered experiences is not just driven by the people seeking them, but also by venues purposely creating them—even if customers might not want them. For example, the live entertainment world has often struggled with two seemingly unrelated problems: how to get people to focus their attention on the performance rather than their phones, and how to prevent people from recording bootleg videos of it.

The company Yondr has created a product that addresses both. Their mobile phone "pouches," which lock devices and prevent their owners from using them, have been gaining popularity at concert venues and comedy clubs. Patrons are required to "lock" their phones in the pouches, which are only unlocked when a performance ends or a patron leaves the venue. Most of the venues using the pouches are primarily interested in locking phones to combat piracy, but they are also encouraging patrons to be more present and enjoy the show with fewer distractions.

Yondr phone-locking platform

The Yondr platform has been so successful that even schools are piloting the use of these pouches to help students focus in class by avoiding the distractions of their phones. In September 2018, a new policy took effect in France,banning students under the age of 15 from bringing mobile phones to school: a bold move to help kids declutter the stimuli that affect their concentration and learning.

## Uncluttering Digital Distractions

The fact that venues and even schools have to physically remove mobile devices to help us avoid their distractions points to a troubling reality: digital clutter may be (and, in some ways, already is) more prevalent and concerning than physical clutter. And it might be far more difficult to get rid of. As this reality becomes clearer to people, it has led to a growing movement toward *digital wellbeing:* the idea that we need to keep the amount of technology we use in check before its detrimental costs (such as its addictive quality) outweigh its benefits.

Google has been trying to develop tools to help people achieve *digital wellbeing*. New features for their latest Android mobile phones include an "app timer" that sets limits on how long a user can spend on a specific app. Another feature is the "Shush" gesture, which switches the phone into "don't disturb" mode when a user puts the phone facedown. Google has even developed a "wind-down" feature that switches a phone to grayscale as soon as the user's predetermined bedtime arrives.

Social media platforms are also proactively investing time and resources into trying to help people declutter the distractions caused by technology. Facebook recently prototyped a tool that allows users to see exactly how long they've spent on the platform. Instagram, meanwhile, now posts a big green checkmark, along with a message "You're all caught up" when a user has scrolled through all new posts from the past 48 hours. This prevents users from wasting time scrolling through posts they might have already seen, or that are old.

## Uncluttering Our Digital Identities

In early 2019, the European Union's highest court will offer a ruling on one of the Internet's most contentious topics: the right to be forgotten, or the right of individuals to request that a website remove their personal data.

In 2018, Google revealed that of the 2.4 million "right to be forgotten" requests they had received from Internet users, it had only complied with less than half (only 43 percent) of them. In many cases, they did not comply with the request because "the page [being requested to take down] contains information which is strongly in the public interest." As Google's response to these requests show, the right to be forgotten touches upon issues of freedom of speech, censorship, privacy, and more.

For the average person, the right to be forgotten is not a question of techno-politics, but rather something far more basic: *do I own the information about me that exists online?* In most cases, the answer is no. However, more social media platforms have taken steps to give people more control over their data.

Google has long offered the ability for users to download the information the company collects about them through a tool called Google Takeout. Facebook, Twitter, and Instagram all offer single buttons that allow users to export and download all the images, status updates, and information they have shared on the platforms in the past. Amazon allows users to see a history of their conversations recorded with voice-activated Alexa devices, and to delete them if you choose ... though they proactively warn that "deleting voice recordings may degrade your Alexa experience."[3]

There are also signs that the desire to declutter digital content about ourselves may be a coping mechanism for social media overload and a desire to have more control over the way we portray ourselves in the online world.

In mid-2016, Jessica Contrera, a reporter for *The Washington Post*, shared an interesting and perhaps slightly worrisome (if you happen to be the parent of a teenager) story of what it was like for a 13-year-old girl growing up with the constant distraction and stresses of social media. At one point in the article, she describes how the teenager self-consciously curates her social media presence. "There are only 25 photos on her page because she deletes most of what she posts," Contrera explains. "The ones that don't get enough likes, don't have good enough lighting or don't show the coolest moments in her life must be deleted."[4]

This is an example of how our fight against digital clutter intersects with our constant battle to define and curate our digital identities. As the tools for controlling our digital identities get better and better, it is not surprising that people will start to use them to cultivate only the side of themselves that they are most comfortable sharing. While adults may be open to sharing their vulnerabilities and "real" selves, teens will often understandably opt to present the side of themselves they find most flattering, or that will gain them so-called "acceptance."

## Decluttering Brand Messages

At Perfumarie, you never know what you are going to smell.

Owner Mindy Yang believes the best way to find your ideal perfume is to try several of them, without knowing the brand or being exposed to any marketing messages about them. Based in New York's SoHo neighborhood, her store features a line of 32 perfumes that consumers can sample "in the dark," so to speak. Once a person identifies their favorite scents, she reveals what the brand behind them are.

The idea behind Perfurmerie's unusual retail experience is that a product's branding, packaging, and imagery can "clutter" a consumer's purchasing decision. By removing the actual brand from product advertising, companies are "decluttering" the buying experience, leading consumers to focus their purchasing decisions on the qualities of the product rather than their brand perception. McDonald's tried such an approach in a bold advertising campaign featuring Mindy Kaling. In these TV spots, the star wears a yellow dress and stands against a red backdrop, recreating the fast-food chain's iconic brand colors. She speaks vaguely about "that place where Coke tastes so good," and never mentions the name McDonald's.

Heineken has taken a similar approach when advertising its popular beers to millennials. Global senior brand director Gianluca Di Tondo told *Fast Company* that the company has chosen to skip taglines in favor of more emotional storytelling, because "taglines are always open to interpretation."[5]

Perhaps the company most invested in this strategy is home-goods maker Brandless, founded by entrepreneurs Tina Sharkey and Ido Leffler. The e-commerce company makes low-priced food, beauty, and personal care products by working directly with manufacturers, cutting out middlemen, and avoiding brand messaging. All items are sold for around $3 in their online store, where the intent is to declutter your purchasing decisions by offering "better stuff for fewer dollars."

Brandless personal care products.

# Why It Matters

Early last year, in a desperate attempt to curb my impulse purchases, I tried a Google Chrome browser plugin called Icebox. Icebox works by replacing the "buy" button on over 400 different popular ecommerce websites, including Amazon and eBay, with a "Put It on Ice" button. This button allows users to save the item and receive a reminder to purchase it a week later. The tool offered an elegant way to help me consider whether I really needed whatever I was about to buy.

In the coming years, as the *Extreme Uncluttering* trend continues to grow, we expect to see more tools and features like IceBox. Consumers will turn to digital solutions to declutter all aspects of their lives—from curbing their impulse to accumulate more stuff to helping to avoid the distractions that keep them from truly enjoying experiences or living the way they want.

Most significantly, the quest to find new ways to declutter our minds and lives will become commonplace, leading us to constantly think differently about how we spend our time and money, the media we consume, and the experiences we choose.

## How to Use This Trend

✓ **Let people opt for less**—As your customers or audiences declutter their lives, they might choose to opt out of all communications or interactions with your brand—unless you give them an alternative. When it comes to email outreach, you can accomplish this by offering subscribers the option to receive less frequent emails rather than unsubscribing altogether. Consider other ways you might be able to remain connected with them while still respecting or even helping them to engage in their own.

✓ **Offer a decluttered experience**—The "Dining Without Noise" movement from Spain is a perfect example of this. How can you create an environment or experience that removes unnecessary distractions and caters to people's increasing desire to declutter? Removing such distractions may end up being the ultimate way to position and distinguish yourself— and the reason people keep coming back to you.

# Deliberate Downgrading

## What's the Trend?

—

As tech-enabled products become overbearing, consumers opt to "downgrade" to simpler, cheaper, or more functional versions instead.

Kyle Wiens is a modern-day superman on a quest to save the world...one broken piece of technology at a time.

In the past several years, he has singlehandedly become the voice of the "fixer movement," and a crusader for any consumer's right to fix the products they buy instead of being forced to throw them away. His weapons of choice are something called a pentalobe screwdriver and a journalist's talent for telling stories to inspire indignation.

The popular blog *Boing Boing* described him as "a culture hero of the 21st century," and he is a frequent contributor to some of the most influential publications in the world including *The Atlantic, Harvard Business Review, The Wall Street Journal,* and *WIRED.*

Why all this attention on a guy whose day job is running a cartoonishly-named company called iFixit? And what the heck is a Pentalobe screwdriver?

The pentalobe screw is the "five-pointed do not enter sign" used on most Apple devices. Shaped a bit like a five-leaf clover, the proprietary screw is meant to prevent consumers from opening up Apple devices to fix or upgrade them. Thanks in part to this barrier, most older Apple devices end up in a landfill. According to Wiens, Apple is one of the biggest enemies of the fixer movement, making devices that are notoriously closed to tinkering by tech-savvy users or any sort of hacker upgrades. To fight back, iFixit was the first to develop its own pentalobe screwdriver and sell it on the Internet.

Pentalobe screw

The move is emblematic of Wiens' personality. He lives to take on large brands and promote the idea that it is every consumer's right to open up the things we own and fix or modify them as we choose. Though it seems like a logical mission, this "right to repair" movement has ballooned into a billion-dollar legal debate. At stake is the very nature of ownership itself, and whether or not we truly own the products we buy.

# Who Owns Your Tractor?

The company propelled to the center of this debate, thanks to a lawsuit in late 2015, was farm equipment manufacturer John Deere. At issue was its fervent legal argument that farmers, in fact, did not own the tractors they had purchased (and sometimes paid close to half a million dollars for), but rather received "an implied license for the life of the vehicle to operate the vehicle."[1]

Incensed by this particular bit of legalese, Wiens did what he does best, and took to the media. In an op-ed published in *WIRED* magazine, he called this high-tech farm equipment a "nightmare" for farmers.[2] In an interview on public radio, he pointed out that that the problem comes down to the law. "Laws that govern the computer and the tractor were written by entertainment lawyers out of L.A. back in the 90s, when they were trying to prevent DVD piracy...it's just time to update some of these laws."[3]

Governments worldwide are tackling exactly this problem with several pieces of legislation, but the problem for many farmers is that they can't afford to wait for the outcome. Most have found an understandable workaround they are returning the new tractors and instead seeking out older tractors with less technology.

We call this *Deliberate Downgrading*, and this desire for older and less tech-enabled products (instead of their more recent replacements) is happening across many other industries, as well.

## Desirably Dumb Devices

When it comes to technology, we generally assume that newer is better.

Computers get faster, cameras add more megapixels, design gets sleeker, and old products aren't built to last - even if we do try to open them up with pentalobe screwdrivers to fix or modify them.

Despite the appeal of shiny new devices, there have been growing signs over the past several years that consumers overwhelmed by the frequent upgrade cycle of technology are actively seeking ways to press the pause button, or even rewind to simpler times populated by more basic devices.

While global sales of smartphones increased by just 2 percent in 2017, sales of "dumb phones" (simple phones without apps or Internet access) rose by 5 percent.[4] In some cases, featureless phones were sought out by people looking to cure their tech addictions, or older people looking for an easier-to-use phone. In other cases, the growth has come from people frustrated by the side effects of smart phone such as the fact that you can barely make it through an entire day of phone usage without your battery dying.

One product that solves this problem is the Punkt MP 01, made by a Swiss startup. Punkt is an "un-smartphone" with no web browsing, no touchscreen, and no camera. It focuses instead on features like a multi-day battery life, high-quality audio, and built-in noise cancellation.

Punkt Phone

The key factor driving the *Deliberate Downgrading* of phones is consumer frustration with things like lower battery life or overly-complicated functionality. In other sectors, this downgrading may be driven less by frustration and more as a matter of preference.

## Why People Still Love Print Books

The death of print books is predicted every year with regularity.

For years, e-book sales had been on the rise consistently every quarter, while sales of print books continued to decline—until they seemed to hit a wall in 2015. Since then, the book industry has been reporting a curious reversal, quantified by industry statistics year after year showing a decline in e-book sales. In the first three quarters of 2018 alone, e-book sales fell 3.9 percent, according to data from the Association of American Publishers, while hardcover book sales *grew* by 6.2 percent in the same time period.[5]

Some blamed the unnecessarily steep e-book price of $9.99 to $14.99 favored by the largest (and greediest) "Big 5" publishers for the decline. Others suspected something more fundamental might be at play. After all, a decline in e-book sales doesn't explain a corresponding rise in print book sales. Was it possible the industry had overestimated how much the younger generation loved to read books in digital format?

That may be exactly the case, accordingly to a Nielsen Books and Consumers Survey, which reluctantly noted that "teens continue to express a preference for print that may seem to be at odds with their perceived digital know-how."[6]

Another study run by the University of Colorado on the evolution of the book industry found that college students, in many cases, actually *preferred* printed textbooks, because they felt that having the print book helped them concentrate better and avoid distraction. "Consumers have an emotional and visceral/sensory attachment to printed books," researchers wrote, "potentially elevating them to a luxury item."[7]

Supporting this theory was the fact that the research showed the top three reasons consumers choose a printed book is because it is easier on the eyes, they prefer the look and feel of paper, and they want the ability to add the book to a personal library.

E-books may offer a superior experience when it comes to the gratification of reading them instantly, but the data suggests that print books remain an indulgent (and perhaps even luxurious) deliberate downgrade. The choice of holding a printed book in your hands still feels and smells and inspires the same way it always has.

## The Return to Vinyl

Another immersive experience going through its own *Deliberate Downgrading* movement is music... specifically, the return of music on vinyl.

British music retailer HMV predicted that turntables would be the "must-have gift" of the past holiday season, and U.K. store John Lewis sold out of eight of the twenty models it stocked in the 2017 holiday season.[8]

Independent music stores across the world are now scrambling to make sure they carry enough record players to support the growing demand. Meanwhile, vinyl sales are at a twenty-year high. While some audiophiles may disagree with my categorization of this choice as a "downgrade," given their preference for the lovably imperfect sound of songs played on vinythe choice to leave behind all the "digital remastery" of modern music in favor of a more authentic listening experience is yet another example of the appeal of this trend.

# The Return Of Paper Voting

In April of 2018, a University of Michigan computer science professor named Alex Halderman posted a video showing exactly how easy it was to hack an electronic voting machine. As a small audience watched, he infected the machine with malware that would guarantee a particular result no matter how the votes came in. The fear of hacking in the political process is a global concern, and one that has made headlines in the U.S. recently thanks to Russian interference in the 2016 Presidential elections.

The solution to the problem is decidedly lo-fi—move back to paper ballots. As Halderman told *The Atlanta Journal-Constitution*, "voting is not as safe as it needs to be. The safest technology is to have voters vote on a piece of paper." It is an opinion shared by many activists around the world and has been leading to a widespread return to paper voting because we live in a time where many people simply don't trust the security of electronic voting anymore.

## Abbreviated Sports

Another reason for the popularity of *Deliberate Downgrading* is time—and the growing desire to optimize how we spend it. This shift toward productivity and the gradual reduction of attention span has created a crisis moment in slow sports that take a long time to play...like golf.

By even the most optimistic numbers, the decline of golf has been pronounced. Down from a high of 30.6 million golfers in 2003, fifteen years later, the National Golf Foundation reported that only an estimated 23.8 million people had played on a golf course, a reduction of almost 20 percent.[9] Even more worrying for the industry is that 63 percent of the playing population of golf is over 34 years old, and almost one-fifth of *that* group is over the age of 65.

The price and time commitment (often up to six hours for a full 18 rounds) are often cited as the most common barrier but there is a movement within the industry to try to appeal to this younger demographic by addressing the time barrier with initiatives such as the industry's "Time For Nine" campaign, focused on enticing younger golfers to come and play an abbreviated half-round of nine holes.

This invitation to enjoy a downgraded and less time-intensive version of a sport also explains the increasingly popular Twenty20 version of the 500-year-old British sport of cricket, which features each team batting for only 20 overs as opposed to the usual 50 overs. The game can be completed in 2-3 hours versus 7-8 hours for a one-day match or a full five days for a test match.

Each of these traditionally long-playing sports is adapting to the fragmented media landscape of today, and offering both younger and older people with shrinking attention spans new ways to downgrade their experiences into shorter and more palatable chunks of time for watching and participation.

## Rejecting GMOs

One final example of *Deliberate Downgrading* applies yet another lens to the trend by considering how an awe-inspiring seed bank and a return to simpler and more natural foods may be an example of choosing to "downgrade" your eating habits to avoid processed or overly-modified foods.

In Europe a few years ago, two thirds of all countries upheld a ban on all genetically modified organisms (GMOs). Despite the disagreements about their safety, the debate itself is leading many people in food-secure countries to select older, more natural, and presumably safer products. For example, there are "seed swaps" taking place among farmers and home gardeners to keep non-GMO crops alive.

These are evidence of the increasing fear that "enhanced" foods may be causing health dangers we don't quite understand. The natural reaction is people choosing to deliberately downgrade to food grown with more simple and human methods, without growth hormones and free from the genetic engineering.

Building on that fear, there is even a vault situated on a tiny remote Norwegian island near the Artic Ocean which holds more than 100 million untainted seeds for nearly 1 million food-crops from around the world. Often dramatically called the "Doomsday Vault," the Svalbard Global Seed Vault's mission is to keep the world's seeds save in the event of global catastrophe, so the survivors might replant the planet.

Svalbard Global Seed Vault (Photo Credit: www.croptrust.org)

While the vault and the scenario it was created for may seem far-fetched, the challenge of increasing our planet's food supply to account for our growing human population is a fierce global debate.

# Why It Matters

The fundamental shift described in this wide-ranging trend is the idea that we, as individuals and consumers, often choose "downgraded" products and experiences that were once described as sub-optimal. Over the past year, the value of these supposedly inferior products and experiences has become multi-faceted, and is causing a reevaluation of which features really matter.

Technology can be too smart, sports can take too long, and crops can be too engineered. Driven by the underlying expectation of empowerment and choice, a greater number of consumers will choose to selectively opt out of innovation they don't value, instead returning to the comfortable past, where food seemed safer, books were tactile, and things just worked.

## How to Use This Trend:

✓ **Offer a "classic mode"**—When Microsoft launches a new operating system, there is usually a way change your interface to use the "classic view" you were used to from the previous version. How could you offer a "classic mode, for your own products and services?

✓ **Respond to the zeitgiest**—The word zeitgeist refers to a prevailing thought that captures the culture of a particular time, and it is often used when talking about new cultural trends. Media seek it out, researchers report on and it offers valuable advice for leveraging this trend, as well. When record players started generating buzz, for example, it created a big opportunity for a certain type of store to begin carrying and selling them. Zeitgeist can be like that: an early predictor of what people will care about. Brands must learn to watch and respond to these early signals.

*This trend was originally named "Strategic Downgrading" and published in the 2016 Non-Obvious Trend Report. It is included in this new trend report with revised examples and new insights.*

# 13

# Enterprise Empathy

## What's the Trend?

—

Empathy becomes a driver of innovation and revenue, and a point of differentiation for products, services, hiring, and experiences.

Over the past several years of researching this report, my team and I have been bullish on the power of empathy. Last year, I wrote extensively about it under the trend prediction of *Virtual Empathy,* which described how technology and art were coming together to help us feel empathy for those unlike ourselves. We saw this trend in everything from the many VR experiences designed to put us in someone else's shoes (*be* a prisoner in solitary confinement!) to pioneering, immersive in-person experiences the evoke empathy (like the powerful *Pollution Pods* in London).[1]

Since then, my team has continued to study the new ways in which empathetic experiences are being delivered to a greater number of people. In many of the stories we came across, we discovered an interesting twist: companies and entrepreneurs were discovering that focusing on empathy can not only improve relationships, but also be surprisingly profitable.

Empathy as a core differentiator is increasingly at the heart of new products and services that are doing very well for their companies, their employees, and the people they ultimately serve. These empathetic products and customer experiences are shifting industries—or even creating new ones—by leveraging (and often monetizing) human emotions.

We call this trend *Enterprise Empathy,* a term that encompasses the growing number of brands, startups, and even large corporations that are benefitting from encouraging more empathy from workers and while also delivering it to customers more regularly. To see *Enterprise Empathy* in action, let's begin by looking at a range of new products designed with empathy built in.

## Made with Empathy

This October, Proctor & Gamble announced a new bottle designed for its Herbal Essences shampoo and conditioners that allow people with vision impairment to distinguish between the two bottles. The design idea was the brainchild of Sumaira "Sam" Latif, a special consultant for inclusive design at P&G.

Latif, who is blind, explains that mistaking the two products is a constant challenge for blind people and those who can't see well. P&G created new bottles to help disabled people live as independently as possible, and the new design was rolled out on selected bottles in January 2019. But as Latif explained

STRIPES = SHAMPOO    CIRCLES = CONDITIONER

to *Quartz*, they didn't do it out of charity, but rather as a business strategy. "We realized we had a massive opportunity," she said. "There are 1.3 billion people with disabilities in the world...and we are not understanding their needs."[2]

Other companies are on a similar quest to appeal to customers previously ignored in the design process.

Recently, IKEA launched a special line of kitchen wares designed for people with limited mobility, such as pregnant women, the elderly, and people who have undergone surgery. Named *Omtanksam* (after the Swedish word for "considerate"), the offering includes anti-slip dishware and easy-to-grip cutlery.

In the U.K., the department store Marks and Spencer announced a new line of clothing for children with disabilities. Their wide range of new apparel include t-shirts with Velcro fasteners on the back and dresses and shirts designed to hide feeding tubes and casts.

And Gillete released the Treo Razer, specially designed for caregivers who need to shave others who no longer can do it for themselves. The design features a handle that makes using the razor feel like gliding a paintbrush. The handle is flexible to maximize control, and the shaving gel is built right into the handle.

Each of these innovative products was designed with empathy and caring for those whose needs had not been considered before. In the process, the companies responsible for them created new categories of products (and revenue) for themselves, as well as a powerful story that generates predictably positive publicity.

## Holographic Companionship

For decades now, Japan has been grappling with a serious social problem: young people are dating and marrying less and less, leading to low birth rates, an aging population, and the prevailing loneliness of many young Japanese salarymen who live alone. In Chapter 6, I discussed this group, known as the *hikikomori,* in more detail.

In an effort to respond to this social shift, a Japanese company called Gatebox released an AI-powered "Holographic Wife" that offers lonely young Japanese salarymen companionship at home. Standing about 8 inches tall inside a glass box, the holographic image is based on an anime character. This holographic wife will text messages asking their husbands how their day is going, thank them at the end of the day, and even watch TV with them. It is now available for sale for about $1,300 USD plus a monthly subscription fee.

The Gatebox "holographic wife"

The loneliness that results in a need for this type of product is not just growing in Japan, either. In an article in the *Harvard Business Review,* former Surgeon General of the United States Vivek Murthy declared that we are experiencing a "loneliness epidemic," with 40 percent of Americans reporting that they feel lonely.[3] As technology moves beyond utility to offer other types of support, like companionship and empathic interactions to respond to our emotional needs, our relationship with this tech is bound to evolve. The companies who provide this type of support, like Gatebox, stand to profit. In fact, the concept of a "holographic wife" may just be evidence of an entirely new industry focused on helping people of all ages and genders deal with the crippling reality of loneliness.

## Caring for Seniors with Empathy

The spiral of loneliness often intersects with getting older, as well. As a result, the challenge of providing care to our aging population with empathy is increasingly the focus of the business models and service innovations we are seeing among the companies that advise the industry as a whole.

Unlike many eldercare facilities, Boulevard Adult Day Care of Flushing, a company that runs several care centers in Queens, New York, specifically customizes their programs—from the food they serve to the décor of their facilities—to their clients' cultural backgrounds. One of their centers, for example, is catered to people who grew up in India, while another is tailored to Hispanic seniors. The centers are thriving, and the people served by this innovation feel greater empathy.

Why do these centers do so well? In an article for *Pacific Standard*, Environmental Gerontology professor Jeffrey Rosenfeld explains that the optimal places for people (and particularly immigrants) to grow old tend to remind them of where they are from. The Indian Boulevard program, for example, was created is and run by a 29-year-old Indian woman named Megha Mehta. In India, all of these elderly residents would have lived with family and been cared by their daughters-in-law, so having a director of Mehta's age and gender running the program makes perfect sense to them.

This is a cultural bias, Mehta acknowledges. But as the article points out, the elderly immigrants are not at a point in their lives where they are going to change their views on such things. Being understanding and sensitive of their cultural preferences and beliefs helps them thrive in their retirement. "The American idea of the melting pot asks individuals to fuse with a greater whole," the article concludes, "but an elderly immigrant has lost enough of themselves already just by moving to an unfamiliar place late in life. Any more melting, and they might dissolve entirely."[4]

Instead of asking its clients to do that, centers like those run by Boulevard offer a different level of empathy on a cultural level that makes all the difference. It also turns out to be a great business model; their centers are packed.

## Digital Friends and Empathetic Avatars

No matter how appealing an eldercare center may be, for millions of people, it will never match the comfort of remaining in their homes. According to AARP, nearly 90 percent of people over the age of 65 would prefer to age at home.[5] And there is ample medical evidence to suggest that if they do, they might have better health, as well.[6] But family members aren't always able to take care of elderly relatives at home or hire someone to help them. A startup called care.coach has built an ingenious digital solution to this challenge by automating some aspects of in-home care without sacrificing the empathy that a real-life companion would offer.

Their service is a 24/7 assistant of sorts: a digital avatar (usually in the shape of a cute animated pet) that appears on a tablet screen and interacts with clients. This pet avatar reminds them to take medications, to drink water so they stay hydrated, and when their next appointment is coming up. And they also engage the client in conversation. But here's the thing: the avatar is staffed by a *real person* who operates the voice behind the scenes.

Digital avatar example from care.coach

The tablet has one-way video mode enabled so the care.coach team members at the other end can keep an eye on their clients. If they see one fall or in need of medical attention, they can quickly call for help. More importantly, care.coach team members engage with those they are caring for in a meaningful way, encouraging them to share memories, listening to their stories, reading to them, and offering companionship. For the clients, the avatar becomes like a cross between a pet and a friend—continually checking on them and helping them with whatever they need.

Although care.coach relies on some predictive artificial intelligence, it operates on the belief that no technology today can truly anticipate everything that an elderly customer may need the way a real human caregiver might. Like Boulevard's eldercare centers, care.coach's deeply personalized service works because it responds not just to the basic care needs of their clients, but because it considers their *emotional* needs—like their desire to live in a familiar, safe place, or talk to someone who understands them—with empathy.

The market for eldercare services is a perfect example of why this trend of *Enterprise Empathy* matters. Nothing could require more compassion than the products or services that come into the home to provide care for our aging loved ones (and ourselves, one day)—whether at home or at a familiar place that *feels* like home.

## Making Death a Positive Experience

Talking about death is taboo in most cultures because it is uncomfortable. Most of us go to great lengths to avoid discussing it—usually because it can be scary, and because most of try to spend as little time thinking about our own mortality as we can. It can be depressing.

Yet there is a movement taking shape of people who are not only brave enough to encourage us all to talk more openly about death, but crazy enough to want to turn it into a *positive* experience instead. In 2003, a social worker in New York named Henry Ferkso-Weiss became disillusioned with the care and support dying people were receiving from the medical community. In contrast, he noticed that the care provided for birth through doulas and dedicated professionals was vastly more empathetic. Determined to change this, he created a certification program for "end-of-life doulas," and started the International End of Life Doula Association (INELDA). The doulas certified through his program do not provide medical care, but rather attend to the emotional needs of the dying (and their families) with empathy.[7]

Since then, a movement of end-of-life doulas—also known as death doulas, end-life coaches, and death midwives—has risen significantly. While some death doulas serve in the community as volunteers, others are setting up their own private practices, charging from $40 to $100 an hour. The growing need has blossomed into a new profession and industry—a powerful example of the *Enterprise Empathy* trend in action.

Just as death and empathy have spawned an entirely new field of doulas here in the U.S., in Japan, they have brought about a different and unexpected industry: cleanout professionals.

For the past seven years, the number of deaths in Japan has outpaced that of births. As the population continues to decline, many older people die without anyone to pass their belongings on to, or with families living far away. The job of these cleanout professionals is to fill the gap.

When someone passes away, they are hired to come to the home of the deceased and help clear out their possessions. Sometimes, a widow or widower who doesn't have anyone else to turn to for help will hire them as a partner to take on the sad task no one else is able to do. At other times, they are hired by a grief-stricken family who can't bear to do the job themselves.

No matter what the situation, it is a job that requires patience and plenty of empathy, as they go through possessions and decide what to do with them. In fact, empathy is often the reason why one professional gets hired instead of another. It is central to the entire experience because of the level of compassion and discernment involved.

According to a trade group representing the industry, its 8,000 member companies generate a combined revenue of $4.5 billion annually, and the association estimates that its membership could double in less than five years, which already seems like a conservative estimate.

## Empathetic Work and Customer Experiences

Two years ago, Starbucks opened its first-ever sign-language-only store in Malaysia, staffed entirely by employees who were either deaf or hard of hearing. This past October, the coffee chain opened another location, this time in downtown Washington, D.C., just a few blocks from Gallaudet University, a 150-year-old institution of learning, teaching, and research for deaf and hard-of-hearing students.

Starbucks "Signing Store" - Washington, D.C. (Image courtesy of Starbucks)

Like Starbucks, many companies are leading with empathy and creating more inclusive workplaces, hiring practices, and customer experiences that accommodate people with special needs.

Software giant SAP estimates that it may fill up to 1 percent of its entire workforce (over 600 people) with people who have autism. They are one of many companies adopting the practice of hiring "neurodiverse" individuals—people who are on the autism spectrum or who have another neurological condition—for their unique abilities, which often include handling technical data and being able to focus on repetitive tasks. Other large organizations, from Microsoft to JP Morgan, have all made similar commitments to diversifying their workforces.

Beyond creating more inclusive workplaces, many companies are creating empathic customer experiences, as well. Tesco, the U.K.-based grocery chain, has already implemented a "slow lane" checkout for the elderly or anyone else who needs a bit of extra time. And another U.K. grocery chain offers quiet hours for shoppers who need or a prefer to shop without as many distractions or announcements over the loudspeaker. This year, even the National Basketball Association (NBA) made its flagship store on Fifth Avenue more accommodating to customers with sensory sensitivities by offering them noise-cancelling headphones, weighted lap bands, and other conveniences while they shop.

## Why It Matters

Over the past decade, we've seen empathy shift from being perceived as something we taught our kids in kindergarten or expected only from therapists to the key to our emotional intelligence and well-being. Later, as empathy was adopted in the business world as a critical ingredient in effective leadership and teamwork, practicing empathy became something that "evolved" organizations aspired to for innovation, productivity, workplace harmony, and the well-being of the organization.

Today, this prediction of *Enterprise Empathy* is moving empathy itself from a "nice to have" into a business imperative, and even a competitive differentiator. In a growing number of examples, empathy has become the driving force in products, services, and customer experiences that people want, and that generate higher revenue, as well. All of this makes a powerful business case for the use of empathy as a strategic way to think more innovatively, drive higher employee engagement, better meet customer needs, and drive a deeper and more loyal customer base, as well.

## How to Use This Trend:

✓ **"Made With Empathy" as a strategy**—As more automation is added to many experiences, from customer-care phone conversations to retail checkouts, refocusing on empathy is already a business necessity. For some organizations, this will mean complementing investments in innovation along with training in greater empathy in order to bridge the gap between the two. Doing this well builds a stronger innovation culture, and can foster a keener ability to see non-obvious needs and find deeper solutions for them.

✓ **Deliver empathy at scale**—To encourage more empathy across a large organization, the best place to start is often with internal success metrics. Some of the most famously empathetic workplaces, for example, have policies that allow employees to spend an *unlimited* amount of time with a customer. Part of delivering empathy at scale is creating a workplace culture that encourages workers to be real people first, and treat their customers like family instead of transactions.

# 14

## Innovation Envy

## What's the Trend?

—

Fear leads entrepreneurs, businesses, and institutions to envy competitors and approach innovation with admiration or desperation.

In 2016, one of our Non-Obvious trend predictions was, at the time, moving at lightning speed: *Insourced Incubation*. The term described the increasing number of companies who felt the need to bring more innovative thinking into their organizations.

Some companies solved this challenge by hosting innovation competitions, like hackathons. Unilever created a platform, Unilever Foundry, to connect startups with its 400+ brands and find ways to leverage their innovations. Coke launched a commercialization program for startups called The Bridge. The goal of these competitions and collaborative partnerships was to bring much-needed "outside" thinking into these companies in order to tackle the big challenges they were facing.

Other organizations chose to launch ambitious in-house innovation programs dedicated to driving disruptive thinking internally, instead. Wells Fargo, Visa, and Citi created high-touch innovation labs designed to both showcase their technology and serve as internal ideation studios. Worldwide shopping center owner the Westfield Group converted a floor of its San Francisco mall into a showroom to pilot new retail concepts. Even fast-food retailer Wendy's got into the innovation lab craze, building its own innovation center to develop and test technologies like mobile payments and ordering kiosks.

As we reported back then, brands in all sorts of industries were desperately trying to find new strategies to innovate and proactively disrupt themselves and their industries, before a startup they didn't see coming rendered them obsolete.

What we underestimated at the time was just how much fear was driving these big investments into innovation.

## The Culture of Fear

In workshop after workshop that my team and I conducted with some of the biggest and most innovative brands in the world, we encountered a genuine desire to find the "next big thing." What we only discovered later was just how much these same companies were also deeply motivated by an all-consuming fear that nothing less than a complete overhaul of their business would be necessary in order to assure their relevance and survival.

Disruption was the elusive prize that everyone was seeking, and those who seemed to find it first were universally envied (even by those outside their industry) as the ideal to which everyone else should aspire. Netflix disrupted their DVD rental business, and moved entirely into streaming content. Uber made taxis irrelevant by offering an on-demand ride service that exploded in popularity.

Warby Parker chose to skip stocking eyewear at retail locations, and instead sold eyewear through an innovative online portal at a deeply discounted rate. They later decided to open their own retail stores to support the online business.

These disruptive companies have transformed entire industries, leaving in their wake countless competitors and admirers who desperately want to think, act, and be like them. It has inspired this non-obvious trend we call *Innovation Envy* to describe the increasing number of entrepreneurs, companies, and governments who look to others in their sector with envy, leading them to act: sometimes out of admiration, sometimes out of fearful desperation, and sometimes even both.

## Why Some Companies Envy Others

In the 2018 book *Lab Rats: How Silicon Valley Made Work Miserable for Rest of Us,* former *Newsweek* reporter Dan Lyons shares a story of being invited to the storied Detroit offices of Ford to speak at a two-day event where the company was also hosting a hackathon. Lyons realized right away just how important it was for the legacy automaker to demonstrate that they were adjusting to the times. "Ford wants us to know that it's in the midst of a huge transformation, and that it's not falling behind," he wrote. "[But] the truth is, I feel bad for these guys. I understand why they want to look hip, but holding a hackathon just makes them look scared."[1]

It is perhaps unsurprising that Lyons would be skeptical of this approach. A few years ago, he wrote a profoundly funny and cranky book called *Disrupted* about his time as a 51-year-old employee at a growing content marketing tech startup staffed almost entirely by twenty-somethings. His cutting brand of humor which likely made the book a bestseller was honed by his time as a staff writer for the hit HBO show *Silicon Valley*. Writing for the show likely drove him to write this new book, which offered several fascinating stories that were tempting to include in our exploration of the *Innovation Envy* trend. The most compelling of these was his experience at Ford.

In the book, Lyons likens Ford's attempts to keep up with the times to his experience at *Newsweek* years earlier, when the magazine's core business was being threatened by "shitty websites like Huffington Post and Buzzfeed." The leadership of their group at the time promised to fight back with innovation. "[*Newsweek*] invested loads of money into hype and marketing—like Ford, holding this hackathon—trying to create a new image for ourselves, to convince people we were 'reinventing' the company and carrying out a radical transformation," Lyons recalls. "What we should have done was forget about marketing, forget about trying to get followers on Facebook, and just invest in our core business, which was journalism. We should have just kept doing what we did best."

By 2010, *Newsweek* had merged with *The Daily Beast*, ceased publication of its print edition, and was eventually acquired by IBT Media in 2013. In 2018, it was criticized for publishing inaccurate stories.

But the underlying point of his story illustrates very clearly how *Innovation Envy* was a contributor to their demise. Out of fear, *Newsweek* looked at the success of its competitors and sought to copy them. It impulsively invested in innovations that ultimately proved useless.

If you work (or have worked) in a company or industry struggling to stay relevant, Lyons' conclusion that *Newsweek* should have just kept doing what it did best might seem overly simplistic. For every company that "overcorrected" trying to disrupt itself, there were more than twice as many who faded away *because* they were not simply not evolving, and stubbornly stuck to doing what they had always done. Inaction is not a viable alternative either—a point that we can clearly illustrate in the fortunes of a brand that was once considered unbeatable in their category.

## The Desperate Innovation of Victoria's Secret

For an industry leader, Victoria's Secret has been desperately trying to update its own brand approach for quite some time. Their problem comes down to a shift in the world of fashion, where competitors are increasingly focusing on more natural looks and including bodies of all sizes in their advertising. In contrast, Victoria's Secret is a brand best known for their over-the-top runway fashion show that one critic recently described as "porny."[2]

The brand has been struggling for years, and its stock was down 41 percent in 2018 alone. In late November 2018, lingerie division CEO Jan Singer stepped down amidst controversy over the brand's tone, direction, and long decline. Citi analyst Paul Lejuez even suggested that the brand may be losing because it is out of touch with real consumers: "Women don't want to be viewed as stereotypical sexy supermodels buying lingerie just to impress men."[3]

In a bid to try and change this perception, the brand took several small steps to rethink the approach to their 2018 Fashion Show. The show's hairstylist, Anthony Turner, told *People*: *"This* is the most undone the hair has ever been. We're playing with each girl's own hair texture, and making them better versions of themselves."[4]

Laying aside the obvious irony of promoting "natural beauty" while still trying to make already beautiful models into "better versions of themselves," the highly selective show has been trying to evolve. This year, they also made the unusually evolved casting decision to include model Winnie Harlow.

Harlow, a former participant in America's Top Next Model, has vitiligo, a skin condition in which the pigment cells in parts of the skin die or stop functioning, leading to loss of skin color in patches. Her inclusion was rightly praised as a positive step in the right direction for the brand. Time will tell if small moves like this and a leadership change are enough to reverse its fortune.

Older companies like Victoria's Secret (founded in 1977) and *Newsweek* (founded in 1933) are most susceptible to falling prey to our *Innovation Envy* trend prediction. They often look at younger industry entrants, and, envious of their rapid success, try to reinvent themselves in their image instead of remembering and focusing on what made them great in the first place. Envy and fear, therefore, become major factors in the short-sightedness that holds many companies back, and, ironically, dooms others to faster obsolescence by wasting their time, budgets, and effort on miscalibrated attempts to become innovators.

## The Lure of Incubators

While envy can lead to unstrategic copycat thinking and confused or unnecessary innovation that misses the mark, it doesn't *always* have undesirable consequences. Sometimes, observing and admiring what others are doing or how they are disrupting can be a source of inspiration and motivation. In the right situation, envy can inspire people and organizations to act more quickly and take important, necessary risks that they otherwise might not. Some places—like startup incubators—are even *designed* to foster this type of envy as a motivating factor.

In my work as advisor to nearly a dozen startups over the past several years, along with advising organizations on how to set up internal innovation centers, I have seen (and come to appreciate) how incubators support entrepreneurs in growing their network, bringing out their best, and sharing it with others.

The Camp is one such place: a secluded coworking facility in the south of France started by entrepreneur Frédéric Chevalier, who tragically died in a motorcycle accident just two months before the project opened. The unique thing about The Camp, aside from its manicured seven-hectare campus that took close to $45 million to build, is a residency program known as the Hive, which offers a six-month residency where 20 young innovators can live on-site and pursue an open-ended challenge to come up with something great.

This latent belief in the power of serendipity is something that drives an increasing number of coworking and networking destinations around the world. The Ministry, for example, is a combination of shared workspace and members' club in the heart of London that handpicks members based upon their profiles in order to ensure diversity of thought and experience. The Battery in San Francisco is another, similarly exclusive club and workspace.

By bringing together entrepreneurs with different experiences, interests, and projects, incubators and coworking spaces such as The Camp, The Ministry, and The Battery allow participants to watch how others innovate and overcome challenges, inspiring them to come up with their own solutions.

## Amazon's Embarrassing Beauty Contest

In September of 2017, Amazon announced it was starting a search for a home for its second headquarters outside of Seattle. The new headquarters, it was promised, would house close to 50,000 employees, and likely result in an economic boom for whatever city was lucky enough to win the bid.

What followed was an embarrassing spectacle of state politicians desperately doing whatever their could imagine to entice Amazon to consider their cities. One critic even described it as the "Amazon Hunger Games."[5] In the end, more than 230 cities submitted bids for Amazon to consider. Many included unprecedented tax incentives worth billions of dollars, and more than one desperate city offered to change its name to "Amazon City" (or some variation thereof) if they were selected.

In November of 2018, after a fourteen-month deliberation period, Amazon announced it would be splitting its second headquarters between two predictable and already comparatively wealthy cities: Arlington, Virginia (a close suburb of Washington, D.C.) and Long Island City, in Queens, New York. The decision drew almost unanimous criticism–even from people within the winning locations. People wondered, was such a theatrical search really required to arrive at such a safe and unsurprising choice? And was offering such costly incentives to a corporation really the best allocation of government funds? Given the recency of the announcement at the time of this publication, it is clear that the debate is only just beginning.

## The Maltese Passport Scheme

Around the same time the Amazon search drama was unfolding, *BusinessWeek* published a fascinating story about another set of politicians from a tiny country in Europe who offered a bold and unprecedented incentive in a desperate ploy to attract investment from wealthy individuals. The incentive was something many felt should never be offered for sale: a European passport.[6]

The country was Malta, a nation of less than half a million people that was formally admitted to the European Union in 2004. In the years since, Malta has driven its growth primarily by offering aggressive financial incentives to foreign investors, including an effective corporate tax rate as low as 5 percent, compared to over 20 percent for most other European countries. In 2013, the government made a brazen attempt to lure even more foreign investment by creating the *Malta Individual Investor Program*, a program that offered a Maltese passport to any foreigner willing to pay €650,000 and make a €150,000 investment in government bonds.

Why did Malta and the 230 cities that bid to become Amazon's new home feel so compelled to offer desperate enticements to lure investors and the giant retailer? One likely reason is the proliferation of link-bait-style lists that rank cities, countries, and places: "The Best Places to Live," or "Most Livable Cities in the World."

These lists drive a ton of media attention, and generate envy from city administrators and politicians who enviously watch their successful neighbors who've made the list attract investment and resources. Fearful of being left behind, they do whatever is necessary to position their countries and municipalities as the next hot, growing destination where everyone wants to live, investors are clamoring to spend, and businesses want to relocate.

The more pressure cities and countries feel to emulate their successful neighbors, the more likely they are to succumb to *Innovation Envy* by offering short-sighted incentives like drastic tax cuts, or compromising their moral standards by doing things like selling passports—instead of following a more non-obvious path, and finding new ways to refocus upon what makes them a unique and desirable destination.

## Why It Matters

The fear of being disrupted and becoming obsolete looms in most executives' administrators' minds in every industry, and drives businesses to constantly innovate. In addition, social media and the increasing transparency with which businesses operate have made it fairly easy for people, entrepreneurs, and companies to see what others are doing in real time. Just as a growing addiction to social media can create a sense of envy and a perception that everyone is living a better life than we are, this transparency is leading people and companies to experience their own envy of more successful or innovative competitors.

*Innovation Envy* can manifest itself as either a positive or negative motivator. On the negative side, as companies become envious of their competitors, they scramble to innovate unnecessarily, expend tremendous resources in unfruitful innovation programs, frustrate employees or move away from their core competencies—forgetting what has made them successful in the first place. On the positive side, this envy can be channeled into motivation and a drive to improve, become more competitive, and earn the same attention their competitor seems to be getting.

Like many of our non-obvious trend predictions over the years, *Innovation Envy* is itself neither a positive nor a negative trend. It is how you end up using it that matters most.

## How To Use This Trend

✓ **Play offense with innovation**—If you try to innovate from a defensive, survival-driven mindset, you will struggle to succeed. Instead, one of the things we often do when leading innovation workshops is help groups focus on the positive and adopt a growth mindset. One effective way to do this is to start by uncovering unique strengths and talents, while positioning your your legacy first. Then you can build new approaches and an innovation program based upon a shared understanding of what it is you do best, and the understanding that a core component of the strategy must incorporate this and never leave it behind.

✓ **Assess your innovation readiness**—Are you asking the right questions to get your organization ready to innovate from a positive place, instead of starting by looking at someone else? To help you ask those questions, my team and I put together an assessment of Innovation Readiness. You can download this assessment from the online resources center, along with some useful tips on how to use it. You can download it here: www.nonobviousbook.com/2019/resources.

# Robot Renaissance

## What's the Trend?

—

As robots adopt more human-like interfaces and micro-personalities, they are raising new questions and issues about how we relate to technology.

The European Renaissance was a time of rapid evolution in human thought and culture in which people started to reevaluate long-held beliefs about the way the world worked and their own place in it. Today, the world is at a similar inflection point. It would be easy to credit technology, or even the Internet, with the pace of this shift, yet they alone have not caused widespread introspection about humanity's place in the world.

Until recently. The evolution of robots beyond the factory and into our workplaces and homes is creating a new age of global self-reflection. The more innovation we see in the use of robots, the more we see a corresponding rise in questions about how we, as humans, will relate to these robots, how humanlike they will be, and what sorts of ethical questions this might raise around our master-servant relationship to robots over the short and long term. The technology revolution of what robots can do for us is driving an important corresponding debate about whether they should be enlisted to take those actions, and what moral consequences might result.

This reevaluation is a trend we first introduced in 2016, and originally called the *Robot Renaissance:* a way to describe how our growing reliance on robots to do the things we cannot or will not do is leading to a new period of enlightenment about our relationship to technology, how much control to cede to it, and what that might mean for organizations, corporations, and our own humanity.

This year, we have seen so many more stories and evolved uses of this technology that many of the questions we first identified three years ago have become more commonplace—and more urgent, as well. Seeing this provided the motivation for us to bring back this trend in our 2019 report, and to revisit its implications for the future.

## Robot Explorers & Builders

The original mission of the Star Trek science fiction series was enshrined in its optimistic challenge to "boldly go where no one has gone before." Today, we have robots to do this for us.

Robots like Boeing's Unmanned Undersea Vehicle (UUV), a 51-foot long hybrid-charging craft with a 7,500 mile range that can stay underwater for up to six months. The UUV is the largest such device ever built, and works autonomously, without a human crew to do everything from providing maritime surveillance to surveying the ocean floor.

On space missions to Mars, NASA is using a series of autonomous robot-controlled landers to collect samples from the surface of the Red Planet. The future of space exploration relies heavily on robotic explorers that can work and survive in conditions that would be far more difficult, and sometimes even impossible, for humans.

Here on Earth, the Japanese brand Komatsu is leading the adoption of autonomous construction equipment, thanks to a unique confluence of factors in Japan creating the necessity for autonomous building far more quickly than anywhere else in the world. Over the past few years, parts of Japan, and particularly Tokyo, have experienced a short-term boom in the need for new construction leading up to the 2020 Olympics. At the same time, there is a serious labor shortage in Japan due to the country's aging population and the relative scarcity of young people left to support the economy.

As the second largest construction company in the world, Komatsu is uniquely positioned to solve this problem solution involves "Smart Construction," the brand's tagline to describe its increasing range of robotic heavy machinery, controlled aerially by a fleet of drones that create 3D maps of the area and track construction progress.

If you consider these examples from NASA, Boeing, and Komatsu together, there is a clear pattern of reliance on robotic technology to make exploration and construction projects easier in space, on earth, and beneath the ocean. These uses, in turn, are already widening our understanding of what robots can do, and offering a necessity-driven use case for them to get smarter and more autonomous as they become our explorers and adventurers: to places we could not otherwise go, to help make discoveries we otherwise could not make.

# Jibo Bot With Personality

If you were imagining the robot of the future, you might have pictured a category of robots known as "service bots," developed mainly to take over doing the things that none of us want to do...often more quietly and efficiently than you could do yourself. The Roomba vacuum cleaner introduced many people to the concept of having a robot in the home. Startups like RoboMow and LawnBot offer robot lawnmowing devices that are growing in popularity.

Apart from everyday-cleaning or housework bots, there have also been interesting experiments with robots in non-obvious ways in unexpected locations—often from the travel and hospitality industry. Royal Caribbean's Quantam of the Seas cruise ship, for example, set sail with a duo of robotic bartenders trained to mix and pour up to two cocktails a minute. Las Vegas has the "Tipsy Robot:" a bar staffed entirely by robots that makes mixed drinks for passersby on the Miracle Mile Shops inside the Planet Hollywood complex.

The robotics startup Savioke has been working with more than a dozen hotels to provide a robot named Relay as an "autonomous butler" that can deliver items from the front desk to guest rooms. The bots have been so popular that front-desk staff at their partner hotels report that people are calling with requests just to see the bot in action.

This is the useful and utilitarian world of service bots, which are adept at handling small details, nuances, quirks, and inconveniences, but only aspire to do these tasks as quietly and efficiently as possible. They are the foundation of the *Robot Renaissance,* created to solve problems and laser-focused on the tasks they were built for.

And then there was Jibo.

# Robots With Personality

Promoted as the "first social robot for the home," Jibo was a robot with personality. Designed to look a bit like the animated desk lamp from the Pixar animated short Jibo used two high-res cameras to track faces and capture photos, learn your preferences, and use natural and social cues to act in more human ways.

Jibo - a social robot

After running for six years and burning through nearly $73 million in funding the team behind Jibo significantly downsized around the end of 2018, and seems to be on its last legs at the time of this publication. Fellow pioneer in the social robotics category Mayfield Robotics (makers of the Kuri robot) has already shut down sales and operations.[1]

Perhaps they were both products ahead of their time, and, at close to $1,000 each, sold at a price too high to appeal to the mass market they needed. Yet the category of social robots with personality that they pioneered is soldiering on.

In late 2018, the home robotics company Anki released their own home robot called Vector, with a tongue-in-cheek marketing campaign that poked fun at all the ways people were increasingly afraid that over-zealous robots might take over. The marketing taglines for the new bot entertainingly made the point that Vector was different: "Smart enough to take over the world. Nice enough not to."

Vector - The Good Robot

Like many other robots built with human-like personality traits, Vector is closer to a functional toy than a serious human companion or workplace colleague. A Japanese robot named Pepper, on the other hand, looks exactly the way science-fiction authors have long imagined a working robot might look.

## Pepper: Your First Robotic Co-Worker

Pepper has a humanoid-looking head, two eyes, and a touchpad on his (yes, his gender has officially been named male) chest to input commands. The promotional website about him from Japanese maker Softbank Robotics describes him in humanlike terms:"

Pepper is a human-shaped robot. He is kindly, endearing, and surprising. Pleasant and likeable, Pepper is much more than a robot; he is a genuine humanoid companion created to communicate with you in the most natural and intuitive way, through his body movements and his voice. We have designed Pepper to be a genuine day-to-day companion, whose number- one quality is his ability to perceive emotions."

Pepper The Robot

When brought into the home, Pepper is described as having been "adopted" by his host family "buy" him for a flat fee, then make monthly payments to keep him updated and active. Designed to interact with humans, Pepper can express himself through the color of his eyes, his tablet, or his tone of voice.

Outside of the home, Pepper is also being trialed in pilot programs across the world to greet customers and provide information. For example, in April of 2018, the Smithsonian museum complex in Washington, D.C. put several Pepper robots in museums to sense when people were close by and engage them in conversation. The aim of the program was to learn how an automated guide like Pepper could perhaps bring people to under-attended galleries, or offer deeper engagement by doing things like translating inscriptions or explaining the history of artwork.

While Pepper has certainly captured significant attention, he is a conservative example when compared to those in a controversial category increasingly being described as "companion robots."

## Sentbots and Robot Citizenship

This new breed of robots fits what Sirius XM founder Martine Rothblatt calls "sentbots." No stranger to being a trailblazer herself as the first transgender female CEO of a major company, she recently shared in an interview, "The Roomba is to the sentbots of tomorrow kind of like the luggable compact computer is to the smartphone of today."[2]

Rothblatt commissioned a robotics company called Hanson Robotics to create the first of these "sentbots" with features and a personality inspired by her wife, Mina. The resulting robot, called Mina48, is bilingual, and even spoke at a Ted Talk in Havana. Rothenblatt believes future robots will be customizable, with personalities that can be "uploaded" via access to your social media profiles, such as Facebook and Instagram.

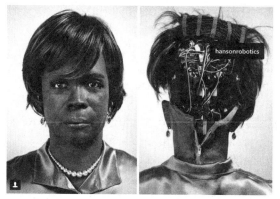

Bina48 Sentbot (Photo Credit: @hansonrobotics on Instagram)

Hanson Robotics also built Sophia, who is widely considered one of the most advanced of the human-like robots ever made. In October 2017, in what was mostly a well-calculated publicity stunt, Saudi Arabia became the first country to grant citizenship to a robot when Sophia was conferred the honor in a ceremony during the Future Investment Initiative Conference in Riyadh.

In 2019, Sophia will even have her own "surreality show" entitled *Being Sophia.* We will be able to watch "Sophia's emerging life, adventures, experiences, and her quest to learn and develop into a super-intelligent, benevolent being."[3]

## Love in a Time of Sexbots

For some, the relationship with robots will soon offer a more physical option. *Realdoll* is a company that sells human-like robots for sex encounters. With their own custom-built Artificial Intelligence engine, the company already has a subscription-based app that allows customers to create their own virtual girlfriend on their phones and converse with her. For the affluent fan who wants a more...personal encounter, male and female versions of the dolls are for sale. And for curious consumers who are not quite ready to buy, a Toronto-based company called Kinky S Dolls has already opened the world's first robotic brothel, and has announced plans to open a second one in Houston.

This entire category and the evolution of this sector will be seen by many readers as clearly crossing the line. Do we really need or want people to be able to enter into these types of encounters with robots? Is it even ethical to do so? Right now, these are open questions, and will remain so as this *Robot Renaissance* continues.

## Why It Matters

Robots have been the subject of science-fiction speculation for decades, and every year, it's easy to think that it will be the "year of the robot." In the process of curating trends, I probably read at least one article a year making that exact prediction—all of which makes me more reluctant than most to have any trend focused solely on robotics. Yet the truth, supported by numbers and technology, is that we do seem to be at a tipping point in our consciousness around robots and their role in society.

We are asking big questions about how we should be treating these robots in our midst. We are training ourselves how to interact most effectively with them. And non-obvious innovators are increasingly building them in our own likeness to reflect us, make them engaging to interact with, and offer companionship of all kinds.

## How to Use This Trend

✓ **Make friends with robots**—As more robots are built with learning personalities, we will need to consider which lessons our behaviors might be teaching them—both intentional and unintentional. Much like a child gets its first impressions on how to act from its parents, robots, too, may soon be imprinted with these sorts of manners from humans. This is an opportunity as well as a threat, but the first step is learning to embrace robots in the right situations and treat them not with fear or contempt, but with curiosity and yes, perhaps even friendship.

✓ **Explore robots across your value chain**—Every organization must periodically expand its thinking to include non-obvious ways of utilizing robots, whether human-like or chatbot, in every aspect of its value chain for customers—from the end experience to the sourcing and creation of products. In some cases, this may mean greater automation of things previously done by humans as a business necessity.

# 16

## Good Speed

## What's the Trend?

—

The urgency of the problems facing humanity is inspiring corporations, entrepreneurs, and individuals to find ways of doing good (and generating results) faster.

In the middle of the ocean, a patch of garbage covering a geographic area nearly the size of Mexico is expanding every day. The "Great Pacific Garbage Patch," as it is widely known, is made up mostly of one material—plastic, an estimated 1.8 trillion pieces of it. Given its size and the severity of its environmental impact, the Patch is a perfect example of what appears to be an unsolvable global problem.

These types of intractable problems—particularly related to the environment—seem to be all around us. For example, in early October 2018, a landmark report from the United Nations' scientific panel on climate change concluded that humans may reach severe climate-change consequences as early as 2040. In recent years, we have also seen countries around the world, from the U.S. to Brazil, elect leaders who either deny climate change is real or are politically unwilling to do anything about it.

When you consider these dire predictions along with the scale of the environmental problems facing us, it's no wonder many feel pessimistic about our future. *WIRED* magazine co-founder Louis Rosetto described all of us a "prisoners of unrelenting pessimism."[1]

Boyan Slat isn't someone who feels this pessimism. Just a few weeks before that scary United Nations report was released, the 24-year-old Dutch social entrepreneur launched a test for the most ambitious project to remove plastic from the ocean ever. Called simply *The Ocean Cleanup*, Slat's solution consists of deploying a nearly 2,000-foot-long tube attached to a plastic netting into the Great Pacific Garbage Patch.

The idea is that plastic will float into the net, which would then be collected and brought to shore for recycling every few months. Using this method, Slat hopes to remove 90 percent of the plastic that is currently in our oceans by the year 2040, and has plenty of financial support to try to make his ambitious idea work.

How The Ocean Cleanup works (Illustration courtesy of The Ocean Cleanup)

As the challenges we face—from helping those who are less fortunate than ourselves to saving our shared planet—are becoming larger and more complex, pioneering entrepreneurs and leaders of responsible companies are responding to them with increased urgency, inspired innovation, and speed. This trend, which we are calling *Good Speed,* describes how all of this good is happening at a pace that is faster than ever before.

The speed is helping drive a new form of what Rosetto calls "militant optimism," a force that has the power to ensure we don't lose hope, even in the face of such large global challenges. From all the stories we uncovered in researching this chapter, it is hard to disagree.

———

*"If we really want to make a better world for our children, we need to believe that the future will be better."*
— LOUIS ROSETTO, Co-founder, *WIRED* magazine

———

# Brands Doing Good—and Doing It Fast

The worldwide concern about the impact that plastic and other waste is having in our environment is not restricted to nonprofit or environmental groups. For-profit companies are taking the challenge head on, as well, and sometimes in wonderfully proactive ways.

LEGO, for example, has launched a massive initiative to find a more sustainable material with which to manufacture its iconic product. The Danish brand is investing more than $150 million more than 100 people to work on this challenge.[2]

Their devotion to finding new and sustainable ways to make their products is noteworthy in itself. But what is even more impressive is that they seem to be doing it unprompted by regulations or public pressure.

No one asked LEGO to change their bricks. There is no widespread consumer demand for eco-friendlier LEGOs. If anything, most of their customers would prefer LEGO bricks to stay exactly the same–unless they can somehow find a way to make them less painful when one steps on them early in the morning. LEGO recognized the effects its products were having on the environment, and wanted to act as quickly as possible to try and do better.

They are not alone. Another brand making it a priority to help the environment by reconsidering their practices—and doing so on a relatively fast timetable—is Swedish retailer Ikea.

The world's producer of the most disposable furniture in the world wants customers to stop throwing away the furniture they buy from them when they no longer want it. The company has found that people have a perception that the low price of their furniture makes it acceptable to only use it once and then throw it away, rather than selling, donating, or recycling it as they might with more expensive furniture.

To counter this misperception, the brand has launched several pilot programs across the world to encourage consumers to bring their used furniture back into the store. The store then either recycles or sells the furniture "as-is." In exchange, customers receive a voucher to be used against new purchases.

This is a similar idea to what mission-driven outdoor retailer Patagonia has done for years with their outdoor gear: encouraging their customers to save and recycle them, and even creating their own online marketplace called "Worn Wear" for customers to resell their used gear for others to enjoy.

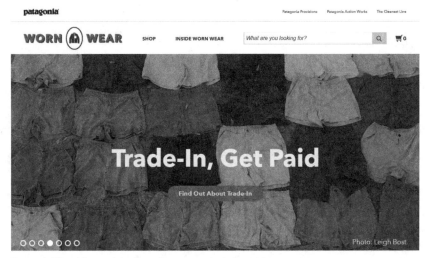

Patagonia Worn Wear website (http://wornwear.patagonia.com)

## Goodpreneurs

Unfortunately, not every business is focused on creating quite so much long lasting utility. In the past few years, far too many Silicon Valley startups have been justifiably ridiculed for creating impractical innovations that solved non-existent problems—like the $400 Juicero (an unnecessarily expensive way to squeeze fruit) or the Pause Pod (an indoor tent for office workers needing quiet time).

Partly as a way to counter these exercises in frivolous invention, just over a decade ago,, entrepreneur Ankur Jain founded a fund called Kairos (named for the Greek word for *opportunity*). Its mission is simple: helping young entrepreneurs innovate solutions to problems that people in the real world face. This mission has inspired its entrepreneurs, who are almost all under the age of 30, to create more affordable urban housing, healthy baby food for low-income families, and solutions for providing better eldercare. Every few months, the fund launches a new startup, and its success has been enviable: the last group of Kairos companies raised $600 million in funding, and is currently valued at $2.5 billion.

Large companies are also encouraging and supporting entrepreneurs to tackle big environmental challenges, usually through contests and initiatives that bring ideas together, and are offering them funding and visibility to implement and hopefully generate results.

Fast fashion retailer H&M, for example, hosts an annual contest for startups developing technologies to help make fashion greener. The winners share a €1 million prize. Recent winners include Smart Stitch, a company that makes a thread that dissolves at high temperatures to make recycling easier, and Crop-A-Porter, a startup that spins yarn out of field waste from banana and pineapple plantations.

In another recent example, two of the largest retailers in the world, Starbucks and McDonald's, teamed up to create the NextGen Cup Challenge, which tasks entrepreneurs to design a new, fully recyclable and compostable drink cup within the next three years. A key element of doing good faster is doing it at *scale*. When we talk about *Good Speed*–change is certainly happening faster. It is an equally important element of this trend to note that we are describing the growing examples in the world (like these) in which change is being *implemented* faster, thanks to these large-scale efforts.

# Every Person–and Every Donation–Counts

Celebrity chef Jose Andrés doesn't spend much time thinking about how he can help in the face of a tragedy. He just goes wherever he is needed. Long known for his pioneering cuisine using molecular gastronomy, he has also become a symbol of how much difference one person can make. After Hurricane Maria hit Puerto Rico, Andrés was on the ground cooking meals for people and encouraging them to rebuild their lives through food-related businesses, like starting a bakery or creating a coffee-roasting collective. He even wrote a bestselling book about the experience.

Plenty of celebrities help with disaster recovery. But Andrés' style is different. As *Fast Company* writes: "Andrés's spontaneity makes him unique. Through his prolific use of social media, his lack of filter, and his impulse to go where the action is, Andrés is pioneering a rapid-response model of leadership. This is no fully vetted corporate social responsibility effort. It's one man acting on instinct, adjusting on the fly, and observing as things tend to fall into place behind him."[3]

Andrés' approach is emblematic of the Good Speed trend. Today, everyday heroes who have the desire to do good are finding ways to make it happen faster and with greater impact—often using little more than the force of their personality to inspire people and spontaneously make things happen.

One way these individual heroes can scale their efforts is through "microdonations," small donations between $0.25 and $10 made online or via mobile apps. Platforms like Roundup or Good Street have sprung up to offer easy—and instant—ways for people to make such donations, simply by using their mobile devices or computers. For years, DonorsChoose.org has offered this capability by allowing teachers to post projects to the site and individual donors to fund them directly. Today, voice- activated assistants like Alexa are making it even more seamless by letting people easily make donations to the causes they care about simply by saying that they would like to do so out loud.

Technologies that facilitate microdonations have the potential to transform how people give. Not only do they make it easier for people to spontaneously give and make an impact (regardless of the size of their wallets), but because they often send prompts to people encouraging them to make microdonations in the moment, they can make giving a habit.

## Immediate Impact through Everyday Spending & Investing

In the past, it was hard for consumers to know exactly how the companies they were buying from or investing in were actually doing business. Were these companies taking care of the environment? Were they mistreating their workers in Third-World countries or supporting dictatorial governments?

Today, this information is much more widely available. Not only can consumers determine which organizations they want to support, they can also make real-time and long-term spending decisions based on this information.

And they are doing so in droves. For example, more individuals are engaging in what is widely known as "ESG" investing, the practice of making investment decisions by looking at a combination of environmental, social and governance factors. By reviewing everything from how an organization is responding to climate change to their treatment of workers and animals, people can selectively support the companies that share their values and concerns for social and environmental issues.

It has also become easier to measure how your spending impacts the world around you—and make necessary changes in your investment and spending mix so it better reflects your values. Aspiration is one example of a new checking-account app that measures and scores the environmental and ethical practices of over 5,000 companies. The app compares users' spending habits against these companies to generate an "Aspiration Impact Measurement" (AIM) score. The score effectively quantifies the impact someone is making in the world based upon what she spends.

What's interesting about ESG investing and apps like Aspiration is that they allow individuals to measure the impact of their choices and "bake in" support for the causes they care about in real time. They allow each of us to do good almost instantly with every transaction and investment decision we make.

## Doing Good Fast by Reducing Waste

This past year, the public declared war against the plastic straw. The inspiration for this movement was widely credited to video marine biologist Christine Figgener and her team filmed removing a plastic straw from a sea turtle's nose. As Figgener told *Time* in an interview, "Definitely that was an object that passed through human hands and made its way to the ocean."[4]

**VISIT THE NON-OBVIOUS RESOURCES CENTER ONLINE TO:**

Watch this full video online!

Seattle banned plastic straws in July, Starbucks is phasing them out over the next couple of years, and McDonalds announced that they will no longer provide them in their U.K. and Ireland locations. But none of these efforts would have happened had it not been for public outcry against plastic straws and people demanding that companies reduce plastic waste by not making them available. Very few societal shifts that will have an impact on our planet have taken hold of the public consciousness quite so quickly as the campaign against plastic straws.

Why did this backlash against a common item grow so quickly? For one thing, straws are rarely necessary, and most people feel that they are fairly easy to do without. While some people like them, when they were presented with the facts about their negative impact on the environment, many were willing to immediately change their everyday behavior to reduce waste. (It didn't hurt that any retail establishment that bans and stops stocking them would stand to save money by doing so).

Another way individuals are responding with urgency to reduce waste is through "upcycling:" creatively reusing items that might otherwise be thrown away. The market for secondhand goods from Japan, for example, has been exploding in the last few years.[5] After Japanese consumers clean out their belongings, these are collected and exported to other Southeast Asian destinations for resale. Reusing has become so popular than even apps are getting in on it.

Both Olio and Too Good to Go are apps dedicated to the unique mission of helping restaurants and individuals share their leftover food with their neighbors in real time to avoid waste and to help feed each other.

This idea of doing good individually is certainly not new, but what is different today is the speed with which a new idea can take off and shift our beliefs and behaviors in a relatively short time. This is *Good Speed,* and judging from the examples we have explored in this section, the ideal situation may involve a change that is relatively easy for people to make—and one that enjoys widespread support from enterprise.

# Why It Matters

As consumers increasingly demand that organizations demonstrate corporate social responsibility, more innovation around this non-obvious trend of *Good Speed* can provide a powerful way to make a bigger impact in the world and generate greater loyalty with customers in the process.

*Good Speed* also builds on the fact that the past decade has been marked by an ongoing shift toward impatience. We now expect everything to get delivered faster, companies to respond to our complaints in real time, ride-sharing cars to pick us up within minutes, and people to respond to our text messages instantly. While it is easy to blame our on-demand economy for the obsessive tendencies, it encourages within each us, this trend suggests there's a silver lining in this shift: brands and organizations that can deliver good faster can be big winners.

The companies investing in socially-responsible practices, the startups creating world-changing innovations, and the consumers who are increasingly voting with their wallets are all making good happen *faster*. Rosetto was right. Given the urgency with which environmental and societal problems are threatening our well-being (and sometimes our very existence), the *Good Speed* trend is, indeed, cause for "militant optimism," as he suggested.

# How to Use This Trend

✓ **Work in Phases**—When it comes to tackling big problems, sometimes the best way to achieve ongoing results is to separate the task into phases. While Boyan Slat may be trying to clean the *entire* ocean, he is starting with one pilot program in a small geographic area and taking it from there. While today, we expect results faster, this doesn't mean we need to try to do everything at once. Organizations that employ steady, ongoing efforts to develop their own non-obvious ways of innovating faster while achieving their results in phases will be the surest winners in the future.

✓ **Seek Strategic Collaborations**—One of the most powerful examples of corporations actively reducing waste is the alliance between Starbucks and McDonald's—two huge players who are willing to team up to create a more sustainable coffee cup. Ask yourself, who are your ideal partners, and how might you team up with them to do good faster?

# Overwealthy

## What's the Trend?

—

Growing income inequality leads to more guilt among the affluent, leading them to seek more ways to give back.

In her 2018 documentary *Generation Wealth*, Lauren Greenberg offers a sobering picture of our troubled obsession with wealth and its complicated consequences. From the story of the couple who gives up on the overly ambitious project to build the world's largest house to the strange rise of elective plastic surgery for dogs, the film documents the spending excesses of the extremely wealthy with unusual candor.

The documentary also tries to answer the question of what motivates the desire for so much wealth in the first place, and what that desire means for our society. In a revealing moment, a hedge fund manager tells Greenberg, "I do believe it's un-American to say you can make too much money." In another, Greenberg asks German financier Florian Homm—charged with defrauding investors of more than $200 million—"Does Harvard Business School teach you to be a good person?" Laughing deeply, Homm replies, "No, they teach you to rule the world."[1] Like many of the financiers accused of fraud or precipitating the financial crash in 2008, he generally escaped severe punishment. After serving his short 14-month sentence, he is now a free man, living in Germany.

The comments of the hedge fund manager and Homm expose a winner-take-all mindset that seems common among the Wall Street financial elite. It's the mindset that might be behind growing income inequality around the world. According to the World Inequality Report, income inequality has risen in every region across the world since 1980. The growth in inequality has been fastest in the U.S. and parts of Asia. In India, for example, *Financial Times* journalist James Crabtree, author of *The Billionaire Raj,* notes that the top one percent of the elite ruling class owns nearly 60 percent of the wealth of the entire country.

Greenberg's documentary certainly paints a portrait of a wealthy elite that is completely out of touch with the rest of the world. But the reality is more complicated. Several months before *Generation Wealth* was released, sociologist Rachel Sherman published a book entitled *Uneasy Street: The Anxieties of Affluence,* in which she interviewed a group of affluent New Yorkers—parents in their 50s who were in the midst of costly home renovations—to find out what they would think and say about their wealth. Without exception, she found that her subjects were deeply conflicted about it.

# Why People Struggle with Being Wealthy

In a review of the book, *Businessweek* journalist Drake Bennet explains that many of them went to "great lengths to downplay" their wealth. "Getting rich is an American religion; being rich is clearly more problematic," he writes. "The people Sherman interviewed tend to define themselves not through consumption, conspicuous or otherwise, but as workers...doing work—any work—is important because it allows these people to feel on some level that they deserve their fortune."[2]

The reluctance to be defined by their wealth presents an interesting counterbalance to the consumption excess captured by Greenberg in her documentary. It seems modern wealth is creating two divergent but powerful mindsets. The first is a winner-take-all mentality symbolized by the worst of the Wall Street elite. They see the world as one that is rightly ruled by those with money, and they work to hoard as much of it as they can for themselves. This group would likely never see themselves as *Overwealthy*.

Remember, this is a group that does not believe you can *ever* accumulate too much wealth.

The second is a more enlightened mindset. It is embraced by people who want to enjoy their wealth, but feel moral discomfort about how to handle it; particularly the possibility that it (and they) may be contributing to a widening inequity among the classes. To feel good about their privileged lifestyle, they create a narrative in which they convince themselves that their wealth is justified because of how hard they worked to acquire it. They spend freely on "indulgences" and give to causes at a higher pace.

It is this latter group of individuals that we primarily describe with the trend *Overwealthy*—a term that aims to describe the growing number of people who accumulate wealth readily, yet frequently struggle with how to *be* wealthy and feel morally comfortable with having all that they have.

Though the term *Overwealthy* may seem to cast a negative judgement on those who have wealth, our intent isn't to criticize people who have money—or even those who seek it. Instead, this trend focuses on understanding what happens when a relatively small number of people control the vast majority of wealth and proactively seek ways to feel better about it.

## Extreme Luxury and Why It Works

To better understand how the *Overwealthy* make peace with their wealth and spending, let's take a look at how luxury retailers and service providers are creating products to cater to these conflicted, well-heeled consumers. Some companies today are creating products specially tailored for those who have money to spend, even when it comes to items that border on the ridiculous. For example, the Gläce Luxury Ice Company sells tasteless ice that has been "hand-carved" from large purified blocks, guaranteeing that it won't affect the taste or drinking experience of expensive cocktails and spirits.

At just over $300 for a bag of 50 ice cubes, it promises customers "minimum dilution and maximum cooling," and is promoted to "connoisseurs and collectors of rare and delicious fine spirits."

In Paris's Saint-Germain-des-Pres, renowned department store Le Bon Marché is investing heavily in a renovation of its top floor. Once completed, the new space will not house another high-end boutique for women's dresses. Instead, it will be dedicated entirely to high-end luxury children's clothing.

During a recent business trip to Tokyo, I witnessed this exploding market in action firsthand: while visiting a Bape store, I watched the parents of a two-year-old pay just over $300 for a simple screen-printed Bape-branded kids' t-shirt.

According to Euromonitor, the global childrenswear market is currently worth $1.4 billion. Thanks to the biological fact that children outgrow most clothes quickly, there is consistent demand, and the segment is growing fast. Fflur Roberts, head of luxury goods for Euromonitor, recently told *Monocle* magazine that "Growth in childrenswear is outpacing both men's and women's fashion in terms of retail sales."[3] Famous luxury brands like Balenciaga, Givenchy, Oscar de la Renta and Dior are just a handful of the many high-end brands developing luxury clothing for kids.

It's not just parents who are spending money on luxuries for their loved ones. In Japan, as more couples decide not to have children (or to delay having them), they are pouring their parental instincts, devotion, and money into their dogs, instead. As Takaaki Fukuyama, a lecturer at Yamazaki University of Animal Health Technology explains, "Japanese people want to spoil their dogs, and also love to be fawned over by their dogs."

One sign of this shift is the popularity of competitive grooming. At the Japan International Dog Show, the Annual National Trimming Competition—where the country's top "trimmers" grow their dog's hair for three months and then style it in various creative cuts—is a huge deal. And it captures perfectly the extravagant tastes of pet owners who are willing to invest lots of money to have their dogs perfectly coiffed, including coloring their hair or fur. Around the country, plenty of specialized grooming schools, spas, and stores selling all kinds of accessories have sprung up to cater to the devoted owners of these pampered pets.

What can the rise of extreme luxury spending on products like "hand-carved ice" or luxury dog grooming or expensive toddler fashion teach retailers, product developers, marketers, and any of us who have something we are trying to promote? It is common among the *Overwealthy* to describe spending on these types of unnecessary extravagances as rare indulgences or signs of a connoisseur mindset.

Of course, most people would never spend $300 on ice cubes, but a *real* whiskey enthusiast is a different story. When you are a dedicated enthusiast, the spending is easily justified. The *Overwealthy* might even describe it as a passion—one that they have most certainly earned the right to have because of how hard they worked to earn their money in the first place.

## Extreme Giving

At the same time that we observe the *Overwealthy* readily spending on extravagant luxuries, we also see them making ambitious declarations about wanting to save the world. These declarations are the product of a combination of guilt and the sense of duty they feel as they struggle to find ways to do something good with their money besides spending it. Uncomfortable with their economic status, they seek out ways to contribute to society by using their wealth for positive means.

One extreme manifestation of this, for example, is the Giving Pledge. Billionaires like Bill Gates and Warren Buffet are leading the charge to create a club of billionaires who pledge to donate more than 50 percent of their net worth to charitable causes within their lifetimes or beyond. Just a few years ago, the club had close to a dozen members. Today, over 175 billionaires have taken the pledge, with more joining each year.

Another example of people's desire to use their wealth for positive means is the disparity in philanthropic tendencies between the richest of the *Overwealthy* and others when it comes to alumni giving to universities. A recent survey by Marts & Lundy, a fundraising consulting firm, found that in 2017 "mega-gifts"—those exceeding $10 million—topped $6 billion in total for the first time. Those donors made 194 mega-gifts in 2017, which was also a new high.

Meanwhile, donations from younger alumni or from a wider donor base have been shrinking year after year. One possible reason for this decline, *Inside Philanthropy* contributing writer

Mike Scutari explains, might be these donors' tendency toward "effective altruism," an approach to giving that emphasizes, among other things, measuring the impact of philanthropic giving in terms of "lives saved per dollar."[3]

Using this metric, it might be hard for alumni donors to justify giving money to a university to refurbish a building or fix a football stadium scoreboard when they could instead give that money to a nonprofit helping to improve the environment or provide clean drinking water to impoverished communities.

The *Overwealthy* want their money to have an impact, like everyone else.

## Selfish Selflessness

In 2018, journalist Anand Giridharadas shook the world of philanthropy and social corporate responsibility with the release of his book *Winners Take All: The Elite Charade of Changing the World*. In it, Giridharadas argues that people and institutions who are very wealthy are motivated to give by a deep desire to maintain the status quo and ensure that the current income inequality in the world continues. Much of the charitable giving and big programs intended to help the lower classes might be unnecessary, he argues, if those people were simply better paid by corporations and taken care of by governments in the first place.

At a critical point in the book, he writes of his conflicted experience at the renowned Aspen Institute, where he was invited alongside wealthy business leaders and entrepreneurs to be a Fellow. "It bothered me that the fellowship asked fellows to do virtuous side projects instead of doing their day jobs more honorably," he writes. "Instead of asking [elites] to make their firms less monopolistic, greedy, or harmful to children, it urged them to create side hustles to 'change the world.' I began to feel like a casual participant in—and timid accomplice to, as well as a cowardly beneficiary of—a giant, sweet-lipped lie."[4]

Giridharadas offers a radical idea, and one that is unpopular among some circles of the *Overwealthy* precisely because it exposes the tension that lives within them: the tension between a desire to accumulate and retain wealth and their reluctance or guilt over how to handle the inequity this accumulation of wealth might create. It is also an idea that was put to the test directly last year in Finland, with the entire world watching.

## Finland's Bold Experiment

In 2016, Finland gave a small group of 2,000 citizens the equivalent of $670 a month for two years, with no strings attached. The purpose of the experiment was to understand how that money affected the lives of its recipients, and to decide whether it may be a good idea to roll out this "universal basic income" to the entire country.

There have been several tests of universal basic income in the past, but the results have been generally inconclusive. For one thing, the money typically offered in most tests (including this one in Finland) is not enough to fully replace an annual income. For another, it generally discounts the human psychological need to have a sense of purpose by meaningfully contributing to something–which survey after survey shows to be the key to workplace happiness.[5] Still, many people believe that the pace of automation will significantly shrink the number of jobs in the future. Giving everyone some sort of basic income could ensure that people can live with dignity and maintain their societies.

When Finland looked at the early results of their experiment, they found that some participants chose to go back to school, while others simply used the money to pay debts or ordinary everyday expenses. The more interesting finding, however, emerged when they studied what they would need to do to roll the program out for the entire country. Researchers estimated that to financially support the program, they would have to institute a flat tax of 55 percent on everyone's earnings. According to national polls, support for the idea dropped from 70 percent to below 30 percent almost immediately.

Why did support decline so drastically? As soon as people understood the personal sacrifice that they would be required to make in order to bridge the income inequality gap, the program become nearly impossible to sell. The story speaks to one of the most fundamental issues that the trend of the *Overwealthy* exposes: most affluent people who want to make an impact in the world struggle to maintain their resolve when doing so might challenge the status or financial comfort they currently enjoy.

The struggle is the reaction Giridharadas anticipated when he wrote, "If helping others means making a buck or buffing your reputation, it's fine. But making a sacrifice to help others without getting credit? No way."[6]

## Why It Matters

This is a complex trend because of its two-sided nature. On the one hand, we have the growing elite's mastery of making money and benefiting from leaders around the world, who are erecting policies designed to help them maintain their wealth. On the other is their growing unease about the scale of the inequality which benefits them—and the many people who are being left behind because of it.

Understanding this trend requires self-reflection from many of us. Are you currently *Overwealthy*? What does that mean in terms of how you live or what you choose to consume? How do you make an impact in the world? Are you enabling the inequality to continue? These are not easy questions, and may cause more than their fair share of defensiveness. Of course, none of us wants to see ourselves as part of the problem. Asking the question, however, is the key to doing better as individuals, and also as leaders of companies that have the power to impact the lives of others who are not in the same economic class.

When it comes to organizations, those trying to promote new products, services, and experiences to sell to the *Overwealthy* must find new ways to match their product, price, and experience to the purpose the customer is seeking to fulfill with the purchase. Inside companies, those with *Overwealthy* employees often face a variety of organizational challenges that can lead to conflict between differently-compensated employee groups within a company. To avoid workplace and interpersonal conflicts, resentment, and misunderstanding, it is important to explore and address this issue explicitly.

## How to Use This Trend

✓ **Empathize with the Overwealthy**—If you are selling a luxury experience or catering primarily to help people indulge in an experience, consider what you might do to offer a greater purpose or mission to that experience. Even the Gläce Luxury Ice company donates a portion of their earnings to support drinking water projects in places like Nicaragua and Honduras. Having a bigger mission and doing something positive in the world is more important than ever when you are selling to an audience who is already uneasy about all that they have.

✓ **Demonstrate equitability**—Pay people you interact with and purchase from more, especially those who are not as wealthy. If you don't run your own business or manage a team, this advice might not seem to apply to you. But there are many times in our daily lives when we could choose to give people more money, and don't. How about paying slightly more to the street vendor selling you something? Or tipping the Lyft or Uber driver more for safely and generously getting you to your destination? Each of us finds ourselves in situations in which we can *choose* to share more of our wealth with others. By demonstrating equitability in personal relationships or as leaders in our organizations, we are making a statement and doing our small part to help rebalance the stark disparity between the haves and have nots.

# 18

## Passive Loyalty

## What's the Trend?

—

As switching from brands becomes easier, companies reevaluate who is loyal, who isn't, and how to inspire true loyalty.

What if all loyal customers aren't as loyal as they seem?

Most companies think about customer loyalty as a binary choice: you are either a loyal customer or you are not. In recent years, this bias has become apparent through both the rapid growth of investment in loyalty programs and their often-disappointing results.

In 2017, the biennial loyalty research from marketing research firm Colloquy found that even though U.S. consumers hold 3.8 billion memberships in customer loyalty programs, membership growth slowed to just 15 percent, with 57 percent of consumers reporting that their number-one reason for leaving a loyalty program was because it took too long to earn rewards.[1]

According to the 2018 Maritz-Wise Marketer report, which surveyed more than 2,000 U.S. consumers, 68 percent of consumers identify as "transient" loyalists—which means they say they could be convinced to buy a competitor's brand. In the same survey, only 29 percent of consumers identified as "resolute" loyalists who buy *only* their favorite brands.[2]

Where most of these programs miss the mark is that they fail to account for the fact that there are two forms of loyalty: the loyalty of convenience (passive) and loyalty of belief (active).

In this trend, we focus on the fact that both exist, and that *Passive Loyalty* may account for a far larger percentage of supposedly loyal customers than most businesses realize.

**Passive Loyalty**

✓ Effortless to sign up or switch
✓ Motivated by signup savings and benefit
✓ Focused on rewards
✓ Convenience drives loyalty
✓ No major affinity, referrals, or proactive engagement with company

**Active Loyalty**

✓ Alignment with brand values
✓ Product/service affinity
✓ Promote brand as ambassador
✓ Drives referrals (net promoter)
✓ Values rewards
✓ May go out of way for loyalty
✓ Not prone to switch (even for up-front incentive)

# Why Real Brand Loyalty Might be a Myth

The market for selling automotive insurance is a good industry from which to spotlight the difference between passive and active loyalty.

On the surface, it seems that many companies in this sector have a loyal base of consumers who renew every year. Yet as a widely-cited article on the consumer decision journey from consulting firm McKinsey notes, there is actually "a significant number of customers who are loyal in name only...they remain with their carrier more out of inertia than satisfaction."[3] The McKinsey article goes on to note that the problem with most companies when it comes to earning loyalty is that "they are giving consumers reasons to leave, not excuses to stay."

When seen in this light, the ever-present advertising from insurance brands like GEICO and Progressive, encouraging consumers to comparison-shop in "15 minutes or less" for insurance quotes and switch providers, makes perfect sense.

Part of the reason these messages work is because the friction and cost of switching is getting lower and lower. All sorts of services, from cable companies to credit cards to mortgage loans, have created easy processes to optimize the process of switching from one to another. Today, it can often happen at the push of a button, with a fully automated process that makes it almost seamless and instant.

Because of all the marketing, consumers are being trained to chase better deals, look to save money, and reward businesses who offer short-term incentives—with the expectation that they will quickly move on and offer that same short-term loyalty to another brand, where the same cycle will repeat.

So, the natural question to wonder is whether active loyalty is even possible anymore. The answer is yes, and to see how, let's look at an example of how one company has managed to do it in the highly competitive industry of U.S. wireless carriers.

## The Uncarrier

T-Mobile has a reputation as a disruptor, thanks largely to the unorthodox business strategies of CEO John Legere. The brand was the first to break with industry convention by offering consistent pricing, free roaming while traveling internationally, elimination of predatory overage fees, and even payment of early termination fees (ETFs) from other carriers to buy out the rest of your contract and make it easier for customers to switch (most of which competitors have since copied).

The experience becomes even more customer-friendly *after* you switch. The brand offers free surprise "thank-you gifts" such as free pizzas and discounted concert tickets to customers every week through it's *T-Mobile Tuesdays* program. They also proactively give customers a "kickback" credit on their bill for extra data they are paying for but not using in any given month.

All of these moves are paying off. According to 2018 analyst reporting from the industry firm Consumer Intelligence Research Partners (CIRP), in the past year, T-Mobile topped all wireless carriers with a 19 percent growth rate (30 percent of which came from customers switching from competitors). The carrier also posted the highest retention rate of any wireless carrier at 85-percent.[4]

As T-Mobile is proving, it is possible to create Active Loyalty even in a competitive industry by focusing on delivering a great experience and putting customers first. The same principles can apply when it comes to keeping your best people and improving your *employee* loyalty.

# The Myth of Employee Satisfaction

In April 2016, the results of the MetLife Annual U.S. Employee Benefit Trends Study were released with the optimistic framing that for the first time in years, employee loyalty was on the rise. The "rise" celebrated by the study was from 41% to 45%. To underscore the low standards these numbers illustrate, just consider that when employees were asked whether they planned to stay at their jobs beyond the next 12 months, *only 45 percent answered yes.*[5]

The 2017 edition of the same study found that over half (51 percent) of employees said they would be interested in freelance or contract work in exchange for more flexible hours. These statistics are hardly worthy of celebration. When less than half of your employees want to be there a year from now, and most are dreaming of working freelance instead of full time, is that really the sort of news that should inspire confidence?

Sadly, when the bar for employee loyalty is so low, the honest answer is often yes.

Yet for every statistic indicating that employees are dreaming of leaving and unhappy in their roles, there is another, such as the recent finding from the Society of Human Resource Management (SHRM) that concluded that 89 percent of U.S. employees reported being somewhat or very satisfied with their current job role.[6]

I realize this seems like a strange contradiction. If people are satisfied, why do they seem to be dreaming of leaving, and generally lack loyalty? The fact is, satisfaction is not the same thing as loyalty.

All these "satisfied" employees are just exhibiting the traits of Passive Loyalty. They are loyal...until something better shows up. They don't hate their jobs or their companies, but they don't love them, either. And the moment an opportunity for career advancement, higher pay, or better benefits comes along, they will leave without a second thought.

## Automated Consumerism

Any discussion of loyalty, either from employees or consumers, would be incomplete without looking at the impact of technology on loyalty, as well. To do this, let's consider the rise of voice-enabled assistants like Google Home or Amazon Alexa. Both offer shopping capabilities that allow you to create lists and then use them to decide what to buy.

Amazon, in particular, has invested significantly in creating more ways to automate the experience for their customers. In 2015, they introduced the Amazon Dash, a Bluetooth-enabled ordering button that would stick to any surface and offer an easy way to reorder products like paper towels or laundry detergent.

At the time, it was a cute but underwhelming idea. Many consumers ordered one and never really used it. But the intent was never really about filling your house with these little reorder buttons. Instead, it was testing Amazon's vision of a home in which you could program everything you need to be automatically reordered whenever you needed it.

This is what automated consumerism could look like one day: technology that anticipates what you need, reorders it, and has it delivered to your home without you even thinking about it. Baked into this idea is a sort of forced brand loyalty in which consumers could end up locked into a brand simply because it happens to be the one that was available or most visible at the time when they first placed an order. Or the one offered by the retailer themselves; a distinct possibility, considering how consistently Amazon has been launching its own private-label products.

Loyalty, by extension, would become something that a consumer is *assigned* rather than something they willfully *choose*. It would be passive instead of active by default...and would perhaps always remain that way.

## Why It Matters

For years, marketers and business leaders have misunderstood loyalty as a singular concept. Today, we are starting to understand that there is more nuance in the idea of loyalty, and examples of passive loyalty are all around us: in our jobs, the things we buy, and how we engage (or don't engage) with brands.

To better drive loyalty, brands will need to rethink their overly complex yet often ineffective loyalty programs, and instead dream up new methods to reward customers that do truly drive brand loyalty. Satisfied customers are not the same as loyal customers. Satisfied employees who perform well are not the same as loyal employees.

Rather than seeing this as a negative, though, smart leaders and organizations understand that passive loyalty is just another stage of the journey toward active loyalty. Passively loyal customers are better than disloyal customers, haters, or the indifferent, who have no idea you exist. The business opportunity is to operationalize ways to transform these people—whether they are consumers or employees—into being actively loyal instead.

## How To Use This Trend:

✓ **Segment into passively and actively loyal**—If you can't tell your truly loyal customers or employees from the ones who would leave the first time they get a better offer, this is the first place you need to focus. Of course, making this distinction isn't easy, and it doesn't always match up nicely with tenure or spend. There are behaviors, indicators, and analytics to understand or even predict the migration down to passive or up to active loyalty. Instead, you need to build your own "ultimate questions" to help you measure this. One example might be asking, "If we could keep your business for the next two years, what would we need to do?" These sorts of questions can help you get a deeper sense of who's actually loyal and who is going to leave they next chance they get.

✓ **Earn loyalty, not sales**—If you preorder a book on Amazon. com and the price drops, they will send you a refund, even if it happens to be 17 cents. This consistency of unsolicited follow-up builds intense trust among customers. There are many people who would never preorder a book from anyone else. And each time Amazon proactively sends back a few cents when a price drops, they continue to earn this loyalty. That's the difference between doing something worthy of loyalty and simply focusing on selling a product once.

*Note: This trend was originally published in the 2017 Non-Obvious Trend Report, and is included in this new trend report with revised examples and new insights.*

## PART III

—

# The Trend
# Action Guide

# 19

## INTERSECTION THINKING

# How to Apply Trends To Your Business

—

*"Discovery consists of seeing what everybody has seen and thinking what nobody has thought."*
— ALBERT SZENT-GYÖRGYI, Nobel Prize–winning Physician

Nearly ten years ago, Tom Maas, a former marketing executive for distiller Jim Beam, finally created his perfect drink. For years, he had been working on developing and promoting a new cream liquor based on the popular traditional milky cinnamon-and-almond beverage from Latin America known as *horchata*.

His new drink was a mixture of light rum, dairy cream, and spices like cinnamon and vanilla that he christened "RumChata" in honor of the drink that inspired its flavors. Unfortunately, RumChata was not an instant hit.

It was only when some creative sales people first started likening its taste to the milk at the bottom of a bowl of Cinnamon Toast Crunch cereal that RumChata began to gain momentum. Bartenders started using the liquor to create inspired blends, which led to more liquor distributors and retailers ordering it. Inventive promotions like "cereal shooter bowls" also helped encourage bars to serve RumChata-based drinks.

Eventually, this creativity began to translate to higher sales.

By 2014, the drink had taken one-fifth of the market share in the $1 billion U.S. market for cream-based liquors, and even started outselling the longstanding leader, Diageo's Baileys Irish Cream, in certain regions. By 2017, it was also the most popular spirits brand on social media, with new videos on its YouTube channel routinely getting more than 2 million views.[1]

More importantly, experts described the drink as a crossover game changer due to its popularity as a mixer *and* as an ingredient for food and baking recipes.

## How to Create a Game-Changing Product

RumChata is a perfect example of the type of success that can come from putting the power of observation together with an understanding for the intersection of consumer behavior and the open space in a market.

While Maas may not have been thinking about trend curation when he came up with his product idea, we can still find some lessons in the example.

When you look backward, there are three cultural signals that may explain some of RumChata's success:

1. A growing consumer desire for authentic products with interesting backstories;

2. The rising prevalence of food entertainment programming on television inspiring more creativity in home cooking;

3. The increased interest across the United States in Hispanic culture and heritage.

In retrospect, these observations support the arrival of a product like RumChata. Of course, putting the dots together looking backward is easy.

The real question is: How can you do this predictably in a way that helps you create your own success in the future?

## An Introduction to Intersection Thinking

Trends are big ideas describing the accelerating world around us. Unfortunately, the value of big ideas is not always easily understood when it comes to applying them to real life.

Trend forecaster Chris Sanderson from the Future Laboratory describes trends as "profits waiting to happen." As tempting as that sounds, achieving those profits takes more than skill at uncovering, curating, and describing a trend. You need to know what to do next.

# Trends only have value if you can learn to act on them.

Is a trend telling you to abandon an existing product line? Or to pivot the focus of your business? Or to stay the course in a direction that hasn't yet paid off? These are the kinds of big questions that leaders often face and they aren't easy to answer.

Learning to curate trends can help you benefit from an outside perspective and prompt you to think about your business in a way that your competitors aren't. Doing this always starts with using "intersection thinking."

# Intersection thinking is a method for connecting ideas in order to generate new ideas, directions, and strategies.

After helping dozens of organizations and thousands of people learn to curate trends and then apply them, I always start by teaching this skill.

To do it, the analogy I use most often is this one:[2]

**PLUM** + **APRICOT** = **PLUOT**

Trends can be exactly like pluots: only valuable if you take the time to put multiple things together and experiment with them. This is intersection thinking, and doing it requires you to embrace four mindsets.

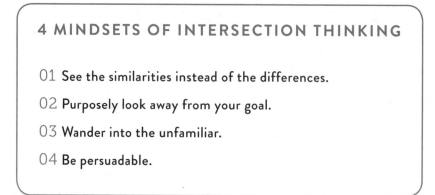

### 4 MINDSETS OF INTERSECTION THINKING

01 **See the similarities instead of the differences.**

02 **Purposely look away from your goal.**

03 **Wander into the unfamiliar.**

04 **Be persuadable.**

## Mindset 1  SEE THE SIMILARITIES

Paolo Nagari is an intercultural intelligence specialist who teaches expat executives the skills they need to succeed while living and working abroad. Unlike many other experts, however, his model doesn't rely on teaching the "dos and don'ts" of a given culture. His belief is that succeeding in a culture other than your own takes more than memorizing lists.

Nagari's first rule for executives is all about learning to focus on the many similarities in cultures instead of the differences. It's a valuable lesson when considering how to embrace unfamiliar ideas in business as well.

When former Coca-Cola executive Jeff Dunn became president of Bolthouse Farms, for example, he walked into a billion-dollar agricultural company that had literally reinvented the carrot industry by creating "baby carrots."[3]

By the time Dunn took over, sales of carrots (and baby carrots) were experiencing a slump and he needed a solution, so he turned to advertising agency Crispin Porter + Bogusky (CP+B).

During their preparation, the agency was inspired by a unique idea based on a simple consumer insight: people love snacking on junk food and hate being told to eat healthier.

As CP+B creative director Omid Farhang shares, "the truth about baby carrots is they possess many of the defining characteristics of our favorite junk food. They're neon orange, they're crunchy, they're dippable, they're kind of addictive."[4]

Using this insight, CP+B built a new campaign that enticed consumers to "Eat 'Em Like Junk Food," inspired by the marketing tactics of other consumer packaged goods companies (like Coca-Cola). Baby carrots were packaged and promoted like junk food, including cutting them in a "crinkle cut" style to make them look more like potato chips.

In campaign test markets, sales immediately went up between 10% and 12%, all thanks to a campaign built from seeing the similarities between the marketing tactics for junk food and applying those to marketing baby carrots instead.

### Mindset 2 **PURPOSELY LOOK AWAY FROM YOUR GOAL**

In early 2017, Starbucks founder Howard Schultz finally realized his thirty-four-year-long dream to open a Starbucks location in the place that started it all: Milan.

More than three decades earlier, his now-legendary spark of insight about what Starbucks could become happened on a walk from his hotel to a convention center. He'd been sent to a trade show in Milan to represent Starbucks, which at the time was a supplier of high-end home brewing equipment.

On that trip, he experienced firsthand the dominance of Italian espresso coffee shops on every street corner and how these might offer a "third place" (after work and home). He returned and persuaded the owners to create a retail coffee shop. Years later he purchased the brand from the original owners and took it global.

The growth of Starbucks is interesting, but what I found most inspiring about this was how it all started—with a curious walk that had nothing to do with focusing on a trade show or business purpose. Schultz's story is a perfect illustration of the power of looking away from your main purpose to discover bigger ideas that may be waiting around the corner (literally in his case!).

### Mindset 3 **WANDER INTO THE UNFAMILIAR**

If you happen to be walking the streets of Bangkok around 6:00 p.m. on any day, you'll see people stop in their tracks for seemingly inexplicable reasons. Ask anyone afterward and you'll quickly learn that there are two times every day when the

Thai national anthem is played (8:00 a.m. and 6:00 p.m.) and all citizens stop what they're doing and observe a moment of silence out of respect.

Once you see this cultural practice in action, it's impossible to forget. Travel experiences are like this—whether they happen across the world from your home, or simply during a visit to a nearby yet unfamiliar place. Wandering is a form of exploration that we often think to embrace only when traveling, but it has great value on a more daily basis.

In a world where we have a mobile map in our pocket, ready to assist us with turn-by-turn directions to anywhere, wandering must be a choice. It's the perfect metaphor for why intersection thinking matters, and why it can be difficult as well.

Sometimes we must choose to leave our maps behind.

## Mindset 4  BE PERSUADABLE

In the first edition of this book, this was not one of the original mindsets. I added it this year because it has become more necessary than ever. The world conspires in many ways to encourage each of us to burrow further into the chasms of our own beliefs. Algorithms on social media serve up stories we agree with. Website cookies aim to segment us to predict what we'll like to see or what we might click on to buy. Polarizing politicians remind us that "truth" comes with the necessity for someone to be wrong so we can be right, and tell us that person should be treated like the enemy. Instead, what if we could be brave enough to change our minds?

What if we could be persuadable[5]—to the point where hearing a compelling argument that we don't initially agree with might sway us to adapt our beliefs or at least allow for the possibility that someone who sees the world in a way other than ours might not be a complete idiot?

# Why Workshops Are So Powerful

A workshop is a gathering or meeting where an individual or a group of people focus their conversation and ideation on solving a challenge or thinking in new, innovative ways.

While it may seem hard or unnecessary to bring the right people together in a room for something like a workshop (and just plain silly if you're doing it alone or with just one other person), there are several reasons to consider taking a workshop-driven approach to applying trends or any other kind of new ideas.

The first is that workshops can help to focus your attention. We're all busy and usually don't have the time to be sitting around thinking about trends all day. To ensure you can have the right focused attention, it's valuable to block out a set period, even if it happens to be short. Just the act of making sure this time is scheduled and separate from your usual daily activities can help ensure that it feels significant. It will also help you to get the right people in the room, because blocking out a set time ensures they have notice and will not (hopefully) schedule something else for that time.

The second key to effectively using a workshop is to set a clear objective. While you usually don't need a step-by-step map, it's always useful to have a purpose or desired outcome defined. There are many ways to engineer the structure of what you do in a workshop. I share four common structures later in this chapter. Whichever you choose, the important thing is, like any good meeting, your workshop has a purpose so participants know what you aim to accomplish.

Finally, you need to be sure to establish accountability. Another critical reason that workshops can be so effective is that they force people to make commitments about what to do next.

# 5 Keys to Running a Great Trend Workshop

### Key #1 PREPARE LIKE A PRO

Take the time to familiarize yourself with the background of an issue, what has already been tried, what the needs of the group are, and what questions need to be asked in order to push the group toward real change.

### Key #2 CAPTURE FIRST, CRITIQUE LATER

People say, "there are no bad ideas in a brainstorm." That's not true. Unfortunately, it's impossible to tell good ideas from bad ones in real time. For that reason, encourage all participants to openly share ideas, and don't waste time and energy trying to immediately critique them. Save that for later.

### Key #3 ADOPT A "YES AND" MINDSET

Improv actors always talk about the importance of collaborating with others in a scene by going with the flow and building upon one another's ideas. This additive approach is one of the hallmarks of great and effective workshops as well.

## Key #4 ALWAYS HAVE AN UNBIASED FACILITATOR

It's easy to assume that the person closest to the issue is the best leader, but this is often untrue. Instead, the best workshop facilitators are individuals who can lead a discussion, keep a conversation on track, and ask provocative questions without bias.

## Key #5 RECAP AND SUMMARIZE

It's the role of the facilitator to summarize the conversation, recap any action items, and ensure that everyone who spent their precious time participating understands what they collectively achieved and what will need to happen next.

---

### 4 MODELS OF TREND WORKSHOPS

01 **Customer Journey Mapping Trend Workshop.**
Building a step-by-step understanding of how your customers interact with you so you can apply trends to each step of the process.

02 **Brand Storytelling Trend Workshop.**
Developing a powerful brand story or message designed to resonate with customers, based on understanding and using current trends.

03 **Business Strategy Trend Workshop.**
Creating a new go-to-market or product-launch strategy or making changes to a business model or revenue model informed by current trends and new competitive situations.

04 **Company Culture Trend Workshop.**
Planning your career or optimizing and improving an internal company culture and team based on current trends.

---

In the original 2015 hardcover edition of Non-Obvious, each workshop was outlined in detail through four additional chapters. For the sake of brevity, those chapters are not included in this edition. They are still available online completely for free for download at www.nonobviousbook.com/resources.

## Note for Small Teams and Solopreneurs

Although most of this chapter and the bonus PDF are specifically written from the point of view of having multiple participants in each type of workshop, many of the lessons in these chapters can be easily applied to small teams (or by individual innovators) as well.

Just because you don't have a large group of team members doesn't mean you can't use the benefits of intersection thinking and workshops to power your business. There's never a bad time to break from your normal routine and dedicate time through a workshop, to strategize for the future.

# 20

# 5 BOOKS ON TRENDS WORTH READING
## (and 15 Websites to Bookmark)

---

Despite the skepticism with which I often approach trend reports from so-called gurus, there are a handful of valuable, well-written resources for trend forecasting and techniques that I've drawn upon heavily over the years. This includes a short list of books and a longer list of websites that I routinely consult for story ideas. While some have already been cited elsewhere in this book, that chapter includes a full list of some of my favorites.

## 1. *Megatrends*, by John Naisbitt (1982)

There's a reason why this book about trends and the future has been a bestseller for the past three decades. Naisbitt paints a fascinating future portrait of the world as he saw it back in the early '80s. Despite the many years that have passed since it was first published, *Megatrends* remains a valuable read both for the prescience of Naisbitt's ideas and how he manages to capture the spirit of his time while also producing a startlingly accurate vision of the future.

## 2. *The Trend Forecaster's Handbook*, by Martin Raymond (2010)

This full-color, large-format volume is the closest thing you can find to a textbook on how to predict trends. Like most textbooks, it has a hefty price tag (used copies currently go for about $100), but the content is beautifully organized and it includes a dictionary-style compilation of everything you need to know about trend forecasting. From interviews with top futurists to highly useful sidebars (like how to select and interview an expert panel), this book shares so much insight that it belongs on your bookshelf.

### 3. *Trend-Driven Innovation*, by Henry Mason, David Mattin, Maxwell Luthy, and Delia Dumitrescu (2015)

The methodology for this book is based on the work of the team behind Trendwatching.com and features a behind-the-scenes look at some of the trends they have predicted over the years. The book is highly visual, easy to read, and a model for not only learning to see trends, but also how to talk about and present them.

### 4. *Superforecasting*, by Philip E. Tetlock & Dan Gardner (2015)

The most mainstream book on the list, Superforecasting was heavily praised when it first came out—named a "Best Book of 2015" by The Economist and "Editor's Choice" by the New York Times. The book uses powerful stories and years of research into what makes good (and accurate) forecasting to offer a model for how anyone can learn to use better foresight to understand the future.

### 5. *The Trend Management Toolkit*, by Anne Lise Kjaer (2014)

This book from longtime futurist and speaker Kjaer offers a somewhat academic description of methodologies used for predicting trends, and is therefore a tougher read than some of the other recommended books in this section. The section on creating and using a Trend Atlas and trend mapping is the most useful element in the book, and is the "toolkit" alluded to in the title. This technique is one which has been borrowed, adapted, and leveraged by many other experts and companies and is worth reading from the original source.

# What Else To Read...

Every year, my team and I receive dozens of books to review, and we purchase dozens more on our own. All of these provide sources of input for the coming year's trend research, but they also are featured in an annual book awards program released every December called the "Non-Obvious Book Awards."

Fifteen shortlist winners and five gold-medal category winners are featured and presented every year in December to coincide with the release of this book. You can see the full list of previous winners along with all the newest winners for the 2018 calendar year online: www.nonobviousbook.com/resources

## 15 Websites to Bookmark

This collection of online resources is a just a fraction of the 100+ sources of news that I subscribe to via RSS and use every week to source ideas both for my weekly newsletter, as well as for this annual book of trends. Below you will find some of my favorite sites, along with a quick one sentence description for each. You can also see this full list and click the links directly at www.nonobviousbook.com/resources.

1. **Trendwatching** (www.trendwatching.com) This is hands-down the most useful trend and forecasting resource online featuring insights curated from a network of thousands of spotters all over the world.

2. **PSFK** (www.psfk.com) A collection of smart daily blog posts and sometimes sponsored research reports on the future of big topics such as retail and healthcare.

3. **Cool Hunting** (www.coolhunting.com) This site has just enough stories to spark new ideas that make wading through the crowded and haphazard site design worthwhile.

4.  **Monocle** (www.monocle.com) While this is best consumed as a print magazine, the site features plenty of non-U.S. examples and will help you learn not only about the business world, but also about lifestyle, culture, and much more.

5.  **Springwise** (www.springwise.com) This is a subscription-based site, so the best information is only available to subscribers, but the collection of stories is valuable and worth paying for.

6.  **Verve** (www.verve.com) The quick takes and daily blog posts on this site are worth reading to keep up with current news.

7.  **Business Insider** (www.businessinsider.com) A prolific site that publishes business articles constantly and quickly.

8.  **Gerd Leonhard** (www.futuristgerd.com/blog) The personal blog of a futurist whose work is consistently useful and insightful.

9.  **The Future Hunters** (www.thefuturehunters.com) Most of their research is presented and discussed in quarterly meetings for clients only, but there's a useful collection of terms and recent white papers available on the site for free.

10. **Trend Hunter** (www.trendhunter.com) A dictionary for interesting stories from around the world shared by a small army of idea spotters. This is a useful resource to find ideas.

11. **Shelly Palmer** (www.shellypalmer.com/blog) This weekly blog from technology expert Shelly Palmer is thoughtful, well-written and offers a new take on the role of technology in our world that will make you think.

12. **JWTIntelligence** (www.jwtintelligence.com) While every agency and consulting group tries to create "thought leadership," this collection of insights from JWT is forward-looking, well-researched, and worth bookmarking.

13. **The Guardian** (www.theguardian.com) The only mainstream news source to make my list, I always appreciate the combination of strong reporting and global view they present.

14. **Slideshare** (www.slideshare.com) This site is filled with deep, insightful presentations and a good amount of useless garbage. Still, the sheer volume of all of it means you may find some interesting ideas, and even the odd internal corporate document that probably shouldn't have been shared publicly.

15. **Cool Hunter** (www.thecoolhunter.net) A collection of neatly organized posts on topics from "Amazing Places" to "Architecture."

# ANTI-TRENDS

# The Flip Side of Trends

—

*"There are trivial truths and there are great truths.*
*The opposite of a trivial truth is plainly false.*
*The opposite of a great truth is also true."*
— NIELS BOHR, Nobel Prize–Winning Physicist

From the end of September until the beginning of November, the Piedmont region of Italy is one of the most popular foodie destinations in the world for two reasons. The first is the famous Barolo wines, which are produced from the native Nebbiolo grape, and the second comes in October, when the town of Alba hosts its annual White Truffle Fair.

Truffles are a favorite decadent ingredient for top chefs, and white truffles are the rarest—sometimes costing as much as $2,000 per pound. Truffles from Alba are often described by chefs as "sublime" and "unlike anything else in the world." The Barolo wines, too, are considered Italy's best, called the "King of Wines" for centuries.

Yet, as amazing as these two Piedmont region delicacies are, there is one critical problem the region can't control: because they require opposite kinds of weather, they are never at their relative prime at the same time.

Truffles are best after a wet summer, while a dry and hot summer is optimal for grapes. As a result, summer cannot be equally good for both wine and truffles. In any given year, one will always be better.

## Flip Thinking and Anti-Trends

In this book I have shared a process for uncovering trends that affect the world around us along with advice on how to use them to power your business and career. Perhaps while reading one of these trends you thought of an example that seemed to do the exact opposite of what the trend was describing.

It's easy to think that finding an outlier to a trend would make it less valuable—similar to the truffles and wine.

Just like Piedmont's delicacies, though, there is often an opposing force that balances out trends, and it comes from people and companies that see what everyone else is doing and choose to do the opposite.

Sometimes, we hear it called "flip thinking," a term used most popularly by author Dan Pink. In one instance, he used it to describe a teacher who "flipped" the classroom by assigning math lectures via YouTube video as homework and doing the problems together in class.[1]

Flip thinking will always be present, and for every trend someone will usually find an example of the exact opposite. These are anti-trends and they can come up often. This is not a flaw in the art of curating trends, but it would be natural to wonder: If we have invested all this work into curating and describing trends, how can we be sure they matter when it seems so easy to find examples of the opposite?

# Breaking Trends

Trends are not like mathematical theories. They are describing a behavior or occurrence that is accelerating and will matter more and more, but they are not unbreakable rules of culture or behavior. There will always be outliers.

The point of curating trends is to see what others don't and to predict a future that can inspire new thinking. There is an interesting opportunity, though, that arises from being able to use this technique of "flip thinking."

Understanding trends not only empowers you to use them positively, but also to intentionally break them and do the opposite when it's an appropriate way to stand out.

Pablo Picasso famously declared that each of us should aim to "learn the rules like a pro so you can break them like an artist."

The clown in an ice-skating show, for example, often needs to be the most talented in order to execute fake jumps and falls while still remaining under control. Similarly, your ability to know the trends may give you the insight you need to bend or break them strategically.

This is, after all, a book about thinking in new and different ways. Taking a trend and aiming to embrace its opposite certainly qualifies.

## PART IV

# Previous Trend Report Summaries (2011-2018)

## OVERVIEW:

# How to Read These Past Trend Reports

—

*"The events of the past can be made to prove anything
if they are arranged in a suitable pattern."*
— A. J. P. TAYLOR, Historian

There was a moment several years ago when I was on stage after having just presented a talk about trends and how to predict the future when a skeptical gentleman stood up to ask me a question. "It must be easy," he started "to publish your trend report when you get to change them every year. How do you know whether any of them were actually right?"

His question was a fair one. After all, there is plenty of evidence to suggest the experts routinely miss predictions and are often just plain wrong. What makes my method or the past trends my team and I have curated any different? The only truthful way to answer that is to take a look backward.

In this section, you'll see a candid review of every one of my previously predicted trends from the past eight years of the Non-Obvious Trend Report. While some of the original descriptions have been edited for space considerations, none of the intentions or meanings have been updated or revisited since the trend was first published.

Each trend is accompanied by a "Trend Longevity Rating" which aims to measure how much the trend as originally described still applies or will have value in 2019. Predictably, the more recent trends fared better than the older trends—but the process of going backward and taking an honest look at past research was illuminating.

In assessing these trends, the aim was to treat them in as unbiased a way as possible. Where one did not accelerate as predicted, I did my best to admit that openly. It is, of course, nearly impossible to grade yourself in isolation—so I have also gathered the feedback from thousands of professionals who have listened to me share my "Haystack Method" and the trends that resulted from it in keynotes and workshops around the world. I took notes as they participated in workshops trying to apply these trends to their own businesses, and recorded some of their probing questions about each trend.

In addition, I made it a habit within our team to also save new stories and examples of trends that we had already published—so we could see just how many more relevant examples would come up since it was originally curated. This story gathering is also what helped decide which five of the previous trends to revisit in this new edition.

If there is anything that has helped this curated list of trends get better year after year, it is this annual ritual of reviewing, grading and critiquing past trends. We learn from our mistakes as much as we celebrate our successes.

As I shared early in this book, the beautiful thing about trends is that new trends don't replace old ones. Rather, they all present an evolving view of the world and individual "non-obvious" trends either become more obvious (and commonly understood) over time, or they fail to accelerate and sometimes fade away.

Either way, the best-case usage for trends is as a spark for new ideas and as an instigator for innovation.

I hope you enjoy this look backward at past years of the Non-Obvious Trend Report.

# PREVIOUSLY PREDICTED TREND SUMMARIES 2011-2018

## 2011
### Non-Obvious Trends

Likeonomics
Approachable Celebrity
Desperate Simplification
Essential Integration
Rise of Curation
Visualized Data
Crowdsourced Innovation
Instant PR & Customer Service
App-ification of the web
Re-imagining Charity
Employees as Heroes
Location Casting
Brutal Transparency
Addictive Randomness
Culting of Retail

## 2012
### Non-Obvious Trends

Corporate Humanism
Ethnomimicry
Social Loneliness
Pointillist Filmmaking
Measuring Life
Co-Curation
Charitable Engagement
Medici Marketing
Digital Afterlife
Real-Time Logistics
Social Artivism
Civic Engagement 2.0
Tagging Reality
Changesourcing
Retail Theater

## 2013
### Non-Obvious Trends

Optimistic Aging
Human Banking
Mefunding
Branded Inspiration
Backstorytelling
Healthy Content
Degree-Free Learning
Precious Print
Partnership Publishing
Microinnovation
Social Visualization
Heroic Design
Hyper-Local Commerce
Powered By Women
Shoptimization

## 2014
### Non-Obvious Trends

Desperate Detox
Media Binging
Obsessive Productivity
Lovable Unperfection
Branded Utility
Shareable Humanity
Curated Sensationalism
Distributed Expertise
Anti-Stereotyping
Privacy Paranoia
Overquantified Life
Microdesign
Subscription Commerce
Instant Entrepreneurs
Collaborative Economy

## 2015
### Non-Obvious Trends

Everyday Stardom
Selfie Confidence
Mainstream Mindfulness
Branded Benevolence
Reverse Retail
Reluctant Marketing
Glanceable Content
Mood Matching
Experimedia
Unperfection
Predictive Protection
Engineered Addiction
Small Data
Disruptive Distribution
Micro Consumption

## 2016
### Non-Obvious Trends

E-mpulse Buying
Strategic Downgrading
Optimistic Aging
B2Beyond
Personality Mapping
Branded Utility
Mainstream Multiculturalism
Earned Consumption
Anti-Stereotyping
Virtual Empathy
Data Overflow
Heroic Design
Insourced Incubation
Automated Adulthood
Obsessive Productivity

## 2017
### Non-Obvious Trends

Fierce Femininity
Side Quirks
Desperate Detox
Passive Loyalty
Authentic Fameseekers
Lovable Unperfection
Preserved Past
Deep Diving
Precious Print
Invisible Technology
Robot Renaissance
Self-Aware Data
Moonshot Entrepreneurship
Outrageous Outsiders
Mainstream Mindfulness

## 2018
### Non-Obvious Trends

Truthing
Enlightened Consumption
Ungendered
Brand Stand
Backstorytelling
Overtargeting
Manipulated Outrage
Light-Speed Learning
Virtual Empathy
Predictive Protection
Human Mode
Data Pollution
Approachable Luxury
Disruptive Distribution
Touchworthy

## The 2011 Non-Obvious
## Trend Report Overview

Original Publication Date: January 2, 2011
Original Format: Visual Presentation Only
Full Book: www.nonobviousbook.com/2011

## THE BACKSTORY

This first edition of the Non-Obvious Trend Report was inspired by five years of blogging. I released it exclusively in a visual presentation format and heavily featured marketing and social media trends that I had written about throughout 2010. The trends were far more limited in scope than later editions of the trend report and featured less description and less actionable advice. They were also not separated into subcategories. This report quickly went viral when it was first released, being viewed over 100,000 times on Slideshare.

## RETROSPECTIVE: HOW ACCURATE WAS THIS REPORT?

The report was one of the first to predict the rise in importance of content marketing and also correctly predicted the rapid growth of real- time customer service through social media. It analyzed the increasing number of marketing campaigns featuring employees as a sign of corporate humanity, and introduced the idea of how social media was making unreachable celebrities more connected and approachable. Overall, there were relatively few big misses or trends that completely imploded or reversed themselves. The biggest idea from the report was undoubtedly the first trend of *Likeonomics,* which ultimately inspired me to write a book of the same name (released in 2012).

*NOTE—There were no icons for trends in this report, and so the individual trend longevity ratings for this year are not included in this book. You can still see the full assessments by visiting the URL at the top of this page.*

# The 2012 Non-Obvious
# Trend Report Overview

Original Publication Date: January 2, 2012
Original Format: Visual Presentation Only
Full Book: www.nonobviousbook.com/2012

## THE BACKSTORY

This second year of the trend report featured a broader look at business beyond marketing or social media. Like the first report, it was released exclusively in visual presentation format online. Topics covered in this report included the sensitive yet emerging field of the digital afterlife of loved ones, as well as the steady rise of social loneliness. In moving farther away from marketing, this report took a more human tone as many of the trends featured cultural shifts and described consumer behavior.

## RETROSPECTIVE: HOW ACCURATE WAS THIS REPORT?

The 2012 report had a few big hits and several big misses. The overall trends that centered on the growth of humanity in companies and consumers stood the test of time. This report was one of the first to explore the potential of big data to impact everything from optimizing supply chain logistics to measuring and quantifying every aspect of our lives. On the flip side, some trends from this year were overly quirky niche concepts like *Pointillist Filmmaking* or *Social Artivism* did not quantifiably catch fire, either in adoption or in the behaviors they described.

*NOTE—There were no icons for trends in this report, and so the individual trend longevity ratings for this year are not included in this book. You can still see the full assessments by visiting the URL at the top of this page.*

# 2013 NON-OBVIOUS TRENDS OVERVIEW

**What is a trend?** *A trend is a unique curated observation about the accelerating present.*

**Culture & Consumer Behavior:** Trends in how we see ourselves and patterns in popular culture.

**OPTIMISTIC AGING**

**HUMAN BANKING**

**MEFUNDING**

**Marketing & Social Media:** Trends in how brands are trying to influence and engage consumers.

**BRANDED INSPIRATION**

**BACKSTORYTELLING**

**HEALTHY CONTENT**

**Media & Education:** Trends in information impacting how we learn, think or are entertained.

**DEGREE-FREE LEARNING**

**PRECIOUS PRINT**

**PARTNERSHIP PUBLISHING**

**Technology & Design:** Trends in innovation, technology and product design impacting our behavior.

**MICROINNOVATION**

**SOCIAL VISUALIZATION**

**HEROIC DESIGN**

**Economics & Entrepreneurship:** Trends in business models, industry or the future of work or money.

**HYPER-LOCAL COMMERCE**

**POWERED BY WOMEN**

**SHOPTIMIZATION**

Original Publication Date: December 10, 2012
Original Format: eBook + Visual Presentation
Full Book: www.nonobviousbook.com/2013

## THE BACKSTORY

In the third year of producing the trend report, the level of detail exploded from about 20 trend overview pages to well over 100 featuring more real life examples. While this edition of the Non-Obvious Trend Report did not originally use the five categories, for alignment we retroactively applied them and created icons.

The report was still delivered primarily in a visual presentation format, but this year an accompanying ebook was released exclusively on Amazon.com with tips on how to put the trends into action.

Thanks to the audience built from the first two editions, this third edition ebook was an instant best seller on Amazon, remaining the number-one book in the market research category for eight straight weeks after launch and was viewed more than 200,000 times online.

## RETROSPECTIVE: HOW ACCURATE WAS THIS REPORT?

Developing the trends for 2013 was a more deliberate process requiring more research and a higher standard of proof before including any particular trend in the report. Trends which resonated most from the 2013 report included *Partnership Publishing, Rise of Women, Human Banking, and Hyper-Local Commerce*. The insights from the report around the rising power of women in business, how large organizations were thinking about being more authentic and innovation on a smaller scale, were all trends that continue to this day.

**OPTIMISTIC AGING**

### What's the Trend?

A wealth of online content and new social networks inspire people of all ages to feel more optimistic about getting older.

### Trend Longevity Rating:

*This trend was important enough for me to select and bring back in my 2016 report—but as I shared in the rating for this trend from that year, the sense of optimism about what will be achievable in life has remained for the older population but over the past year it was tempered by increasing fears about the macro future of things like the environment, politics, the economy and security.*

B

**HUMAN BANKING**

### What's the Trend?

Aiming to change years of growing distrust, banks finally uncover their human side by taking a more simple and direct approach to services and communication and develop real relationships with their customers.

### Trend Longevity Rating:

*Every new financial crisis underscores the importance of more human interactions between us and our financial institutions. At the same time, growing inequality and distrust of banks has created a crisis of trust that remains hard to overcome.*

B+

**MEFUNDING**

### What's the Trend?

Crowdfunding evolves beyond films or budding entrepreneurs to offer anyone the opportunity to seek financial support to do anything from taking a life-changing trip to paying for a college education.

### Trend Longevity Rating:

*While the many sites featured as part of this trend remain available for people to use, the widespread use of tools to raise personal funding has not materialized the way we anticipated.*

C

**BRANDED
INSPIRATION**

**What's the Trend?**

Brands create awe-inspiring moments, innovative ideas and dramatic stunts to capture attention and sometimes demonstrate their values to the world.

**Trend Longevity Rating:**

*While this original trend was about using big moments for inspiration, this year we saw a resurgence in the use of theatrical stunts, which impacted our choice to introduce the Strategic Spectacle trend this year.*

**BACKSTORYTELLING**

**What's the Trend?**

Organizations discover that taking people behind the scenes of their brand and history is one of the most powerful ways to inspire loyalty.

**Trend Longevity Rating:**

*As social platforms splinter but also grow in popularity, the necessity for brands to share their backstory in multiple ways continues to grow. A good Backstory can offer a reason to believe in a brand's mission and share it with others.*

**HEALTHY
CONTENT**

**What's the Trend?**

Crowdfunding evolves beyond films or budding entrepreneurs to offer anyone the opportunity to seek financial support to do anything from taking a life-changing trip to paying for a college education.

**Trend Longevity Rating:**

*While the many sites featured as part of this trend remain available for people to use, the widespread use of tools to raise personal funding has not materialized the way we anticipated.*

**DEGREE-FREE LEARNING**

### What's the Trend?

The quality of e-learning content explodes as more students consider alternatives to traditional college educations.

### Trend Longevity Rating:

*Learning and higher education are simultaneously changed by this growth of people who choose to learn new skills and industries without requiring a degree to display at the end of it. While this has not overtaken traditional degree-granting programs, it continues to gain in popularity.*

**PRECIOUS PRINT**

### What's the Trend?

With an ever increasing digital culture, the few interactions we have ith the print medium become ever more valuable.

### Trend Longevity Rating:

*The basic human behavior outlined in this trend—that we place even more value on the things that are printed because they are so much more rare—continues year after year ... so much so that this trend returned in 2017 as it relates to the updated trend of Touchworthy.*

**PARTNERSHIP PUBLISHING**

### What's the Trend?

Aspiring authors, lacking a platform, and seasoned publishing professionals, in need of partners and content, team up to create a new "do-it-together" model of publishing.

### Trend Longevity Rating:

*This trend eventually inspired me to start Ideapress Publishing as a new venture to bring together some of the top tier freelance publishing talent and authors. There were plenty of other similar ventures to explore this idea as well—leading to a resurgence in publishing that has surprised some.*

### What's the Trend?

Thinking small becomes the new competitive advantage as slight changes to features or benefits creates big value.

### Trend Longevity Rating:

*If anything, this trend has accelerated in recent years as more brands adopt a lean startup mentality that encourages them to make incremental changes to products in ways that can deliver value. The quest to do this in a meaningful way is ongoing, particularly in the technology industry.*

**MICROINNOVATION**

A-

---

### What's the Trend?

In an attempt to make data more accessible, new tools and technologies allow people to visualize content as part of their social profiles and online conversations.

### Trend Longevity Rating:

*Visual interfaces continue to be commonplace and popular. This is one of those trends that was emerging at the time when it was first written but today more than five years later it seems obvious —which is the best sign of success for any trend over time.*

**SOCIAL VISUALIZATION**

A

---

### What's the Trend?

Design takes a leading role in the introduction of new products, ideas and campaigns to help change the world

### Trend Longevity Rating:

*The growth of design thinking as well as an increasingly reliance from the global community on seeing solutions to global problems posed by designers led us to bring this trend back for the 2016 report. Since that time, the importance of design serving a "heroic" purpose to solve society's biggest challenges has continued.*

**HEROIC DESIGN**

A

## HYPER LOCAL COMMERCE

**What's the Trend?**

New services and technology make it easier for anyone to invest in local businesses and buy from local merchants.

**Trend Longevity Rating:**

*Whether you examine this trend in relation to the growth of local commerce or as fueled by investment and interest in mobile commerce platforms and experience, the fact is consumer experiences continue to become more local more custom and more personal ... and so this trend is likely to continue.*

## POWERED BY WOMEN

**What's the Trend?**

Business leaders, pop-culture, and ground-breaking new research intersect to prove that our ideal future will be led by strong and innovative women working on the front lines.

**Trend Longevity Rating:**

*There is no denying the role of women in business, culture and politics has grown year after year. Today there are more female leaders, role models and celebrated citizens than ever before—and it is a wonderful thing leading to interesting related trends, like 2017's Fierce Femininity trend.*

## SHOPTIMIZATION

**What's the Trend?**

The proliferation of smart phones coupled with new mobile apps and startups let consumers optimize and enhance the process of online shopping for faster purchases of everything from fashion, to home goods to medical prescriptions.

**Trend Longevity Rating:**

*Thanks to increasing competition among retailers and a rising tide of new productivity tools online, the task of optimizing each of our shopping experiences has continued to be a top priority leading to better mobile first interfaces, one button shopping apps, and the ability to buy anything anywhere at the touch of a button.*

**What is a trend?** *A trend is a unique curated observation about the accelerating present.*

**Culture & Consumer Behavior:** Trends in how we see ourselves and patterns in popular culture.

**DESPERATE DETOX**

**MEDIA BINGING**

**OBSESSIVE PRODUCTIVITY**

**Marketing & Social Media:** Trends in how brands are trying to influence and engage consumers.

**LOVABLE IMPERFECTION**

**BRANDED UTILITY**

**SHAREABLE HUMANITY**

**Media & Education:** Trends in information impacting how we learn, think or are entertained.

**CURATED SENSATIONALISM**

**DISTRIBUTED EXPERTISE**

**ANTI- STEREOTYPING**

**Technology & Design:** Trends in innovation, technology and product design impacting our behavior.

**PRIVACY PARANOIA**

**OVERQUANTIFIED LIFE**

**MICRODESIGN**

**Economics & Entrepreneurship:** Trends in business models, industry or the future of work or money.

**SUBSCRIPTION COMMERCE**

**INSTANT ENTREPRENEURS**

**COLLABORATIVE ECONOMY**

## The 2014 Non-Obvious
## Trend Report Overview

Original Publication Date: February 18, 2014
Original Format: eBook + Visual Presentation
Full Book: www.nonobviousbook.com/2014

### THE BACKSTORY

This fourth edition of the Non-Obvious Trend Report was expanded to feature categories for trends for the first time instead of simply listing 15 in random order. Those categories are the ones used in every consecutive report since then.

In an effort to build visibility, in 2014 the full report was freely available online with a bonus ebook available for sale on Amazon.

This edition also corresponded with an exponential growth in the volume of public speaking and workshops I was being invited to deliver and was also the year that I left my role Ogilvy (after 8 years) to start my own consulting group focusing on trend research, keynote speaking, consulting and teaching.

### RETROSPECTIVE: HOW ACCURATE WAS THIS REPORT?

Due to this new category driven approach, our predictions had more discipline around their curation, and began to have more longevity. *Desperate Detox, Subscription Commerce, Collaborative Economy, Obsessive Productivity, Branded Utility* and *Curated Sensationalism* were all big trends that described entire movements and they received a lot of attention. This report also incorporated some of the healthcare specific trend research that my co-author Fard Johnmar and I published that same year in our industry vertical book about trends in health called *ePatient 2015*.

### What's the Trend?

Consumers try to more authentically connect with others and seek out moments of reflection by intentionally disconnecting from the technology surrounding them.

### Trend Longevity Rating:

*Technology is only becoming more omnipresent in our lives, and this trend was so impactful that it was an easy selection as one to bring back in 2017 to include in this year's report.*

**DESPERATE DETOX**

---

### What's the Trend?

As more media and entertainment is available on any device on demand, consumers binge and are willing to pay extra for the convenience.

### Trend Longevity Rating:

*Streaming options continue to expand yet this past year saw some fatigue with the idea of binge-watching where consumers felt overloaded or obligated to watch.*

**MEDIA BINGING**

---

### What's the Trend?

With thousands of life-optimizing apps and instant advice from social media–savvy self-help gurus, becoming more productive has become the ultimate obsession.

### Trend Longevity Rating:

*The past few years have brought plenty of new bestselling books talking about optimizing your life, hacking your daily chores and saving time. To say people continue to obsess over their own productivity is an understatement.*

**OBSESSIVE PRODUCTIVITY**

# 2014 Marketing & Social Media Trends

## LOVABLE IMPERFECTION

### What's the Trend?
Consumers seek out true authenticity and reward minor imperfections in products, personalities and brands by showing greater loyalty and trust.

### Trend Longevity Rating:
*While this was the first year that this trend was predicted, it was so powerful that a version of it was included in the 2015 report (Unperfection) and made another appearance in the 2018 report. It continues to be one of our most popular trends.*

## BRANDED UTILITY

### What's the Trend?
Brands use content marketing and greater integration between marketing and operations centers to augment promotions with real ways to add value to customer's lives.

### Trend Longevity Rating:
*As content marketing continues to change the way that marketers communicate with their audiences, there have been dozens more examples of brands using this trend. Its impact was also important enough to bring it back to include in my 2016 Trend Report.*

## SHAREABLE HUMANITY

### What's the Trend?
Content shared on social media gets more emotional as people share amazing examples of humanity and brands inject more of it into marketing communications efforts.

### Trend Longevity Rating:
*This was one of the trends from the previous year that was negatively affected by the fatigue some media consumers are starting to experience from overly dramatic media stories and click-baiting headlines. Though we continue to find human stories irresistible to read and share, this trend no longer has the impact it once did when first predicted.*

# 2014 Media & Entertainment Trends

### CURATED SENSATIONALISM

**What's the Trend?**
As the line between news and entertainment blurs, smart curation displaces journalism as engaging content is paired with sensational headlines to drive millions of views.

**Trend Longevity Rating:**
*Media continues to deliver over-the-top headlines and sensationalism which made this trend a precursor to many that followed, including Truthing and Manipulated Outrage in 2018, as well as Strategic Spectacle this year.*

---

### DISTRIBUTED EXPERTISE

**What's the Trend?**
The idea of expertise itself shifts to become more inclusive, less academic and more widely available on demand and in real time.

**Trend Longevity Rating:**
*Learning through experts online in many formats is still a big trend and one that is powering some of the fastest growing learning platforms online today (including many profiled in this original trend). We have on demand access to experts in more ways than ever and this shows no signs of slowing down.*

---

### ANTI-STEREOTYPING

**What's the Trend?**
Across media and entertainment, traditional gender roles are being reversed, assumptions about alternative lifestyles are being challenged, and perceptions of how people are defined evolve in new ways.

**Trend Longevity Rating:**
*The reversing of gender roles continues to be a big opportunity for brands to get their messaging right or wrong, when it comes to speaking to these diverse groups through marketing and communications—but the broader aspects of this trend were what encouraged us to bring it back in 2016 as well.*

## PRIVACY PARANOIA

### What's the Trend?

New data breaches are leading to a new global sense of paranoia about what governments and brands know about us—and how they might use this big data in potentially harmful ways.

### Trend Longevity Rating:

*As more tools enter the market to help consumers protect their information and take back control of their privacy, this paranoia is shifting to empowerment. All the warnings and attention on privacy are leading some people to ignore the warnings while others take back control. Either way, "paranoia" no longer seems like the ideal term to describe our relationship to privacy.*

## OVERQUANTIFIED LIFE

### What's the Trend?

As big data leads brands to overload data with cute infographics and superficial analysis, they also add more confusion about what all this data really means, and how it can inform decisions in real life.

### Trend Longevity Rating:

*Connecting all the data we collect on ourselves in a meaningful way continues to be a challenge, and we are indeed still "overquantified." In this year's report, the Overtargeting trend from 2018 takes this idea further to explore how it impacts business and marketing.*

## MICRODESIGN

### What's the Trend?

As communication becomes more visual, design gains more respect and becomes an everyday business requirement. At the same time, demand for design skills also explodes, leading to easier access to bite-sized chunks of design expertise.

### Trend Longevity Rating:

*The need for design expertise continues to grow, and this trend is still an important one for any type of organization. In addition, design thinking has exploded as a category of learning and insights. As a result, this trend continues to sit at the intersection of several others.*

# 2014 Economics & Entrepreneurship Trends

## SUBSCRIPTION COMMERCE

**What's the Trend?**
More businesses and retailers use subscriptions to sell recurring services or products to customers instead of focusing on the one-time sale.

**Trend Longevity Rating:**
More industries and brands turn to the lessons of subscription commerce, but as I wrote about in the 2018 trend report, it has also led to significant burnout among consumers. There will likely be more trials and failures from those trying to leverage this trend, which we already write about in this year's Fad Fatigue trend.

## INSTANT ENTREPRENEURS

**What's the Trend?**
As the barriers to starting a new business begin to disappear, incentives and tools mean anyone with an idea can launch a startup knowing that the costs and risks of failure are not as high as they once were.

**Trend Longevity Rating:**
The shift in many industries from full-time employee to entrepreneur continues to take shape as top professionals continue to branch out on their own. In addition, it is a global priority among national governments to make the process of entrepreneurship faster and easier because of the widespread understanding that entrepreneurs drive economies forward.

## COLLABORATIVE ECONOMY

**What's the Trend?**
New business models and tools allow consumers and brands to tap the power of sharing and collaborative consumption to find new ways to buy, sell and consume products and services.

**Trend Longevity Rating:**
While growing last year, the shared or collaborative economy has become well understood, a symbol of its continued rapid acceleration. While it may be "obvious" now, the impact of it and just how much attention brands are paying to the space justifies its continued ranking among the top trends for its longevity over the years.

**What is a trend?** *A trend is a unique curated observation about the accelerating present.*

**Culture & Consumer Behavior:** Trends in how we see ourselves and patterns in popular culture.

**EVERYDAY STARDOM**      **SELFIE CONFIDENCE**      **MAINSTREAM MINDFULNESS**

**Marketing & Social Media:** Trends in how brands are trying to influence and engage consumers.

**BRANDED BENEVOLENCE**      **REVERSE RETAIL**      **RELUCTANT MARKETER**

**Media & Education:** Trends in information impacting how we learn, think or are entertained.

**GLANCEABLE CONTENT**      **MOOD MATCHING**      **EXPERIMEDIA**

**Technology & Design:** Trends in innovation, technology and product design impacting our behavior.

**UNPERFECTION**      **PREDICTIVE PROTECTION**      **ENGINEERED ADDICTION**

**Economics & Entrepreneurship:** Trends in business models, industry or the future of work or money.

**SMALL DATA**      **DISRUPTIVE DISTRIBUTION**      **MICRO CONSUMPTION**

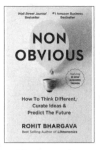

NON OBVIOUS

How To Think Different,
Curate Ideas &
Predict The Future

ROHIT BHARGAVA
Best Selling Author of Likeonomics

# The 2015 Non-Obvious Trend Report Overview

Original Publication Date: March 1, 2015
Original Format: Hardcover + eBook
Full Book: www.nonobviousbook.com/2015

## THE BACKSTORY

After four years of growing an audience by publishing the Non-Obvious Trend Report only a digital format, in 2015 I decided to work with my team to expand the content into a full length book. I spent most of the year writing about the technique we used to curate ideas which would eventually be honed into trends. I created a "formula" for how anyone could predict the future (the Haystack Method), and published the new book along with the signature list of 15 trends as usual. The result was *Non-Obvious* released as a full length hardcover book for the first time.

The book hit #1 in the entire business category on Amazon and made it up to #27 in ALL Kindle books within 48 hours. The popularity of the book drove it to hit the *Wall Street Journal* Best Seller list the week it launched, but it also introduced the idea of trend curation to a much wider audience. Over the course of the next year, the book was contracted for six translated editions and my speaking and workshops continued—with more global invitations.

## RETROSPECTIVE: HOW ACCURATE WAS THIS REPORT?

The trends that year described culture in a way that many people started talking about—from *Everyday Stardom* exploring how consumer expectations were rising to *Selfie Confidence* describing the role social media plays in building self-esteem. Other popular trends from this year included *Small Data*—which offered a counter idea to the growing discussions of "big data" and media trends such as *Experimedia* or *Glanceable Content* to describe our shifting attention spans.

**EVERYDAY STARDOM**

### What's the Trend?
The growth of personalization leads more consumers to expect everyday interactions to be transformed into "celebrity experiences" with them as the stars of the show.

### Trend Longevity Rating:
*As the opportunities for companies to use big data to personalize experiences for customers continue to grow, this expectation from consumers to be treated like superstars has only continued to grow and is even more of a necessity for brands today than it was when this trend was first introduced. ort.*

**SELFIE CONFIDENCE**

### What's the Trend?
The ability to share a carefully crafted online persona allows more people to use social content such as selfies as a way to build their own self confidence.

### Trend Longevity Rating:
*Selfies are a misunderstood medium. They were when this trend was first written, and perhaps are even more so today ... yet this trend took the optimistic view that those selfies were an important part of how kids build self-esteem today and that remains true three years later, even as self expression has broadened to include more video and broaden beyond just selfies.*

**MAINSTREAM MINDFULNESS**

### What's the Trend?
Meditation, yoga and quiet contemplation become powerful tools for individuals and organizations to improve performance, health and motivation.

### Trend Longevity Rating:
*Not only did we bring this trend back as a featured trend in 2017, but it has come to describe entire industries, new ways of thinking for organizations and a powerful new movement towards improving ourselves at home and at work.*

**BRANDED
BENEVOLENCE**

### What's the Trend?

Companies increasingly put purpose at the center of their businesses to show a deeper commitment to doing good that goes beyond just donating money or getting positive PR.

### Trend Longevity Rating:

*Brands continue to focus on purpose and big initiatives to demonstrate a commitment to the environment, social issues, and ethical business practices. This trend directly inspired the 2018 trend of Enlightened Consumption.*

**REVERSE
RETAIL**

### What's the Trend?

Brands increasingly invest in high-touch in-store experiences as a way to build brand affinity and educate customers, while seamlessly integrating with their online channels to complete actual purchases and fulfill orders.

### Trend Longevity Rating:

*The original inspiration for this trend was the rapid growth of "showcase stores" that were being used by brands to offer experiences to consumers. Since then retailers continue to focus on the experiential side, a fact we also explore in this year's Strategic Spectacle trend.*

**RELUCTANT
MARKETER**

### What's the Trend?

As marketing shifts away from pure promotion, leaders and organizations abandon traditional silos, embrace content marketing and invest in the customer experience.

### Trend Longevity Rating:

*As content marketing becomes a greater part of the marketing mix, organizations see themselves doing more than just "marketing." This shift away from promotional marketing and toward being useful, providing utility and answering questions continues to grow.*

## GLANCEABLE CONTENT

**What's the Trend?**

Our shrinking attention spans and the explosion of all forms of content online lead creators to optimize stories for rapid consumption at a glance.

**Trend Longevity Rating:**

*As much as I would love to say this trend disappeared as people started engaging with content longer (see 2017's Deep Diving trend), this behavior remains true and much of daily or hourly content does need to be glanceable still in order to receive any sort of attention.*

## MOOD MATCHING

**What's the Trend?**

As tracking technology becomes more sophisticated, media, advertising and immersive experiences like gaming and learning can be tailored to match consumer moods.

**Trend Longevity Rating:**

*Automated sentiment filters and new technologies like eye tracking and vocal analysis are letting consumers have even bigger expectations about how technology will cater to them. That said, this trend always described something that was only really relevant in some situations and therefore not as broad or wide-ranging as many of the other trends.*

## EXPERIMEDIA

**What's the Trend?**

Content creators use social experiments and real life interactions to study human behavior in unique new ways to ultimately build more realistic and entertaining narratives.

**Trend Longevity Rating:**

*For a time it seemed that media featuring social experiments was a hot new practice likely to continue for a long time. Over the past few years, though, this trend has slowed down significantly and even though there are still some examples of this happening, it is not at the volumes it once was.*

# 2015 Technology & Design Trends

**UNPERFECTION**

### What's the Trend?

As people seek out more personal and human experiences, brands and creators intentionally focus on using personality, quirkiness and intentional imperfections to be more human and desirable.

### Trend Longevity Rating:

*One of my favorite trends for what it described when it was first curated, this trend was partially brought back in the 2017 report along with Lovable Imperfection from 2014. The idea that brands and leaders are showing vulnerability and building trust through their willingness to share flaws continues to have resonance.*

---

**PREDICTIVE PROTECTION**

### What's the Trend?

A growing concern for privacy coupled with elevated expectations technology's role in our lives leads to more intuitive products, services and features to help us live better, safer, and more efficient lives.

### Trend Longevity Rating:

*The need for the type of proactive protection that this trend continues to grow each day influencing several later predictions, such as Robot Renaissance and Self Aware Data. This trend was also revisited in this past year's report.*

---

**ENGINEERED ADDICTION**

### What's the Trend?

Greater understanding of the behavioral science behind habit formation leads to more designers and engineers intentionally creating addictive experiences that capture consumers' time, money and loyalty.

### Trend Longevity Rating:

*If you consider the growth of everything from packaged foods to fantasy sports, this trend is still central to how new experiences are conceived and the way that experiences can now be engineered to be irresistible whether they are good for us or not.*

# 2015 Economics & Entrepreneurship Trends

**SMALL DATA**

### What's the Trend?

As consumers increasingly collect their own data from online activities brand-owned big data becomes less valuable than small data.

### Trend Longevity Rating:

*Since the publication of this trend, a best-selling book from Martin Lindstrom of the same title and growing sophistication of technology to personalize experiences has led this trend to be even more relevant today than when it was first curated*

---

**DISRUPTIVE DISTRIBUTION**

### What's the Trend?

Creators and makers use new models for distribution to disrupt the usual channels, cut out middlemen, and build more direct connections with fans and buyers.

### Trend Longevity Rating:

*This trend has exploded in recent years and is likely to impact even more industries in the near future. As a result, we brought it back in the 2018 trend report.*

---

**MICRO-CONSUMPTION**

### What's the Trend?

As new payment models, products and experiences become available in bite-sized portions, multiple industries will experiment with new micro-sized forms of pricing and payments.

### Trend Longevity Rating:

*While this trend will likely continue, it has not accelerated as initially predicted with the same industry-defining pace as several others.*

# 2016 NON-OBVIOUS TRENDS OVERVIEW

**What is a trend?** *A trend is a unique curated observation about the accelerating present.*

**Culture & Consumer Behavior:** Trends in how we see ourselves and patterns in popular culture.

**E-MPULSE BUYING**

**STRATEGIC DOWNGRADING**

**OPTIMISTIC AGING**

**Marketing & Social Media:** Trends in how brands are trying to influence and engage consumers.

**B2BEYOND**

**PERSONALITY MAPPING**

**BRANDED UTILITY**

**Media & Education:** Trends in information impacting how we learn, think or are entertained.

**MAINSTREAM MULTICULTURALISM**

**EARNED CONSUMPTION**

**ANTI-STEREOTYPING**

**Technology & Design:** Trends in innovation, technology and product design impacting our behavior.

**VIRTUAL EMPATHY**

**DATA OVERFLOW**

**HEROIC DESIGN**

**Economics & Entrepreneurship:** Trends in business models, industry or the future of work or money.

**INSOURCED INCUBATION**

**AUTOMATED ADULTHOOD**

**OBSESSIVE PRODUCTIVITY**

# The 2016 Non-Obvious Trend Report Overview

Original Publication Date: January 25, 2016
Original Format: Paperback + eBook
Full Book: www.nonobviousbook.com/2016

## THE BACKSTORY

Given the success of the first year that *Non-Obvious* was available in print (in 2015), we had high expectations for this sixth edition. Looking backward over the previous trend predictions each year, we realized that many past predictions still had a lot of relevance for business and a year seemed too short to really see how some of them would evolve.

As a result, for the first time this year we decided to only publish ten NEW trends and include five PAST trends in the report (one per category). These past trends would include all new examples as well as analysis on what had changed and why we chose to bring it back. The other thing this report featured was an in-depth analysis of the previous year's trends (2015) and how they had evolved over the past year—a model that was later adapted to the shorter analysis and more visual grading that you now see in this section.

## RETROSPECTIVE: HOW ACCURATE WAS THIS REPORT?

The most popular trends from this year's report included *Earned Consumption, Strategic Downgrading* and *Virtual Empathy* (which was revisited in 2018). While the series maintained its popularity, the report this year underperformed for a number of reasons mainly related to timing. The report was released late, and failed to include the year boldly on the cover, which created confusion among readers as to whether the content was actually new or not. These were all issues we corrected in 2017!

**E-MPULSE BUYING**

### What's the Trend?

Despite fears that the e-commerce might kill impulse buying, the growing integration of mobile devices into the shopping experience is opening new possibilities for real time marketing to entice consumers to make split second emotional buying decisions once again.

### Trend Longevity Rating:

*Over the past year ecommerce retailers have gotten even more adept at encouraging impulse purchases through their interfaces, and one button ordering is growing in availability. Throughout this year, it is likely more and more retailers will continually add more features designed to encourage impulse buying.*

**STRATEGIC DOWNGRADING**

### What's the Trend?

As more products become Internet-enabled and digitally remastered, consumers start selectively rejecting these supposedly improved products and services–opting to strategically downgrade to simpler, cheaper and sometimes more functional versions instead.

### Trend Longevity Rating:

*A sense of nostalgia remains a high influencing factor for this trend as "retro"products continue to be launched successfully. This trend was also brought back this year (and renamed) as Deliberate Downgrading, and influenced the RetroTrust trend as well.*

**OPTIMISTIC AGING**

(Originally Curated 2013)

### What's the Trend?

After years of being sold anti-aging solutions–a new generation of newly aging adults are embracing the upside of getting older and finding cause for optimism in the growing opportunities, financial freedom, respect and time that their "third age" can offer.

### Trend Longevity Rating:

*The sense of optimism about what will be achievable in life has remained for the older population but over the past year it was tempered by increasing fears about the macro future of things like the environment, politics, the economy and security. These big issues are casting a distant but significant cloud over the optimism that older people otherwise feel.*

## B2BEYOND MARKETING

**What's the Trend?**
Brands used to promoting their products or services to other businesses embrace their humanity, take inspiration from other sectors and think more broadly about effectively marketing to decision makers as people first, and buyers second.

**Trend Longevity Rating:**
The steady shift in B2B marketing best practices is continuing to take shape thanks to high visibility examples, leading us to decide to bring the trend back this year to explore new ways that is has evolved.

## PERSONALITY MAPPING

**What's the Trend?**
As behavioral measurement tools build a detailed map of our personalities, multiple industries will be able to use this information to bring likeminded people together and provide more transformative learning and bonding experiences.

**Trend Longevity Rating:**
While organizations are getting much better at using the data that they have, there are growing signs that sometimes this type of customization limits the audience too quickly in a quest to better understand consumer personalities and cater to those. Moving forward the challenge with this trend is to ensure personality mapping is useful, not overdone.

## BRANDED UTILITY
(Originally Curated 2014)

**What's the Trend?**
Brands begin to focus on a combination of content marketing and a greater integration between marketing and operations to provide value through usefulness in customer's lives.

**Trend Longevity Rating:**
As content marketing explodes, this trend is undeniably going along with it. The idea that brands can and should provide more utility for their potential customers is leading brands to invest in creating quality content, shifting marketing spending and creating new ways to offer more than just empty promotions.

## MAINSTREAM MULTICULTURALISM

**What's the Trend?**

After years of being ignored, niche demographics, multicultural citizens and their cultures find new widespread acceptance through a growing integration of diverse ideas and people in entertainment, products and politics.

**Trend Longevity Rating:**

*Even as xenophobic political sentiment lingers in many places around the world, the generational shift towards acceptance and embrace of multiple cultures is allowing this trend to have a continued impact in the business, art, media and culture of today.*

........................................................................................

## EARNED CONSUMPTION

**What's the Trend?**

The desire for authentic experiences leads to a willingness from consumers to earn their right to consume, offering businesses a chance to build more loyalty and engagement by letting consumers "pay" for products or services with more than just money.

**Trend Longevity Rating:**

*There are still many situations where consumers want to earn their chance to be a customer and feel the pride in achieving their place—yet a growing skepticism of experiences and products means that anyone selling anything has to work harder to feel worthy of the time investment.*

........................................................................................

## ANTI-STEREOTYPING
(Originally Curated 2014)

**What's the Trend?**

A fundamental change takes place across media and culture, where traditional gender roles are being reversed, assumptions about alternative lifestyles are challenged, and perceptions of what makes someone belong to a particular gender, ethnicity, or category are being upended.

**Trend Longevity Rating:**

*The number of people who now define themselves with something other than the traditional descriptors of male or female is growing every day —an idea that led directly to the 2018 trend of Ungendered.*

**VIRTUAL EMPATHY**

### What's the Trend?

An improved quality and lower costs for virtual reality allows creators to tell more immersive stories and let people see the world from another point of view—growing their empathy in the process.

### Trend Longevity Rating:

*Over the past year, the examples of virtual reality being used to engage, improve and quantify human empathy were too numerous to count. In bringing this trend back in 2018, we took a fresh look at the impact of the trend and found it more relevant than ever.*

**DATA OVERFLOW**

### What's the Trend?

The combination of growing personal and corporate owned data mixed with open data creates a new challenge for companies to go beyond algorithms for data management and rely on better artificial intelligence, smarter curation, and more startup investment.

### Trend Longevity Rating:

*Data continues to "overflow" and create problems of measurement and analysis, but as the Self-Aware Data trend from 2017 shows, the overflow is no longer the same challenge it once was because of automation. The greater issue is not the volume but the quality of it—an issue we explore in the 2018 trend of Data Pollution.*

**HEROIC DESIGN**
(Originally Curated 2013)

### What's the Trend?

Design takes a leading role in the introduction of new products, ideas, and inspiration to change the world in nuanced, audacious, irreverent, and sometimes unexpectedly heroic ways.

### Trend Longevity Rating:

*The continued presence of design competitions to celebrate new solutions for global problems and a suite of tools to help anyone bring more design thinking to their own jobs means that this trend of putting design on a pedestal and asking it (and designers) to create "heroic" solutions will continue.*

### INSOURCED INCUBATION

**What's the Trend?**

Companies desperate to bring more innovation into their enterprise turn to a new model of intrapreneurship modeled after the best business incubators—bringing innovators in house, providing support and resources, and starting innovation labs.

**Trend Longevity Rating:**

*The slate of Innovation Labs and new efforts chronicled in this trend produced early successes to legitimize the idea and inspire this year's related trend of Innovation Envy. .*

### AUTOMATED ADULTHOOD

**What's the Trend?**

As more people go through a prolonged period of emerging adulthood, a growing range of technology and services help to automate all aspects of their journey to adulthood.

**Trend Longevity Rating:**

*As new tracking products get released to measure everything about life, and tools for automated living continue to be popular, this trend will continue to inspire more co-living arrangements and other facilities that ensure people have partners to help carry them emotionally and physically into adulthood.*

### OBSESSIVE PRODUCTIVITY
(Originally Curated 2014)

**What's the Trend?**

Thanks to our reduced attention spans and "always-on technology," the necessity to be productive in every moment has rapidly evolved into an obsession that underpins every brand interaction or other experience.

**Trend Longevity Rating:**

*To say that technology has made us all very aware of those moments when our time is valued or wasted would be even more of an understatement than when this trend was originally written 3 years ago. Productivity is still an obsession—and looks to stay that way.*

# 2017 NON-OBVIOUS TRENDS OVERVIEW

**What is a trend?** *A trend is a unique curated observation about the accelerating present.*

---

**Culture & Consumer Behavior:** Trends in how we see ourselves and patterns in popular culture.

**FIERCE FEMININITY**      **SIDE QUIRKS**      **DESPERATE DETOX**

---

**Marketing & Social Media:** Trends in how brands are trying to influence and engage consumers.

**PASSIVE LOYALTY**      **AUTHENTIC FAMESEEKERS**      **LOVABLE UNPERFECTION**

---

**Media & Education:** Trends in information impacting how we learn, think or are entertained.

**PRESERVED PAST**      **DEEP DIVING**      **PRECIOUS PRINT**

---

**Technology & Design:** Trends in innovation, technology and product design impacting our behavior.

**INVISIBLE TECHNOLOGY**      **ROBOT RENAISSANCE**      **SELF-AWARE DATA**

---

**Economics & Entrepreneurship:** Trends in business models, industry or the future of work or money.

**MOONSHOT ENTREPRENEURSHIP**      **OUTRAGEOUS OUTSIDERS**      **MAINSTREAM MINDFULNESS**

## The 2017 Non-Obvious Trend Report Overview

Original Publication Date: December 5, 2017
Original Format: Paperback + eBook
Full Book: www.nonobviousbook.com/2017

## THE BACKSTORY

This year was the most extensive report so far, with not only 15 brand new trends predicted but also a newly expanded appendix with full analysis and grading of every previously predicted trend. Some of the most popular trends from this year included *Fierce Femininity, Passive Loyalty, Unperfection, Precious Print, Invisible Technology, Robot Renaissance* and others. Over the year, the volume of keynote speaking I was doing and workshops my team was delivering also increased—which drove even more visibility for the trends. In addition, in this year many of the translated editions of the book started to come out—growing our global audience for the trend report.

## RETROSPECTIVE: HOW ACCURATE WAS THIS REPORT?

Unlike the 2016 edition of the report, this 2017 edition came out a full month earlier and sold extremely well through retail and directly to large organizations to share with their teams. This edition of the book was also awarded the prestigious Axiom Award for Business Books (Silver Medal for Business Theory) and was featured widely in the media. In 2017, multiple foreign editions were also released, including a special edition in China which also featured new regional examples for each trend and an increasingly global point of view. Given the recency of these trends - we spent a lot of time researching whether they were still relevant and ultimately decided all of them had enough examples and acceleration to merit the grades we assigned.

**FIERCE FEMININITY**

### What's the Trend?
Over the past few years the fierce, independent woman has emerged, redefining the concept of femininity and reimagining gender roles.

### Trend Longevity Rating:
*Current events and the political and cultural climate continue to shift how we perceive women's place in modern society. Women are finding more support from men in power. This trend also informed this year's Muddled Masculinity trend.*

**SIDE QUIRKS**

### What's the Trend?
A global shift toward individualism has led to a surge in side businesses and a renewed appreciation for what makes people unique.

### Trend Longevity Rating:
*People continue to create value out of their hobbies, passions, and personality quirks. This desire to pursue "side projects" and the continued global rise of individualism inspired us to bring this trend back in 2019.*

**DESPERATE DETOX**

(Originally Curated 2014)

### What's the Trend?
As technology, media clutter and an overload of gadgets make life increasingly stressful, people are seeking moments of reflection and pause.

### Trend Longevity Rating:
*Tech saturation continues to drive people to seek tech-free havens. There are even apps which help people find connectivity dead zones. Hotels, restaurants and even workplaces now offer an option for guests to "check in" their phones and enjoy some time without technology interruptions.*

## PASSIVE LOYALTY

**What's the Trend?**

A new understanding of loyalty is challenging brands to get smarter about how they can generate brand enthusiasts.

**Trend Longevity Rating:**

*Over the past year, forward looking brands have redesigned their loyalty programs to overcome the challenge of passive loyalty and focus on delivering consistent experiences and rewards. As brands continue to rethink how to engage consumers and drive loyalty, we decided to bring this trend back for 2019.*

## AUTHENTIC FAMESEEKERS

**What's the Trend?**

A new generation of creators are turning to social media to establish their brands, attract eyeballs and become the next big thing.

**Trend Longevity Rating:**

*Influencers continue to be a force online in using social media to drive extreme fan loyalty yet some of the overall fatigue with content combined with this year's trend of Artificial Influence have softened the impact of this trend.*

## LOVABLE UNPERFECTION

(Originally Curated 2014)

**What's the Trend?**

Today, successful marketing campaigns are putting an increasing focus on using the power of personality, quirkiness, and imperfections to create authentic with customers.

**Trend Longevity Rating:**

*Each year that passes, brands continued to learn that consumers connect with real, unfiltered, honest messaging and campaigns. Unretouched photos, "hand-finished" imperfect products and many other brands refocused on taking customers behind the scenes and injecting more reality into their story.*

**PRESERVED
PAST**

### What's the Trend?

Technology is offering new ways to preserve history, changing the way we learn from, experience, and remember the past in the process.

### Trend Longevity Rating:

*Preservation focused groups continue their important work by creating "virtual curations" of artifacts, tracking deteriorations, preserving fragile papers, and even creating 3D libraries of the world's cultural heritage sites before they are damaged in war or consumed by natural disaster.*

**DEEP
DIVING**

### What's the Trend?

While brands compete for our shrinking attention spans with more content than ever, many people prefer to go all in on the topics and experiences that truly capture their interest.

### Trend Longevity Rating:

*People continue to find enjoyment in content and storytelling that takes them deep into interesting topics. Podcasts, investigative journalism, documentary filmmaking and the long-form rants of comedy news anchors remain popular.*

**PRECIOUS
PRINT**

(Originally Curated 2013)

### What's the Trend?

Thanks to the digital revolution, people are developing a more meaningful and emotional relationship with physical objects and printed material.

### Trend Longevity Rating:

*Books, records, and simpler, retro models of cameras, video games and anything that generates nostalgia will strike a chord with people who long for the nostalgia and tangible nature of physical objects and printed materials.*

# 2017 Technology & Design Trends

**INVISIBLE TECHNOLOGY**

### What's the Trend?

As technology becomes more sophisticated, it becomes better at predicting and anticipating needs, protecting us, and providing utility while blending seamlessly into our lives.

### Trend Longevity Rating:

*In the coming year, artificial intelligence, connected objects, machine learning, virtual and augmented reality, will multiply the ways that technology can make everyday tasks, transactions, communication and learning easier, cheaper, and more efficient.*

**ROBOT RENAISSANCE**

### What's the Trend?

As robots' utility moves into the home and the workplace, they adopt more human-like interfaces and even adopt micro-personalities.

### Trend Longevity Rating:

*The true impact of this trend is still at the early stages. How much of our "work" should we cede to technology? Do we need universal income? Will robots take over? These are "renaissance age" questions, and they they led us to include this trend in 2019 once more.*

**SELF-AWARE DATA**

### What's the Trend?

As technology advances, algorithms and artificial intelligence make real-time analysis so fast that it can move from input to insight to action all on its own.

### Trend Longevity Rating:

*Data and real-time analytics will continue to transform how companies get insight. In contrast to the more alarmist trends of Data Overflow and Data Pollution, this trend offers a more positive future vision of a future where data might create value by analyzing itself.*

# 2017 Economics & Entrepreneurship Trends

## MOONSHOT ENTREPRENEURSHIP

**What's the Trend?**

A new generation of entrepreneurs are thinking beyond profit and making social impact, not financial performance, at the center of their organizations' missions.

**Trend Longevity Rating:**

*The world's problems remain complex, and entrepreneurs continue to generate social impact. As they continue to fill the gap left by ineffective governments, this trend inspired the 2019 trend of Good Speed.*

## OUTRAGEOUS OUTSIDERS

**What's the Trend?**

Some of today's most innovative and influential ideas are coming from complete outsiders whose unconventional quirks disrupt entire industries.

**Trend Longevity Rating:**

*The past few years offer plenty of evidence for how outsiders can disrupt entire industries, countries and global orders. We expect that this trend will continue to effect everything from politics to music in the coming year and beyond.*

## MAINSTREAM MINDFULNESS

(Originally Curated 2015)

**What's the Trend?**

The business community is starting to reject the "sleep when you're dead philosophy" in favor of mindfulness in all its forms: yoga, meditation, quiet contemplation and even sleep.

**Trend Longevity Rating:**

*Many professionals continue to desperately seek spaces of quiet to disconnect and improve focus. An increasing number of employers are also incorporating practices that encourage rest, meditation, and healthy sleep.*

# 2018 NON-OBVIOUS TRENDS OVERVIEW

**What is a trend?** *A trend is a unique curated observation about the accelerating present.*

**Culture & Consumer Behavior:** Trends in how we see ourselves and patterns in popular culture.

**TRUTHING**

**UNGENDERED**

**ENLIGHTENED CONSUMPTION**

**Marketing & Social Media:** Trends in how brands are trying to influence and engage consumers.

**OVERTARGETING**

**BRAND STAND**

**BACKSTORYTELLING**

**Media & Education:** Trends in information impacting how we learn, think or are entertained.

**MANIPULATED OUTRAGE**

**LIGHT-SPEED LEARNING**

**VIRTUAL EMPATHY**

**Technology & Design:** Trends in innovation, technology and product design impacting our behavior.

**HUMAN MODE**

**DATA POLLUTION**

**PREDICTIVE PROTECTION**

**Economics & Entrepreneurship:** Trends in business models, industry or the future of work or money.

**APPROACHABLE LUXURY**

**TOUCHWORTHY**

**DISRUPTIVE DISTRIBUTION**

# The 2018 Non-Obvious Trend Report Overview

Original Publication Date: December 5, 2018
Original Format: Paperback + eBook
Full Book: www.nonobviousbook.com/2018

## THE BACKSTORY

This year included a full overhaul of design and layout of the book to make it easier to read and to incorporate color and visuals as well. In addition to the formatting, the trends themselves continued to gain popularity, but looking at all of the predictions of the years started to get difficult for my team in workshops. To help create more of a sense of continuity and encourage people to take a bigger view of the trends, we partnered with Microsoft this year to also create an interactive trend experience and also launched an ambitious website that featured extended content about every past trend.

## RETROSPECTIVE: HOW ACCURATE WAS THIS REPORT?

This edition continued to gain more visibility in the industry and was a frequent winner of major book awards, including the Eric Hoffer Book Award, INDIE Book Award Gold Medal and being selected as a finalist for the Leonard L. Berry Marketing Book Prize sponsored by the American Marketing Association. As for the trends themselves, there were several that captured reader and media attention. *Manipulated Outrage* was a big winner, describing a phenomena that many people recognized - and other popular trends from this report included *Brand Stand, Truthing, Approachable Luxury* and *Human Mode.*

**TRUTHING**

**What's the Trend?**

*As a consequence of eroding trust in media and institutions, people are engaging in a personal quest for the truth based on direct observation and face-to-face interaction.*

**Trend Longevity Rating:**

*As widespread distrust of the media, governments and corporations continues, this trend continues to be important and describe a critical coping mechanism that many people are using to seek out who they can really trust.*

**UNGENDERED**

**What's the Trend?**

*Shifting definitions of traditional gender roles are leading some to reject the notion of gender completely, while others aim to mask gender from products, experiences, and even their own identities.*

**Trend Longevity Rating:**

*The way we understand and describe gender roles continues to shift. In past years we have talked about women, men and this trend - which sits squarely in between. Each continues to describe broad movements and evolving beliefs.*

**ENLIGHTENED CONSUMPTION**

**What's the Trend?**

*Empowered with more information about products and services, people are choosing to make a statement about their values and the world today through what they buy, where they work, and how they invest.*

**Trend Longevity Rating:**

*The speed with which we continue to have access to real time information to evaluate the impact our buying has on the world continue to make this trend a critical one to watch.*

# 2018 Marketing & Social Media Trends

## OVERTARGETING

### What's the Trend?
Lured by the promise of big data, organizations segment audiences too narrowly and unintentionally end up abandoning large groups of potentially lucrative customers.

### Trend Longevity Rating:
While businesses continue to do this frequently and unnecessarily narrow their audience, in many cases it has not turned out create the sort of major issues or challenges that we initially predicted.

## BRAND STAND

### What's the Trend?
Reacting to a polarized media atmosphere, more brands feel compelled to take a stand and highlight their core values rather than try to be all things to all people.

### Trend Longevity Rating:
Over the past year since this trend was first predicted, there have been example after example of brands utilizing this effect to inspire belief, share what they believe and grow loyalty.

## BACKSTORYTELLING

### What's the Trend?
Organizations use the power of stories to share their heritage, mission, and reason for existing with audiences to earn loyalty and position themselves as desirable places to work.

### Trend Longevity Rating:
If there is any trend that could be described as universally important, it would be this one. Though it has been brought back over time, the idea of stories as a way for brands to stand apart continues to be an effective strategy.

# 2018 Media & Entertainment Trends

## MANIPULATED OUTRAGE

### What's the Trend?
*Media, data analytics, and advertising are combining forces to create a perpetual stream of noise that is intended to incite rage and illicit angry reactions on social media and in real life.*

### Trend Longevity Rating:
*Unfortunately, this trend remains sadly important due to the continued use of manipulation by evil corporations and self-centered politicians, exacerbated by the gullible media who help amplify the manipulation much more broadly.*

---

## LIGHT-SPEED LEARNING

### What's the Trend?
*The road to mastery on any topic gets faster through the help of bite-sized learning modules that make education more time efficient, engaging, useful and fun.*

### Trend Longevity Rating:
*This trend has driven real business change and positive results, as we have seen companies use this principle to stand out, educate their customers and help close sales.*

---

## VIRTUAL EMPATHY

### What's the Trend?
*Immersive experiences delivered through technology and personal interactions increase empathy by helping people see the world through foreign and unfamiliar eyes.*

### Trend Longevity Rating:
*The broader take on this trend that we described this year made it even more relevant as we see new examples of installations, art projects, experiences and technology that continue to offer people ways to feel more empathy.*

# 2018 Technology & Design Trends

## HUMAN MODE

### What's the Trend?
As automation increases, people hungry for more personal and authentic experiences begin to put a premium on advice, services, and interaction involving actual humans.

### Trend Longevity Rating:
The more technology continues to evolve and automation happens to experiences and interactions that used to involve people, we will continue to see a rise in the importance of this trend and the counter intuitive importance of humans that it implies.

## DATA POLLUTION

### What's the Trend?
As we create more methods for quantifying the world around us, data gets manipulated, contaminated and sabotaged, making it harder to separate true insights from useless noise.

### Trend Longevity Rating:
There is no doubt the flood of data is continuing to rise and sorting through it to find what really matters continues to be a major problem for corporations that even the smartest artificial intelligence has not yet been able to solve.

## PREDICTIVE PROTECTION

### What's the Trend?
Organizations create smarter connected products, services and features that can proactively protect our safety, health and environment by anticipating our actions or needs.

### Trend Longevity Rating:
One of the side effects of the pace of evolution of technology is just how demanding we have become of that technology. Those high expectations continue to make this trend highly relevant as people want tech to anticipate their needs more than ever.

**APPROACHABLE LUXURY**

### What's the Trend?
*Luxury is no longer defined by scarcity and privilege, but rather through more down-to-earth authentic human experiences that create unforgettable moments worth sharing.*

### Trend Longevity Rating:
*The reckoning amongst luxury brands never quite materialized as deeply as we anticipated. Alongside luxury that was "approachable" was luxury that was even more out of touch, designed for the "Overwealthy" described in our 2019 prediction.*

B+

---

**TOUCHWORTHY**

### What's the Trend?
*Overwhelmed by digital, consumers turn back toward products and experiences that they can touch, feel and sense to deliver a much needed sense of calm, simplicity and humanity.*

### Trend Longevity Rating:
*The more digital things are becoming, the more the importance of tactile experiences continues to be. Our 2019 trend of "Deliberate Downgrading" also relates to this idea that sometimes we just want a more real and tangible non-digital experience.*

A

---

**DISRUPTIVE DISTRIBUTION**

### What's the Trend?
*Traditional models of distribution get reinvented as businesses of all sizes seek more efficiency, build direct connections with consumers and rethink their own business models.*

### Trend Longevity Rating:
*Traditional distribution models continue to be disrupted by new players, innovative aggregators and an ongoing shift in how consumers expect buy and receive just about anything.*

A

# AFTERWORD

—

*"There's no such thing as weird food. Only weird people."*
— FERRAN ADRIÀ, Chef and Molecular Gastronomist

Apparently, the world will end on March 16, 2880.

While putting the final touches on the first edition of Non-Obvious, I came across a news article about a team of scientists who discovered a 0.3% chance the world will end on that day due to a cosmic collision course between Earth and a celestial body known only as Asteroid 1950 DA.

The story immediately struck me as the perfect metaphor for the types of predictions we commonly encounter in the world today... overblown proclamations with dire consequences and relatively little certainty.

One of the aims for this book is to challenge lazy or obvious trend predictions that are, sadly, just like that exaggerated astronomical prediction. Mistaken trend predictions can be even more damaging than a doomsday prophecy, because they lead to flawed decisions today instead of just empty dread for the far future.

A trend is a unique curated observation of the accelerating present.

Non-Obvious intentionally doesn't offer geopolitical arguments for why Denmark is going to become the world's next superpower by 2050 thanks to wind energy production, or optimistic technology predictions about how self-driving cars will enable virtual-reality tourism during daily commutes.

These kinds of predictions are sexy, and some might even come true. Unfortunately, they also include a lot of uncertainty. The future should involve far less guesswork.

Curating trends is certainly about seeing the things others don't. Yet it's also more broadly about a mindset that encourages you to be curious and thoughtful. It's about techniques that help you move from trying to be a speed reader to being a "speed understander," as Isaac Asimov wrote.

The future belongs to those who can learn to use their powers of observation to see the connections between industries, ideas, and behaviors and curate them into a deeper understanding of the world around us.

I'm not saying that this type of thinking can save us from the asteroid 867 years from now, but it can change the way we approach our lives and our businesses in the present.

Preparing for the future starts with filtering out the noise and getting better at understanding today... as it always has.

# RESEARCH:

# Notes, References, & Credits

—

The preparation of this book and the Non-Obvious Trend Report involves scanning tens of thousands of stories every year, interviewing dozens of experts and reviewing more than 100 books. Where relevant, these sources have been cited specifically in an endnote, however this does not reflect the full breadth of sources consulted. On average, each trend includes about 30 stories and links that were used in the development, curation and writing of that chapter. Since inserting a long list of links in a physical book (or even an ebook) has limited value, all of these links are instead shared through a downloadable PDF (where you can click any link which you can access and download). The intent of this list is to offer a useful way for you to visit individual links to stories, to learn more about a trend, or to discover where exactly the ideas and research cited in this book come from.

To download a PDF with active links for this 2019 edition of Non-Obvious, visit this URL: www.nonobviousbook.com/resources

# ENDNOTES

### Chapter 1: The Norwegian Billionaire

1. **Mini Bottle Gallery.** This story is gathered from first-hand conversations with staff at the venue, stories available online about the founding, and literature provided to visitors at the museum.

2. **Trend spotter definition.** This definition was taken from Wisegeek.com, but there were plenty of similarly narrow-minded definitions spread across the Internet I could have picked to share here. The common bias of most of them is that there is some type of special training and industry knowledge required to be a trend expert. There isn't.

3. **Curse of knowledge.** The famous linguist Steven Pinker discusses this "curse of knowledge" in his book *The Sense of Style,* where he notes that the more expertise we have about a topic, the more difficult we tend to find it to simplify or explain it to those who are not as well versed as ourselves.

### Chapter 2: The Curator's Mindset

1. **Mindset.** Carol Dweck's simple yet profound book was first published in 2006.

2. **"Parking ticket not a car wreck."** Dweck's *Mindset* is filled with analogies and anecdotes like this one to illustrate the value of a growth mindset versus a fixed one.

3. **Vogel Collection.** This story was sourced primarily from the *New York Times* profile written about the Vogels after Herbert's death in 2012. http://www.nytimes.com/2012/07/24/arts/design/herbert-vogel-postal-clerk-and-modern-art-collector-dies-at-89.html

4. **The truth about Columbus.** Columbus deserves little of the ceremony he gets and, in fact, he never even set foot in North America during his famous journey in 1492. Listen to the real story: http://www.npr.org/templates/story/story.php?storyId=141164702

5. **Why are traffic signs orange?** The answer took a bit of Googling after my kids asked, but they're orange because testing shows that this is the color most visible from a distance. And everyday cars aren't orange because people care more about picking a color they like than optimizing the color for safety.

### Chapter 3: The Haystack Method

1. **John Naisbitt Interview.** This profile and the quotes are taken from an article and interview published in the *USA Today* around the time that his book *Mind Set!* was published. Full interview: https://usatoday30.usatoday.com/money/books/2006-09-24-naisbitt-usat_x.htm

2. **Non-Obvious Trend Report (1st edition).** This first year of the report was published as a visual presentation and is available online (unedited). More details about this report and how to read it, as well as how the trends fared over time, is all included in the Appendix.

3. **Bliss point.** Michael Moss is a Pulitzer Prize–winning investigative journalist. For a short summary of his story on the scientists who uncovered and exploited the "bliss point," see this excerpt from his book reprinted in the *New York Times*: http://www.nytimes.com/2013/02/24/magazine/the-extraordinary-science-of-junk-food.html

4. **Addicted by Design.** In her book, Schüll explores the idea of a trance-like state she calls the "machine zone," where gambling addicts play not to win but simply to keep playing. When this machine design is combined with casino's focus on "ambience management," addiction is the result.

5. **Philip Tetlock.** The full body of Tetlock's research was originally presented in his 2005 book *Expert Political Judgment: How Good Is It? How Can We Know?* The book was recently republished (August 2017) with a new preface from the author and updated insights.

6. **Oscar Wilde.** This quote is from Wilde's play "An Ideal Husband."

## Chapter 4: Strategic Spectacle

1. **The Humanity Star.** Background story from *The Atlantic* - http://bit.ly/2ziFiUL

2. **Museum of Ice Cream revenue.** Revenue figures come from this Marketwatch article - https://on.mktw.net/2B7aJ5x

3. **"Instagram-optimized funhouses."** Source for quote - http://bit.ly/2K3J741

4. **Casper retail expansion plans.** Source for figures - http://bit.ly/2PZWNm7

5. **"Omnishoppers."** Link to original study that coined this term - http://bit.ly/2K5akmS

6. **Value of Banksy artwork.** This Newsweek article suggests the painting may be worth more after the shredding - http://bit.ly/2zPbDSm

## Chapter 5: Muddled Masculinity

1. **Sweet Valley High.** Archived link to 1986 article from the *LA Times* about the popularity of the teen romance series - https://lat.ms/2DHoDhs

2. **What do men think it means to be a man?** Full survey results and highlights from *FiveThirtyEight* - https://53eig.ht/2DHbqVG

3. **Girl Scout Badges (2018).** Full list of badges available for Girl Scouts in 2018 - http://bit.ly/2DFLKJ7

4. **Modern Masculinity Is Stifling.** Read the full article from Sara Rich published on *The Atlantic* - http://bit.ly/2DExuAc

5. **Toxic Masculinity" (definition).** Full definition from The Good Men Project - http://bit.ly/2DJwICj

6. **Axe Campaign.** Profile piece on the Axe marketing campaign by *Adweek* - http://bit.ly/2DEpeQZ

7. **"The Man Box" Report.** Download and read the full study from Axe/Unilever and Promundo - http://bit.ly/2RWWeqp

8. **Doofus Dads In Ads.** Read the full article on *Adweek* - http://bit.ly/2DHhOML

9. **Men are seen as the financial providers.** Details on the Pew research study citing men are still traditionally seen as financial providers of the family - https://pewrsr.ch/2DFM8r3

10. **Trends in fatherhood imagery.** Read the full article on *Mashable* - http://bit.ly/2DK2UVO

11. **Past 100 years of baby name trends.** Read the full article and name list on *Quartz* - http://bit.ly/2DL3dQm

## Chapter 6: Side Quirks

1. **Etsy global marketing campaign.** Read the full story about Etsy's campaign on Adweek- http://bit.ly/2OGXYC9

2. **Cultural map of the world.** See the full map and research behind it - http://bit.ly/2RXhVXF

3. **Side hustle.** Full article about millennials and the rise of the side hustle - http://bit.ly/2RU79Bj

4. **Hikkimori.** Read the full article and photo essay from *National Geographic* - https://on.natgeo.com/2RUMBbL

5. **Individualism in China.** Read the full article - http://bit.ly/2RUMUTX

6. **Koreans spending time alone.** Read the full article and see the survey data - http://bit.ly/2RUN7Xf

7. **The Twee Revolution.** Full review of the book from *The Atlantic* - http://bit.ly/2RVuUsS

8. Gen Z report. Read the full research report from Sparks & Honey - http://bit.ly/2RVC683

## Chapter 7: Artificial Influence

1. **About Shudu.** Quotes from *Harper's Bazaar* interview with Cameron-James Wilson - http://bit.ly/2PrKUGj

2. **Amy Winehouse hologram announcement.** Read the full article - http://bit.ly/2B6zyi4

3. **Profile of GAN creator Ian Goodfellow.** MIT magazine full profile - http://bit.ly/2Puk14r

4. **Deepfakes in the Philippines.** For more context on the election, read the full article - http://bit.ly/2Pwi1J7

5. **Unilever issues mandate to ad industry.** Full article - http://bit.ly/2qNZAAG

6. **Crowdcasting.** This term is further explained in this *Washington Post* article - https://wapo.st/2z905Kj

7. **Edelman Trust Barometer.** Read the full 2018 edition of the report here - http://bit.ly/2RWJ9h5

**Chapter 8: RetroTrust**

1. **Reinvention of Kodak.** Read the full article - http://bit.ly/2qKNVT0

2. **Arcade bars in Buenos Aires.** Read this for more on the popularity of these destinations - http://bit.ly/2qOfKtW

3. **Board games make a comeback.** Read the full article - http://bit.ly/2OKwQCg

4. **Profile of Mario Talarico.** Read the full profile in National Geographic Traveller - http://bit.ly/2RTmZvQ

5. **Profile of Kari Voutilainen.** Read the full profile in the *NY Times* - https://nyti.ms/2za6Mvm

**Chapter 9: B2Beyond Marketing**

1. **Caterpillar brand strategy.** Read the full story on *Adage* - http://bit.ly/2RWO-pRC

**Chapter 10: Fad Fatigue**

1. **Growth of fitness equipment market.** The numbers cited come from this article - https://on.mktw.net/2Fml1Tr

2. **Exercise fad timeline.** See the full list of annual fads from 1956 to 2018 - http://bit.ly/2B7N3xX

3. **Goat yoga.** Yes, it is real. This is one of many stories about the curious idea - https://n.pr/2zdwAqu

4. **Photo Credit:** Central Washington University, Flickr - https://flic.kr/p/28Z-jp23

5. **Cauliflower has its moment.** Here's a comprehensive article about the rise of this despicable vegetable - http://bit.ly/2DF4VTh

6. **McDonald's Fries Cure Baldness.** Read the full article here - http://bit.ly/2D-EYkZa

7. **Drinking Coffee Could Shrink Women's Breasts.** Read the full article here - http://bit.ly/2zQRzPy

8. **Sitting impacts your long-term health.** Despite being sponsored by a maker of sit-stand desks, the website JustStand.org has a useful compilation of research studies on this topic here - https://www.juststand.org/the-facts/#the_research

**Chapter 11: Extreme Uncluttering**

1. **National Dining Survey.** Read the full results from the Zagat Survey - http://bit.ly/2RZuh1h

2. **Chefs choose simplicity.** Read the full article - http://bit.ly/2RYwyd9

3. **Amazon Alexa Terms.** Read the full terms for Amazon voice search - https://amzn.to/2S4hjQ1

4. **Growing up with social media.** Read the full article on *Washington Post* - https://wapo.st/2RZut0v

5. **Heineken's new brand strategy.** Read the full article on *Fast Company* - http://bit.ly/2RZhfRq

## Chapter 12: Deliberate Downgrading

1. **John Deere copyright guidelines.** Full 2015 guidelines from John Deere - http://bit.ly/2DJUduR

2. **Tractor ownership.** Read the full story on *WIRED* - http://bit.ly/2DLpqxN

3. **Right to repair article.** See the full interview transcript - http://bit.ly/2DLpmhy

4. **"Dumb" phone sales rise.** Read the full article with stats from Daily Mail - https://dailym.ai/2DLoHg4

5. **Publisher revenue statistics.** Sales data from the American Association of Publishers - http://bit.ly/2DLpCNy

6. **Nielsen book sales data.** Read the full report from Nielsen with print book sales data - http://bit.ly/2DMMyMp

7. **Why people prefer print books.** Read the full story - http://bit.ly/2DMmSPY

8. **Popularity of turntables.** Read the full article from *The Guardian* - http://bit.ly/2DMMr3r

9. **2018 Golf Industry Report.** Full 2018 report from the National Golf Foundation - http://bit.ly/2RVf8OC

## Chapter 13: Enterprise Empathy

1. **Pollution Pods.** These were an art exhibit showcased in 2017 and featuring 6 domes that each included some of the world's worst air pollution for people to experience. Read more about the experience - https://cnn.it/2DJkl99

2. **Herbal Essences inclusive shampoo bottle design.** Read the full article - http://bit.ly/2RYANFs

3. **Work and the loneliness epidemic.** Read the full article - http://bit.ly/2RYBgrc

4. **Indian day care center.** Read the full story on *Pacific Standard* - http://bit.ly/2RUX07m

5. **AARP Study: Aging in place.** Read the full study - http://bit.ly/2DJ46J4

6. **Aging in place reduces healthcare costs. Read** the summary of the full study - http://bit.ly/2DI0A1H

7. **End-of-life Doulas.** Profile of the rise of this industry in the *Washington Post* - https://wapo.st/2RYOOTI

## Chapter 14: Innovation Envy

1. **Lyons, Dan.** *Lab Rats: How Silicon Valley Made Work Miserable For The Rest Of Us.* New York: Hatchette Books, 2018 - Page 71-72.

2. **Victoria Secret's "porny" fashion show.** Read the full article by Sangeeta Singh-Kurtz - http://bit.ly/2DNMkoa

3. **Victoria's Secret stock is falling.** Full article from *NY Times* on the struggles of Victoria's Secret - https://nyti.ms/2DMUgG4

4. **Victoria's Secret hairstylist.** Read the full interview in *People* magazine with Anthony Turner - http://bit.ly/2DIHs3H

5. **"Amazon Hunger Games."** Read the full article - http://bit.ly/2DLKqV2

6. **Maltese corruption.** Read the full story on *BusinessWeek* - https://bloom.bg/2DLGWBP

## Chapter 15: Robot Renaissance

1. **Jibo struggling to survive.** Read the full analysis on *The Robot Review* - http://bit.ly/2S0EXg9

2. **Martine Rothblatt interview.** Read the full interview - http://bit.ly/2S1quAu

3. **Being Sophia.** Read the announcement from Hanson Robotics - http://bit.ly/2RVOBAw

## Chapter 16: Good Speed

1. **"Militant optimism."** Read the full article on *WIRED* from Rosetto - http://bit.ly/2DH9499

2. **Lego creates more sustainable bricks.** Full article from *NY Times* - https://nyti.ms/2DHwZp0

3. **Jose Andres helps Puerto Rico.** Full *Fast Company* article referenced - http://bit.ly/2DGhVrJ

4. **Turtle with plastic straw video.** Read the referenced *TIME* article and watch the video - http://bit.ly/2DFIc9L

5. **Japanese used goods industry.** The cited figures about growth come from the Japan Times - http://bit.ly/2DEui7G

## Chapter 17: Overwealthy

1. **As several early readers shared with me,** this is not a perspective shared by most Harvard graduates.

2. **Uneasy Street book review.** Read the full review on *Businessweek* - https://bloom.bg/2S6sMi7

3. **Alumni giving is shrinking.** Read the full article from Inside Philanthropy - http://bit.ly/2S6tXhx

4. **Giridharadas, Anand.** Winners Take All: The Elite Charade of Changing the World. New York: Alfred A. Knopf, 2018 - Page 266.

5. **Meaningful work survey.** Read the full SHRM 2017 Employee Job Satisfaction and Engagement Survey - http://bit.ly/2S0U890

6. **"if helping others ..."** This quote is from an interview with Giridharadas published in *WIRED* magazine. http://bit.ly/2DKzXJv

## Chapter 18: Passive Loyalty

1. **Colloquy loyalty research.** Read the full study–http://bit.ly/2QSSVkd

2. **68% of consumers are transient.** Full study from Maritz - http://bit.ly/2DI-Awnj

3. **The consumer decision journey.** Full article from McKinsey Quarterly - https://mck.co/2DKNtwM

4. **Wireless provider rankings.** Data from CIRP on wireless carrier loyalty rankings cited - http://bit.ly/2DIDR5y

5. **Metlife benefits survey.** Results from the MetLife U.S. Employee Benefits Trend Study - http://bit.ly/2DMtYnA

6. **SHRM job satisfaction survey.** Results from 2017 SHRM Employee Job Satisfaction survey - http://bit.ly/2S0U890

## Chapter 19: Intersection Thinking

1. **RumChata popularity.** These claims are taken from an interview conducted on CNBC by Jim Cramer with RumChata founder Tom Maas. Full story - http://cnb.cx/2giWzU1

2. **Pluot.** While this may seem fabricated, the pluot is indeed a real fruit—and certainly not to be confused with the plumcot, which is different. If the story interests you, read more here: http://bit.ly/pluotstory

3. **Bolthouse Farms.** Bolthouse is generally credited with being the first to introduce "baby carrots" to consumers.

4. **"kind of addictive."** Full story - http://bit.ly/2wCyLR6

5. **Persuadable.** I first encountered this term when reading a book of the same title by author Ali Pittampalli.

## Chapter 21: Anti-Trends

1. **Flip thinking.** This idea was first described in an Op-Ed contributed piece by Dan Pink for The Telegraph. Full story - http://bit.ly/2xoyocu

# ACKNOWLEDGEMENTS

The concept for the book has been many years in the making – and now that it is officially an annual series with a new update every year, the first group of people I need to thank are the many people who have read an earlier edition of this book or one of my Non-Obvious Trend Reports and decided to get in touch and interact with me directly.

As much as anyone, this book is for all of you – and if you happen to be among that group, I want to thank you first.

Aside from this broad group, there are also some individuals who helped with various stages of getting this 2019 update (and previous editions) ready for publication and deserve my specific thanks:

First of all, to Paresh for jumping into the process of trend curation, working on the ideas, becoming a true partner and just being a force for good. Your insights in helping to bring these trends to life this year as well as your leadership in helping us bring them into organizations around the world is helping us to spread the power of non-obvious thinking globally - and it's a beautiful journey.

To Gretchen, Matthew, Terry and Christina for offering an ongoing sounding board of editorial advice and jumping in to provide assistance when needed on updates this year and in previous years as well. This year I also owe significant thanks to Genoveva, who joined and worked tirelessly on the trends to make them stronger. The book benefitted greatly from your thoughtful and well-constructed suggestions ... so thank you!

To Joss, Frank, Anton, and Jessica for all your design smarts and making the visual design of the book as beautiful as it is, and to the entire design team at Faceout for the original inspiration and setting the tone for the series back in the beginning.

To Marleen, Chrys and the foreign rights team for helping to bring the ideas in Non-Obvious to so many diverse audiences around the world in their own language and continuing to grow this list every year.

To Marnie for all your work keeping this and so many other Ideapress projects on track.

To Rich for being a great partner, always working under a crazy time-line and still getting things done like a pro.

To my wife Chhavi, who continually manages to deal with a shifting annual writing process that requires me to disappear to finish off chapters and "visualize" ideas by spreading my notes across entire rooms of the house. You are the first person to tell me when it's good and the first to tell me when it isn't. I love that.

And finally, to my boys Rohan and Jaiden for remaining curious enough about the world to continually inspire me to observe more, judge less and always listen with both ears.

From time to time, we all can use a reminder like that.

# INDEX

elegance of, 24, 32–34, 35
essential habits of, 19–35
fickleness of, 24, 29–31, 35
for fun and profit, 37–38
importance of, 3–4
observation of, 24, 27–29, 35
thinking like, 18
thoughtfulness of, 24, 31–32, 35
*Trend-Driven Innovation (Mason et al.),* 236
*The Trend Foresters's Handbook* (Raymond), 235–236
Trend Hunter (www.trendhunter.com), 238
Trend Longevity Ratings, 247–248
*The Trend Management Toolkit* (Kjaer), 236
Trend predictions
usefulness of, 7–12
as useless, 15–18
Trend Report Summaries (2011-2018), 247–275
from 2011, 249, 251
from 2012, 249, 253
from 2013, 249, 254–261
from 2014, 249, 262–269
from 2015, 249, 270–275
from 2016, 249, 278–285
from 2017, 249, 286–293
from 2018, 249, 293–295
reading, 247–248
Trend spotting, myths of, 12–15
as based on hard data, 13–14
concept of, 13
as hopelessly broad predictions, 14–15
prediction by industry experts, 13
short time span in, 14
Trendwatching (www.

trendwatching.com), 237
Trend workshops
models of, 232
running a great, 231–232
*Truthing,* 294
Turner, Anthony, 175
Tuttle, Richard, 21
Twee, 94–95
*Twee: The Gentle Revolution In Music, Books, Television, Fashion, and Film* (Spitz), 94
Twist, 54
Twitter, 3, 39

U
Uber, 173, 212
Unbiased facilitator, 232
Underappreciated side of data, 11–12
*Uneasy Street: the Anxieties of Affluence* (Sherman), 204
Unfamiliar, wonderingi into the, 228–229
*Ungendered,* 80, 86, 294
Uniliver Foundry, 171
Uniquitous Addiction, 60, 61
Upcycling, 200

V
Value chain, exxploring robots across, 190
Vector, 185
Verve (www.verve.com), 238
Victoria's Secret, 175–176
*Virtual Empathy,* 52, 278, 279, 284, 294
Virtual Reality, 52
Visa, 172
Vitiglio, 175
Vocaloid, 98

# ABOUT THE AUTHOR

Rohit Bhargava is a trend curator, marketing expert, storyteller and the Wall Street Journal best-selling author of six books on topics as wide ranging as the future of business and why leaders never eat cauliflower. Rohit is the founder of the Non-Obvious Company, teaches marketing and storytelling at Georgetown University and has been invited to deliver non-boring keynotes for more than 500 events in 32 countries around the world.

Prior to becoming an entrepreneur, Rohit spent 15 years leading brand strategy at two of the largest marketing agencies in the world (Ogilvy and Leo Burnett). He lives in the Washington DC area with his wife and two boys.

# Can we help your team be non-obvious innovators?

## HERE'S HOW YOU CAN WORK WITH US...

→ Bring your team together for one of our signature **Innovation Day Summits** to learn how to think in non-obvious ways and drive action.

→ Master the art of predicting the future with our hands-on **Trend Prediction Intensive Workshop**.

→ Inspire and persuade others with our signature **Storytelling Masterclass** and training.

→ Get one-on-one **Executive Coaching** with our leadership experts to solve your biggest challenges.

## WE DELIVER INSPIRING AND ACTIONABLE
### WORKSHOPS, KEYNOTES + EXECUTIVE COACHING.

## LEARN MORE:

www.nonobviouscompany.com
OR CONTACT US AT INFO@NONOBVIOUSCOMPANY.COM